No Circuses

James F. O'Callaghan

No Circuses
By James F. O'Callaghan

©2014 by James F. O'Callaghan

Cover Design/Interior Design: Linda Boulanger
www.TellTaleBookCovers.weebly.com

Published by: Tacchino Press
ISBN: 978-0692263921

Also available in eBook publication

PRINTED IN THE UNITED STATES OF AMERICA

Dedication

To Giovanna, without whom there would be little joy in writing or anything else.

Acknowledgements

I thank my wife Giovanna and sons John, Neil, and Louis for laughing as they read various drafts of *No Circuses,* and also friends in the Green River Writers Guild Group and elsewhere. Their suggestions and criticism helped greatly.

Special thanks to son Louis for his proofreading, and to my editor J.K. Kelley for making the manuscript more lean and readable.

I am grateful to all those Americans and Latin Americans who made my experiences in South America so enjoyable, interesting, and surprising. A wonderful and varied group, they live on in fond memory.

Special thanks to Terry Caesar; for nearly fifty years his letters and emails have taught me what words are for.

Any resemblance between the characters in *No Circuses* and any person living or dead is purely coincidental.

Shots Ring Out

The black embassy Impala swung onto Avenida Villacruz at 12:03 PM. Through the thick bulletproof windows, Ambassador Bradford Webster surveyed the dilapidated buildings on either side. His handsome patrician face showed distaste, but no fear. The representative of the United States of America would not be kept from his duties by tabloid scaremongering and indigenous gossip.

Ambassador Webster, having just delivered a no-nonsense speech on trade to the local Chamber of Commerce, was en route to visit an Engañadan-American cultural center in the squalid provincial port of Nueva Alcalá. The center did not interest him, but he was the American Ambassador and in his judgment the job included presence at anything connected with the United States. If he resented that his first ambassadorial assignment was to this backwater, he also knew that aggressive leadership would attract the right sort of attention, leading to an ongoing assignment to a real country.

If matters went awry, however, his career would head downhill. The Center's new director, a guy named Lacey, hadn't made much of an impression upon his Embassy check-in some months before. It was time to see if things were under control. Webster did not think these centers did the U.S. much good, but they had almost limitless potential to produce embarrassment. He intended to prevent any such thing.

Consequently, when the sedan passed the obelisk and the noise began, he felt irritation but not unease.

The obelisk memorialized 'Don Juan Francisco Espejo Suárez.' Webster knew the name well: an oft-exiled anti-American politician. Near it, he saw the first of the

1

demonstrators, and heard the first chants of *¡Espejo, Sí! ¡Yanquis, No!*

"What the hell is this?" he demanded coldly of Jethro Jackson, the Public Affairs Officer seated to his left.

"I dunno, sir," answered Jethro, wiping a bead of sweat from his pink face. "But it looks like trouble to me. Maybe we better just turn 'round get on outta here. Right, Pepe?"

Pepe Martínez, the bodyguard in the front passenger seat, was a heavyset Engañadan on loan from the national police. He seemed not to hear. The driver, also a loaner and subordinate to Pepe, continued on.

"It will take more than one demonstrator to chase me out. Keep going!" came the proud, ill-fated reply, in the same tone Webster had employed as an Army first lieutenant.

Jackson's pink complexion faded to nearly match his flowing white hair. Together with his accent and portly figure, that countenance earned him the nicknames of 'Colonel Sanders' and 'Colonel Chicken' among the Embassy's Marine guards. Jackson regained a little color when he saw a demonstrator waving a placard: "LONG LIVE U.S. – ENGAÑADAN FRIENDSHIP!" If this were some strange sort of welcoming committee, it seemed even stranger when he saw the next placard: "YANKEES OUT!"

The car picked up speed, but not for long, thanks to an abandoned bulldozer blocking the street. Demonstrators surrounded the sedan. Pepe began to look nervous. "Señor Ambassador, with respect, I believe it would be safest if we turned around."

"No. We'll walk if we can't drive." The current administration believed in showing firmness, a policy Webster approved and upheld.

"Mr. Ambassador, this sure don't seem like..."

"Shut up, Jethro."

Pepe exited first. Webster waited for Pepe to open the door for him, then swung out and stood for a moment, staring at the scene as if his tall athletic form, tailored blue suit and distinguished gray-streaked dark brown hair would silence the

2

absurd chant. When it did not, he walked past the bulldozer and glanced in disdain at the demonstrators. *Espejo? Are they nuts?* He angled left to avoid the acrid smoke trail from a burning tire. Jackson and Martínez followed, neither with any enthusiasm.

Ten feet farther on, Webster stopped in disbelief. Ahead of him was a circus wagon cage containing a sleepy-looking ape that scratched her nose and stared dumbly at the U.S. Ambassador. Beyond it he could see some clowns and jugglers, and in the patio of the cultural center itself, three elephants. He stopped to look around in outrage as a Fat Lady waved at him. Then he resumed walking, drawing on his experience with night patrols at Fort Ord. *I was good at those. I'd have done well in Vietnam, if I'd been assigned there. I should have no problem dealing with circus clowns and protesters. Probably university students, children of privilege, never worked in their lives. Gives them leisure to make and wave signs denouncing the CIA, foreign investment, and everything American everywhere. Because, no matter who's really at fault, there's always political capital in blaming anything and everything on the United States.*

Webster noticed the pale figure in the second-story window for only a second. It awakened a memory. Then he heard a bugle call and the sound of gunshots. Knowing that bullets fired even by idiots can be fatal, Webster turned and moved quickly toward the safety of the car. He didn't see the girl with long hair and vacant eyes running after him.

Chapter One: It Can't Be That Bad

Six Months Earlier . . .

"You're gonna love it, just love it. Great for your career!"

Max Lacey frowned, wishing he could believe the tinny voice from Washington. "I'd rather stay in an embassy," he repeated. "I don't know anything about bi-national centers. There's got to be somebody else."

"There's not. And besides, you can go by ship! Not many places left you can do that. So we're set, right?"

"I guess." Max glared northeast toward the cheerful unseen personnel officer who had such power over his life.

"Good. You'll get your orders in a couple of days, and you should leave by the beginning of March or you'll have to fly. Got to be on board there by the fifteenth, latest. And really, Max, you'll love it. Best job in the Foreign Service. You get to do everything."

"I know. You told me."

"Right. Have a good trip, hear?"

Lacey put down the phone and looked out his office window at Mexico City, his home for the past two years. The smog seemed a bit thinner on this windy February day. *And I'll miss it: the smog, the traffic, noise, and crowding that I hated when I got here.*

4

What the hell, you get used to anything. Maybe it won't be so bad.

Speculation was limited by Max's utter ignorance of Engañada. He had no mental picture of the place, no images that might make it seem not so bad, maybe even exotic. Nonetheless, he told himself again, *it can't be that bad.* Maybe George would tell him something helpful. He had a center once.

He walked down the hall to find his boss, Press Attaché George Breen, with his feet on the desk, reading the afternoon tabloids and puffing on a Cuban cigar. In Max's first post, George had been something of a mentor as well as a supervisor.

Max told him about the call from Washington.

"Engañada!" George roared. "You're really going to Engañada! My God!"

Max didn't want to see the joke. "Come on, George, he said I was going–"

"To *love* it! Oh yes, you'll love it all right there in–what? San Genesio?"

"No. Nueva Alcalá. He said that's better than the capital because I'll be out of the embassy and, you know, independent."

"You sure will! No one else knows where it is. Hey, did he say it would be great for your career?" George swung his feet onto the floor and leaned forward, resting his elbows on the desk. The ceiling light now lit up his bald spot.

"He said I can take the boat."

"That works, as long as you don't get off it. But come on: did he give you the spin about how it'd be great for your career? And that you'd love it?"

"George, how could it be good for my career? After working for you, everything else has to be downhill, right?"

"Absolutely. Oh, it will help your career. Sure! After two months in Nueva Alcalá, you'll get out and sell insurance or something, make a bundle. Then you contribute to the right candidate and get made ambassador someplace. I know you'd make a great ambassador. Or maybe you'll get kidnapped; that always gets some sympathy, if you survive. If they notice, you being in Nueva Alcalá." He blew a cloud of blue smoke out of a malicious smile.

"They'd notice," Max answered lamely. "They'd notice if the Director disappeared, surely." As he watched George's eyes widen in delight, Max knew he'd stepped in deeper.

"Riiight! The bi-national center director, a VIP! Look, Max," he went on in a mock-conspiratorial tone, "don't go. Tomorrow, tell the Ambassador that extra-terrestrials are camped in your closet. We'll get you sent to the States, and in a year or two, they'll declare you cured. You could live that down; hell, you might even get compensation or something. You have a better chance of recovering from a bughouse than a bi-national center."

Well, hell. "Thanks, George." He got up to leave.

George eased up. "Hey, come on. Ain't so bad. I mean, I was a center director once."

"I know. Got any advice?"

"Well...keep your head on straight off there by yourself. I mean, don't go native and start wearing flip-flops and Bermudas. Other than that, well, I never did understand what the accountant was saying. Or get along very well with the board. But . . ." He paused, thought. "With any luck the place will run itself. There are always people who have been there forever and know what to do."

"That'll help. Anything else?"

"Don't get involved with any of the women on the staff. Complicates things. They all have large families with knives. And keep the ambassador the hell away, or he'll want you to do a bunch of things you can't, or that don't make sense. He wants to visit, tell him the building's being fumigated or something."

"Thanks, George." Max got up to return to his office.

The voice followed him down the hall: "You're gonna love it, Max! I mean really *love* it!"

Chapter Two: Sailing South

Max left Mexico on the first day of April, as scheduled. He did love the ten-day trip aboard the *Thomas Nast*, a slow freighter carrying a dozen aged passengers. He read, ate, made small talk and played bridge with the others, slept, and lacked only exercise to be wholly content. Healthy but not very athletic, he'd always liked sports anyway, as well as his two summers of ROTC physical training. Then he had nearly blown himself up on a demolition exercise, soured on an Army career, and replaced calisthenics with tennis. He enjoyed the game, and people enjoyed playing against him; he compensated for limited agility with good positioning, forcing the other guy to play his best game. Tennis had been a professional asset in Mexico. By playing a lot of mixed doubles, Max met people, kept in great shape, and got a deep tan to complement his medium-dark hair. Many people mistook him for Latino, at least until he said something in Spanish. But now, after a few days at sea, he felt lethargic and wished the ship had a place to swim or jog.

Some people get nothing from a cruise except seasickness. Some get bored; others become fascinated by the intricacies of navigation and ship routine. And some find the steady throb of the engines and the widening white wake on calm days and nights soothing, almost hypnotic. Max was among the latter. He began to imagine Nueva Alcalá more favorably, letting George's mocking faux enthusiasm fade. His personnel officer had sent him the Foreign Service's *Guide to the Bi-national Center*. Max found it pompous, bureaucratic, exhaustive, and reassuring. Until then, Max had known nothing about such places. Now he thought he knew something.

Bi-national Centers, as the *Guide* taught, were dedicated to mutual understanding. They belonged to their members—mostly local nationals, but usually including some resident Americans—

7

who elected a Board. That body either hired a director, or was loaned a Foreign Service officer by the United States. During World War II, Nelson Rockefeller had taken a goodwill tour of numerous countries. This led to the foundation of many such centers, planned as important vehicles for "telling America's story to the world." Now, in the budget-constrained 1970s, Washington had begun to cut back on the lending of Foreign Service officers.

All bi-national centers offered English classes, combining the aims of understanding and income. If everything went as the *Guide* foresaw, the classes should produce enough revenue to pay all bills and salaries (except that of the loaned American director). It offered detailed chapters on how to make everything run smoothly: course schedules, teacher relations, accounting, purchasing, and maintenance.

I'm not really leaving the Federal bureaucracy at all. I need only follow this program, and it'll work out.

It might even be fun. He would have no nearby superior. The personnel officer in D.C. had assured Max that the Nueva Alcalá Center had been completely remodeled a few years before, and that his predecessor had left it in excellent shape. Max would have leisure to see the country and read the rest of his Hemingway. If George was right, and it had efficient old employees who handled most of what came up, he might only have to work a few hours a day and write a few reports each month. His vision of Nueva Alcalá became an amalgam of *The Sun Also Rises, A Farewell to Arms, Casablanca,* and *South Pacific*. In Mexico, walking through the old city, Max had often imagined himself as Zorro, fencing with evil-eyed men across the balconies or in the narrow cobbled streets. Maybe the daydream would work in Nueva Alcalá as well. If not, he'd find another.

The ship's few ports of call promised romance until Max walked around them. Seen from a mile offshore, they looked lush, mysterious, even picturesque. Reality set in beginning at dockside, where squalor overwhelmed mystery. Instead of warm-eyed maidens beckoning from beneath palm trees, he saw hard-eyed men studying him from alleyways. By the time they reached Buenaventura, Max decided to heed the Captain's warning and

8

stay aboard.

He stood at the rail watching the stevedores work, shouting back and forth at the ship's crew. They unloaded more cargo than they took aboard, which made sense; a crewman had told Max that the *Nast* was to return from Nueva Alcalá with a full load of bananas. The fruity smell of previous voyages floated up from the holds and mixed with other damp smells of the dock, the oily water, and the haphazard city. Max was idly calculating in his head the number of bananas the ship could carry when he heard, *"Buenos días."*

It was Luis Gonzales Caballero, a short, dignified Engañadan of Max's earlier casual acquaintance. Gonzales wore an engaging smile and a carefully pressed white suit. Max had watched him climb slowly up the gangway moments before, and returned the greeting.

Max knew little about the small, white-haired old man, save that he had boarded in Panamá and was returning to Engañada after a long absence. The other passengers who had boarded in Mexico, or joined the freighter in San José or Panamá, had been reticent about sharing information about themselves or learning anything about Max. Only Gonzales had reacted at all to Max's mention of his new assignment, joking that he should invoke St. Gabriel, the patron of ambassadors. Max had objected that he was no ambassador, and that he hoped the saint also looked out for bi-national center directors.

"The ports get worse as we go south, don't they?" Gonzales asked.

Max grinned and answered in Spanish. "They don't get prettier."

"Alas, Alcalá is the last port. I think you and I are the only ones going that far?"

"Isn't it '*Nueva Alcalá*'?"

"Yes, properly speaking. But natives usually shorten it to plain 'Alcalá. No one's likely to confuse it with the Spanish city of the same name."

"I see." *If Americans had done this, we'd have the York Yankees. Wouldn't sound right.* "Well, I don't know if anyone else

9

is going there. No one has said anything to me. But you must be eager to get home, to see your family. You've been gone a long time, haven't you?"

"Some years. Yes, I'm glad to get back. My wife, God rest her soul, is buried there. My children mostly live elsewhere, but there are nephews and in-laws enough. And you, Mr. Lacey, are you eager to get to Nueva Alcalá?"

Max knew the diplomatic answer: "Of course."

"Good!" Gonzales laughed. "But seriously, what do you know of Engañada?"

"Not as much as I'd like to, not yet." *Which is kind of embarrassing to admit.* "I read what I could; the State Department's *Country Report* and a couple books, so I hope I learned the basic things. I remember that its full name is *La Republica de Engañada* because the Spanish explorers had been deceived by local guides, or something like that."

"And very appropriate, too. Our guides often deceive us. And you learned also that the capital is San Genesio in the mountains, that it and Alcalá are long-time rivals, that the principal export is bananas, the area is such and such and the population was so many in the last census; that earthquakes are frequent and the climate varies from zone to zone. Yes?" Gonzales' smile flickered playfully.

"Well, yes. That sort of thing. And that the country has had lots of economic problems for several years now."

"Alas, even worse than the norm for our poor impoverished country. More unemployment, worse health and education statistics, and more government corruption. Anything else?"

Max thought for a second. "Also, there was an important battle there during the revolution against Spain. Near Nueva Alcalá."

"Moderately important, and the Spanish won. Very good. I doubt, Mr. Lacey, that fifty Americans know as much. By the way, do you know the difference between the United States and Engañada?"

"I know a number of them, but probably not the one you have in mind."

10

"It's this: no Engañadan about to leave for the United States would have to look it up in an encyclopedia. But not even an encyclopedia can tell you very much, certainly not those things you must know to run that center." He paused, seemed to consider, then put a paternal hand on Max's arm. "You're very young, certainly young enough to need advice, but I hope not so young as to ignore it altogether. Be very careful. Don't believe everything you hear. On the other hand, follow the advice of reliable people. Like Mariana Guzmán. Listen to her."

"Mariana Guzmán?" Max frowned. He'd seen that name somewhere.

"In the cultural center. She's been there for years."

"Right. I should have remembered. I saw her name in some of the things they sent me." *Along with stuff that mentioned, with a touch of pride, occasional anti-American demonstrations at the Center, on the grounds that if the Communists denounced the Center it must be doing something right. All the same, I could do without demonstrations.* "And of course, yourself?" he asked, smiling. "Surely I can trust an old shipmate?"

"Oh, beware old shipmates," laughed Gonzales. "But I'll drop by to see how you're getting on, what fate has in store for you. I hope it will bring you fewer problems than it did to some of your predecessors, or that you manage to deal with them better. Listen to Mariana."

"What kinds of problems?" Max asked.

"Oh, that's a long story, or several long stories. Money problems, of course. And there was one fellow who got involved in an 'affair of skirts' as we say, and snuck aboard a freighter in the middle of the night." Gonzales smiled at the memory, then started toward the staterooms. He turned and said, "I suggest you read the local papers they brought aboard. There are copies in the lounge. You may get, as *you* say, a *head start.*"

Good idea. The humidity is sticking my shirt to my back. Max went down to the cool lounge where there was indeed a stack of fresh periodicals. He sat down in an easy chair and began skimming. The Buenaventura papers were given mostly to murders and robberies, but one of them described what Gonzales must have meant:

> Panamá, April 8. Juan Francisco Espejo Suárez, Engañada's elder statesman, has announced he will return to Engañada and possibly seek the presidency for the thirteenth time if and when the current dictator, General Juan Roberto Madera Gómez, fulfills his promise to hold elections. Espejo Suárez, who was first elected to the presidency in 1925, saw each of his previous administrations end by *coup d'état,* the most recent in 1971.
>
> Former President Espejo, who says he is not superstitious about a thirteenth term, has held Engañada's highest office more often than any other man with the exception of General José Abelardo Suárez O'Connor, who was elected eight times and came to power by *coup* on seven other occasions between 1834 and 1860 for a total of fifteen terms. (Some historians credit Suárez with a sixteenth term in 1861 but most dismiss this "lunchtime presidency" which lasted only three hours.) Mr. Espejo already holds the record for the greatest number of times elected to the presidency (twelve).
>
> Political observers believe Mr. Espejo would have an excellent chance of winning an election despite his advanced age (he will be 86 in July) and the opposition of the powerful landowners who have traditionally resisted him.
>
> The Engañadan Embassy in Panamá had no comment on the Espejo announcement.

Max put down the paper and stared out the window, but didn't focus on the buildings or the cranes that moved back and forth. Instead he saw a fuzzy image of an old man walking through the jungle smiling as scowling generals watched him closely, and people cheering except for fat landowners whispering among themselves. Twelve times elected president! The man must be something other than, or beyond, a politician. The people must love him. Or something. And someone will have to stop the schemes of those landowners and generals.

That was a mission worthy of Zorro.

Or an intrepid American agent.

Chapter Three: Sage Advice

Max awoke to find the Pacific Ocean replaced by a twisting estuary through a thick, quiet jungle. The *Nast*'s engines were but a murmur. No ocean wind or wave broke the silence. Something mysterious and exciting about the scene held him fascinated at the porthole for several minutes, until he remembered that he had best get to breakfast if he didn't want to disembark hungry.

Over coffee and rolls on deck, he again watched the shoreline ease by. Estuaries, wide spots and other openings broke up the shore's dense vegetation now and again. The ship maneuvered around several small islands as thick with trees as was the shoreline. Max tried to project some sense of place into the land, to imagine people living there—or, much harder—to imagine a place with no people, no history, but only the eternal indifferent kingdoms of plant and animal, where time had no meaning and snakes and bugs and trees enjoyed perpetual Eden. When a strange white tree exploded into a thousand flying egrets turning deeper into the forest, their thrashing wings the only sound in the prehistoric stillness, he experienced it almost as a dream.

Then they passed a hut, one solitary thatched *Lord Jim* hut perched high atop thin bamboo legs, and the jungle became a place. Max assumed a pair of dark eyes following the ship, following him. Whether fierce or soft, they allowed him to be there too, to imagine himself a part of something rich and strange. *This,* he thought, *is what the Foreign Service is all about.*

Early in his Mexico tour, he had regretted leaving Washington and his Civil Service job in the General Services Administration. Max had spent two years at the GSA checking vehicle usage forms from six agencies in the Middle Atlantic states, passing each form on to one of a dozen other desks depending upon the form's correctness or allocation code or project number, always with an appropriately initialed slip. It afforded him mind-space to daydream about traveling to exotic places and doing brave romantic things, even if at times he had to restrain his imagination in order to give the forms their due attention. They would, of course, need to pass the scrutiny of superior bureaucrats in other offices. Such dull, regular work and hours had provided what he thought enviable freedom: he did not have to manage his life, but only observe its clear markings. From this secure position, he could indulge in mild sarcasm at his own expense, or at the expense of the administration, the press, or even the bureaucracy itself. He traded jokes with old classmates from Georgetown, now colleagues. He even took the same bus from the family home in Arlington that he had taken to the university, where he had spent four enjoyable years until his credits added up to an English degree. Then there seemed nothing to do but take the Civil Service test, which landed Max and several classmates at the GSA. They discussed the Redskins in the GSA cafeteria, just as they had at the Student Union. He'd been promoted twice in his two years, and even if further promotion could not be expected soon, it was inevitable. Surely it was folly to sacrifice such a life to a daydream, to family pride, or even to slightly better benefits. But life is often determined by disappointment or accidents or mistakes or coincidence. In his case, it was the last two: both Max and his father made the same basic error on the same fateful day.

Florence, Max's former girlfriend, had gone on to law school. On their last date she had chided him for a lack of ambition. The charge had puzzled more than irritated him. *Is ambition necessarily a good thing? Wasn't that why they killed Caesar? And besides, how is setting my sights on a GS-15 lacking in ambition?* But he couldn't argue away the imputation, nor the gnawing awareness that he would never find behind a desk the adventures he imagined for himself. On a certain Tuesday afternoon, as he checked New Jersey light truck maintenance schedules, imagination mixed with the morning report on the latest Middle East crisis. He saw himself inviting Israelis and Palestinians to lunch with the Pope, and by quoting parallel points in the Old Testament and the Koran in flawless Hebrew and Arabic, moving the old antagonists to embrace. He hadn't worked

15

out every aspect of that daydream, especially a suitably important role for His Holiness; one could hardly have a pope just sit there. Maybe the lunch ought not to be in Rome at all. Nonetheless, the fantasy stayed in his head. He let it slip out at dinnertime, commenting that it might be interesting to transfer to the Foreign Service.

His father frowned.

The senior Lacey had grown fat and gray during his long career at the Department of Labor. Whenever he heard of some new diplomatic absurdity, he loved to sneer at the "elite Foreign Service." He thought "diplomats" a bunch of *prima donnas* who enjoyed wholly unjustified benefits in comparison with the civil service. But father, like son, had a predilection for daydreams, and one came on him before he could speak.

While Lacey senior chewed a large forkful of dry pot roast, he imagined himself riding in his carpool and that Tom, from Minimum Wage Statistics, asked what Max was doing lately. "He's in Geneva," Mr. Lacey heard himself answering. "The Secretary asked him to run over and troubleshoot some SALT hang-up." By the time the father managed to swallow his pot roast and respond to the son, he too had confused daydream with possibility. He transposed his daydream to familiar terms: those undeserved Foreign Service benefits. "You could retire at fifty, then get on again with Civil Service, draw two retirements. You get a housing allowance overseas, could save a bunch of money." He gazed thoughtfully at his plate. "Might be worth a shot."

Fantasy began sliding ominously toward reality. It was unnerving to contemplate his life turned upside-down, but Max could hardly tell his father to forget it, explain that it was just a daydream. What son ever suspects that his father also has fantasies? So he said nothing, but worried things would get out of hand. So they had. Ashamed *not* to take the Foreign Service test after suggesting it himself, Max passed it despite feeling confident he wouldn't. Eight months later, after finishing the State Department's orientation and Spanish courses, he was on his way to Mexico City with warnings of smog and traffic and crime ringing in his ears.

He happily learned that the stories about Mexico City had exaggerated the city's problems while ignoring its virtues. The metropolis boasted fine restaurants and a rich history displayed in Aztec ruins and colonial churches. His Spanish improved with daily use. The large embassy differed little from the GSA building, full of offices where typists typed and middle-aged men initialed standard government forms. True, they dealt with trade fairs and visiting pianists and political rumors as well as routine recordkeeping, but the embassy environment was collegial. It might best be described as a little country where social life overlapped with official duties, so Max often found himself at dinners or art exhibits or concerts with co-workers, joining them in conversation with Mexican politicians or businessmen or artists. After a year, he received a promotion. Moreover, he was a diplomat, representing his country! He took increasing pride in doing so, even as he learned to appreciate much that he'd never really noticed about the United States. Mexico had many wonderful qualities, but the poverty and corruption made him thankful he had been born in Virginia.

Of course, Max's activities as an Assistant Cultural and Press Attaché didn't live up to his fantasy of bringing about world peace. Deep down, he hadn't expected them to. Max considered himself fortunate that his parentally-abetted foray across the wall between fantasy and reality had worked out so well.

Yet this morning, watching more huts glide by during his third cup of coffee, Max wondered if Mexico hadn't simply been a more exotic version of the GSA career he had left behind. *Why shouldn't I have a little adventure as a Foreign Service officer? Some safe romance, action, achievement, or at least variety. A jungle instead of a big city—is that too much to ask when you're off on your own, speaking mainly to foreigners in their own language? Maybe Engañada will be different. If Zorro proves too Mexican for Engañada, maybe I'll imagine myself a jungle explorer or guerrilla fighter.*

He joined Gonzales on the starboard walkway, where the scenery of huts had yielded to houses. The *Nast* shared the river with small boats and canoes and a rusty barge that listed to one side. "Much farther?" Max asked.

"No. We're in the Cholo River now. I always enjoy this part of the trip."

"It's very beautiful."

"And very confusing. I doubt I could find my way through this maze even though I've made the trip many times. It's not a bad introduction to Engañada."

A road appeared out of the jungle, then ran parallel to the ship's course. Max watched a truck make its way upriver past burros loaded with high bundles or pulling large-wheeled carts. Farther on, a bus bounced past a clearing where children played in front of a cinderblock school. Then they rounded yet another bend in the river, and before them as far as they could see, lay the principal port and second city of the *Republica de Engañada*: Nueva Alcalá. Both men gazed at it, following the riverfront dotted with docks and warehouses and boats and ships, then the modest-sized buildings gathered in the flat river basin with its eastern edge defined by jungle-green hills. Beyond those cloud-draped hills lay the Andes. Up there was the capital, San Genesio, which housed the embassy and the Ambassador, the one George had cautioned Max to keep far away.

He turned back to the riverfront, determined to find something romantic or at least mysterious about it. Leaning wooden structures overhung the muddy bank. Beneath them, canoes scurried back and forth laden with bananas and goats, chickens and children, poled by short, dark, barefoot men with dirty straw hats and ragged clothes. *A Third World Venice?* The faint smell of fish and sodden vegetation seemed just right here, if not very like the Venice of travelogues: a correct conclusion to the winding journey upriver. The two tall office buildings in the background, clumsy cement-and-glass tourists, seemed out of place. But for those, he might have been with the Spanish when they first furled sail here, looking for fresh water.

Scruffy tugboats maneuvered to hold the *Thomas Nast* against the current and nudge it toward a long wooden pier. The dockworkers went from dots of moving color to short men in colorful shirts, cutoffs, and tennis shoes. A couple threw lines to secure the ship; a forklift dropped the gangway in place with a heavy *clang,* the sudden noise serving to divide the journey from whatever lay beyond it. Max felt a sudden affection for the ship, especially in contrast to the riverside buildings sagging under the scorching sun. One could believe that only the heavy air held those woebegone buildings up. *It's picturesque,* Max told himself.

For some indistinct bureaucratic reason, the passengers could not disembark for two hours. When they were finally allowed to carry their suitcases to the small customs shed on the pier, they had another thirty-minute wait before a sleepy agent appeared to stamp their passports. In the next room, a customs agent noted Max's diplomatic passport with the correct diplomatic visa—officially, he was the Embassy's Branch Cultural Affairs Officer—and waved him through without opening his bags. Behind him, Gonzales shook hands with the agent, asked about his wife and children, and then dragged his own untouched suitcases over to where Max waited. They stepped outside and began walking down the pier, followed closely by the immigration and customs agents who now locked up the shed.

Gonzales and Lacey found a cab quickly enough, a 1950s vintage Ford station wagon that soon became snarled in traffic. As bad as the dust was, closing the windows was unthinkable in the steamy heat. Around them old Chevrolets and even older Dodge trucks belched blue-black smoke from broken mufflers while the newer Japanese cars tried to edge around them. The cab proceeded, inched, halted, nosed in, maneuvered for headway. Max noticed a fat woman in a flowered dress leaning from a second-story balcony and waving a half-plucked chicken, shouting angrily at somebody below. Beggars sat along the sidewalk or worked the street. Max fished a dollar from his pocket and gave it to a youngish man who hobbled over with a crutch under one arm. The ragged fellow scowled at it, muttering something indistinct.

"He says American money isn't worth much anymore," interpreted Gonzales as the taxi leaped forward again.

The city didn't change much as they left the port area. The new office buildings, so impressive from a distance, showed moldiness and neglect similar to that of the old ones. Everything remained crowded: the street, the sidewalks, and the little shops that pushed against one another. In places, bicycles and electric fans made the sidewalks impossible for pedestrian traffic, forcing walkers to dodge cars in the roadway. Every block seemed to have an English Academy, announced by hand-drawn posters promising modern electronic methods: "*Tu puedes hablar el inglés en tres semanas.*" Max nodded toward the sign. "I certainly didn't learn to speak Spanish in three weeks," he observed to Gonzales. "Looks like I have competition."

"Yes, there are even more than before. Well, look at it this way: you're the victim of your own success. When the Center first opened, they had to persuade people to learn English. Now everyone wants to."

"I hope so."

"Besides," Gonzales spoke over the engine and street noise, "the Center has been in crisis for most of its history, about as long as your life. It will probably survive for you, too. Just listen to Mariana."

Probably survive?

They turned onto a broader avenue divided by a strip of dusty forlorn grass, marked every block or so with a bust of someone or statue of a rider on a rearing horse. Max could not read much except the dates carved in large Latin numerals: MDCCCXXXIV, MDCCCLVI, MCMXXVII, etc. All but the last one, 1927, took too long to decode. Farther on, a cement obelisk proclaimed:

Don JUAN FRANCISCO ESPEJO SUÁREZ
Salvador de la Patria
1955

"Isn't that the guy—"

"Of course. We are always in a hurry to put up monuments. But here, we're at your Center."

The taxi swung to the curb and stopped. Gonzales wouldn't allow Max to pay the fare. "He'd only cheat you."

Max thanked him and dragged suitcases from the front seat. As he closed the door, Gonzales held up a finger. "*Cuidado.*"

For a second, Max Lacey felt as if he were seven years old, with his mother warning him yet again to be careful as he ventured into the world.

Chapter Four: Well Begun is Work Half Done

Max turned to survey the odd structure that was his Center. It was U-shaped, part old three-story wooden building resembling those along the river, part four-story modern addition. An ugly swath of cement joined the two portions. The latter portion appeared unfinished, with several of its very large windows replaced by plywood sheets. *Broken by demonstrators, perhaps? At least it looks good compared to the boarded-up ruin next door.* A beggar lazed in the sun on that edifice's broken steps.

Max picked his way through the courtyard of the U, stepping around scraps of lumber and concrete chunks. An unfinished reflecting pool in the middle sported wooden forms around its perimeter, awaiting concrete. If the thing were ever finished, the pool's water would wash against an eight-foot tall piece of twisty metal. *I guess that's a sculpture of Great Significance. But hey, how hard can it be to clean the place up and pour some concrete? There's opportunity here. I can see myself on a Saturday morning in the courtyard, watching enthusiastic volunteers washing and sweeping, inspired by new-found pride and purpose. The Director, American friendship personified, jokes benevolently in jeans with a brush in his hand. Buys beer for all. University students who came to demonstrate stay to paint. Photographers arrive. The wire services pick up the story and the* Washington Post *runs it on a slow day, with the Director's image smiling across the columns at the President.* He walked briskly, carrying his fantasy up the stairs into reality.

Peering through the double glass doors, Max thought he saw

someone waving at him, maybe in welcome. Max pushed the handle forcefully and stepped forward.

The door fell flat in front of him and shattered.

"*La otra! Le dije la otra!*" shouted a fat little man with rumpled black-gray hair and an unbuttoned dirty shirt. Max's smile went from glad to witless.

"The other?" he echoed, stupidly.

"Yes, the other! Can't you see this one's broken? I told you to use the other! It's not my fault! I was fixing the hinge like Señorita Rosa told me and you broke it! Are you blind that you didn't see me tell you to use the other door? Juan! Didn't I tell him to use the other?"

A tall figure lounging on a bench by the wall controlled his laughing long enough to answer, "Oh, yes, Don Manuel, you told him! Now tell Miss Rosa!"

Miss Rosa? Who the hell? I thought they answered to this famous Mariana.

A door opened to the right. Juan stopped laughing and tried to look concerned as a pretty young woman came out, her dark eyes sweeping the lobby. "*Que...?*" she began to ask. Seeing the door, she turned on Manuel and Juan. "*Idiotas!* I ask you to do one little thing and you break the door! *Por Diós!* What do we do now? How do you fix *that*?"

Manuel hurried to explain that he had told "this gentleman" or alternately, "that fool" to use the other door, thus the gentleman/fool was to blame. The young woman turned to face Max. Behind her, Juan suppressed his laughter.

"Did you break the door?" she demanded.

"*Bueno,* I guess maybe I did. Sort of. I just opened it and it fell down and, well, seems to have broken there so..." His Spanish had issues, but she seemed to understand it, just as he understood most of what she said despite her rapid Alcalá accent.

"If you broke it, you'll have to pay for it," she cut in, her voice hard and determined. Manuel nodded agreement.

This is not going well, Max thought, wondering how to announce himself and get control of the situation.

Still irate, Rosa turned and walked to a large counter beneath a sign: *Informaciones*. Two girls leaned against the other side, giggling. Watching Rosa obtain pen and paper at the counter was not visually painful; she had fierce yet soft eyes, a small nose and full lips. Her black hair fell well over and past her shoulders. She glared at Max. "Name, and where you work?"

"Lacey, Max Lacey," he answered. "And I work, well, here. In the Center. I'm the new Director."

Juan covered his face with his hands while Manuel looked behind himself as if he'd lost something. Rosa stared with her mouth half open, the pen poised over the paper on which she had written 'Leci.' Her face showed a rapid succession of surprise, fear, shame, anger, resignation, and finally, pride. "The door's still broken," she noted, her voice only somewhat softened.

"Yes." Max was encouraged by the sudden silence. The girls behind the counter had shut up, as had Juan. Rosa looked not so much cowed as slightly off balance. "We'll worry about the door a little later," Max said, trying for assertiveness. "Though I suppose we might clean up the glass now."

Manuel began a strange dance toward the back of the lobby, trying to make haste without turning his back on the new Director. Amid frequent turnabouts and incomprehensible apologies to the *Señor Director*, he fetched a broom. Max did catch one phrase: "It was probably the door's time anyway." Juan shuffled after him, loose sandals slapping the gray linoleum.

Max took a moment to survey the lobby. It was cleaner than the patio, with doors identified in English as Administration or Library or Cafeteria leading off in different directions. A wide stairway rose to the left.

"I guess you want to see your office," said Rosa shyly, pushing her long hair back over her shoulder. "Are those your suitcases outside? Juan! Get the suitcases before someone steals them!"

"Thank you."

Blushing and avoiding eye contact, Rosa showed him through the Administration door from which she had entered. It led down a corridor with four doors marked Cultural Assistant, Activities Director, Executive Assistant, and at the end the largest one:

Director. Max began to wonder which was Mariana's, but only until Rosa's swaying bright skirt, a pattern of red and white birds and fish on a blue background, captured his attention.

Wonder how serious George was about advising me not to get mixed up with the secretaries. I suppose she has a big family.

His office had one interior wall and three glass window sides, squarely within the Center's newer addition. The ragged but sturdy furniture included an elaborate desk, a living room set, and a conference table. Several paintings hung on the interior wall. His desk offered views of the patio and two streets, except for the pane that had been replaced with plywood. Most of it was tatty, but remarkably clean.

"We try to keep it neat," said Rosa, "but no one knew what to do with all this." She walked behind the desk and picked up an armful of envelopes and files from a pile neatly hidden there. "There are some letters here for you. Personal letters."

She handed him a small pile of things that had been forwarded from Mexico via the diplomatic mail. Max flipped through the stack quickly, wondering how much it had cost to forward the junk. One envelope, from his parents, he put in his pocket.

"Things have been sort of confused," Rosa went on, "and we didn't know when you were coming. Dr. Ramírez—he is the President of the Board—got a letter last month from the Embassy, but it didn't say when."

"Oh. Well. That's all right. I mean, I see..." What now? The enormity was starting to sink in. Each of Max's previous jobs had begun with someone telling him where, when, how and at what to work. Here, he was to set the tone and direction for all the Center's employees and activities, beginning with the employee before him.

"How about a coffee break?" he suggested.

Her eyes widened. "Of course. I'm sorry. I should have done it."

"No, I don't mean that." Now it was his turn to blush at his clumsiness, his embarrassing her for having forgot that most Latin of customs, a cup of coffee before discussing anything. He had spent long enough in Mexico to have learned to do his best never to embarrass a Latino, much less a Latina. "I mean," he stumbled on, "maybe a beer would be better? It's pretty hot in here." The back of his shirt was soaked.

"The air conditioning doesn't work today. Maybe it will tomorrow. It's never really worked right and lately it's just strange. But there's no money to fix it again. Maybe it just can't be fixed." She picked up the phone, dialed three numbers and told someone the Director wanted a beer. She listened a second, snapped "Don't be stupid!" and hung up.

"No money," Max echoed. "Is that why the window hasn't been replaced?" He nodded toward the plywood sheet.

"Yes. Glass is very expensive."

Max wondered how much it would cost to replace the door he'd just broken as he sat on one of the easy chairs while Rosa balanced herself modestly on the edge of the soft couch. "Let's see now," he began, "you're Rosa..."

"Fuentes Serena. I'm a secretary here."

"Yes. And you...live with your large family, do you?"

"Yes," she answered, puzzled. "We're nine. My brothers work with my father, transporting things for people with his old truck, or in the neighbor's butcher shop."

"Ah. Well, I understand there's an Executive Assistant as well, Mariana Guzmán?"

"No, not now. She was here for years but she quit."

"She quit?" *What? From what Gonzales told me, Mariana Guzmán was the key mover and shaker, as permanent as the Center itself, holding it all together. My right-hand employee, to whom I should listen to avoid problems, is not here.*

"She left two months ago," Rosa explained, "and that's why things are so confused. She was in charge after Mr. Grimaldi left, but then at the last Board meeting something happened, and she quit. Or, really, retired. She could have retired a long time ago."

"Do you know why she quit? Was she mad or something?"

Rosa hesitated an instant. "Yes. She was mad and unhappy. She was crying when she left."

Max gazed out at the patio past the plywood sheet that danced against the frame as the wind came up. *Maybe she'd come back if I asked her nicely,* he thought. "How can I contact her? If nothing else, I'd like to talk to her about how things are. At the Center."

"She went to the United States after she left. She'd never been there and now she has the chance. She came here to say goodbye."

"Two months? Surely she should be back soon."

"I don't think so. She said she wanted to see everything."

Max sighed. "Well, who's in charge now? I mean, who has been in charge?"

Rosa shrugged. "Gloria, Gloria Angelita Córdova Medellín, is still in charge of cultural programs. Washington Maldonado is in charge of Activities. Luis–"

"What activities?"

"I don't know. No one seems to. Anyway, Luis Verde is the accountant and Bertram Braden is American and the Academic Director, and Carmen Jaramillo is the Librarian, but no one is in charge of everybody. I use Mariana's desk," nodding toward the adjacent door labeled Executive Assistant, "and sort of tell the other girls in the office what to do. You saw them at the information desk outside, Cecelia and Maria. I also give tasks to the janitors. I've been here the longest, of the girls at least, two years."

Max wanted to ask what he should do now, but couldn't. He was supposed to decide that, for himself and everyone else, even though he knew less about the place than any of them. Irrelevant thoughts about names popped into his head: *the Activities guy is named Washington, so it's like Mexico where they name children for great men like Washington or Lincoln or Bolívar or Lenin. What if the children don't follow their parents' politics, so a Lincoln grows up to be a Communist, or a Lenin turns into a free-market enthusiast?*

A knock at the door banished his wanderings. Manuel entered carrying a bottle of beer and a glass on a tray, smiling and bowing. He placed the glass neatly on the coffee table and filled it.

"Thank you," Max said, reaching for it. Manuel turned to leave, kicked the table and knocked half the beer onto the table, the floor, and Max's arm.

"Perdón, perdón," he mumbled, dropping the tray. It bounced off the table onto the floor. He ran through a small door and returned with a handful of paper towels and began mopping everything, including Max, all the while pouring out continuous apologies. Rosa stared glumly out the window.

"Bueno, there's everything clean again," Manuel announced as he wiped the last drops from the floor. "Everything in perfect order."

"Yes. Very good. Thank you...Manuel, isn't it?"

"Yes. Manuel San Martín Echeverría, at your orders." He gave a jerky bow. "I am now with the Cultural Center thirty-one years since its foundation and worked with the first Director, the *caballero* Don Jorge Machala del Rio, a very great gentleman for whom, I believe, my performance was wholly satisfactory, as also for the esteemed first American Director, Mr. Smeet, whom we all remember with great fondness. Allow me to take this opportunity to welcome you to Alcalá and to the Center, and to assure you that whatever thing you wish done, I am here at your disposition."

A great virtue of Spanish is its dignity, which can lend presence to the humblest citizen and impose formality in the midst of chaos. Max had found comfort in this virtue ever since he had begun to learn the language.

"Thank you, Manuel. I'm sure I will find your services as invaluable as did my several illustrious predecessors."

"I have total assurance that it will be so, *Señor* Director. And now I beg your permission to absent myself to see to other duties, the discharge of which cannot longer be delayed."

"Of course."

"Then, *con permiso. Señorita.*" He bowed to both of them and left, smiling and nodding as he backed out the door. Max drank the remaining beer quickly. *Quite good. I'm liking Engañada better already.* He noticed Rosa watching and cursed himself for forgetting his manners.

"Would you like a glass as well?"

She looked at the door and said, "No...please!" They both laughed. Max noticed a photo on the wall above her head: a smiling American wearing one of the local shirts, posing with Center employees. Manuel was one. Looking at his own wet sleeve, Max asked, "Do directors usually wear suits?"

"Just for big meetings and such." She had noticed his gaze. "That's Mr. Grimaldi. He always wore a *guayabera.* I think most directors did."

"I think I'll have to get some. This suit is just too warm."

"Yes, unless the air conditioning ever starts working right!"

"Even then. It's hot outside. Well, then, where were we? No one's in charge of everything. Or no one has been. Then I suppose the first thing I should do is..." He tried to remember if the *Guide* had said anything about the first day. At last, the obvious occurred to him. "Let's call the Embassy!"

"You want to talk to San Genesio? Now?"

"Yes. I guess I could talk to Jackson there."

"Jethro Jackson?" She pronounced the name as *Hetro,* and with distaste.

"Right. He's the one we work for, I guess."

"We do? He certainly doesn't pay us anything, and he hasn't even called all this time we were waiting for a Director." Rosa pushed her hair over her shoulder again, lips tight. Max thought even her pouting cute.

"Well, I work for him. Officially, at least."

"That's true," Rosa said, as if acknowledging a serious illness. "But the Embassy's closed now. They only work until five, but we can try tomorrow. Sometimes it takes a while to get a call through."

Max looked at his watch, surprised that it was already five-thirty. "How late do we work?" he asked.

"The office is open until eight, though classes run until ten. And when we have an art exhibit or movie or something, we stay until midnight or later. I mean, you do. The office people always leave at eight."

Twelve-hour days? "You must take a long lunch?"

"The usual: one to four."

Obviously. La siesta. Good for tropical afternoons. "Good," he said. "Sounds fine. Now why don't you show me around the

Center so I can meet everybody?"

"All right." Rosa's voice betrayed reluctance. "Be careful."

Careful of what? Max twisted his sleeve to hide the beer stain, then followed Rosa on his introductory procession through the building. All were delighted that he had arrived. One after another, each employee promised readiness to do whatever thing at whatever hour the Director might deem convenient. Absent were Gloria Córdova and Washington Maldonado; "I haven't seen her for a couple of days," said Rosa, "and Washington said he was taking his vacation a week ago." Only the accountant, Luis Verde, offered a restrained greeting: a polite reception of a man thirty years his junior. He introduced his two bookkeepers, Mario Fuentes and Inés Suárez.

Something about Verde made Max vaguely uneasy but he dismissed the feeling and marveled instead at the number of employees: half a dozen secretaries and clerks; five janitors, a cafeteria supervisor and four helpers, a librarian and two assistants. That was just the ground floor. His confidence went up a bit upon seeing all the help available to him, but he also felt a burden. Given Engañada's chronically high unemployment, these people depended upon *El Señor* Director to hold the place together, to prevent their being thrown onto the street. At the same time he wondered if they were really all needed, and what they added to the overhead.

On the second floor, Rosa showed him two conference rooms, both dusty with several fluorescent tubes burnt out. Max found two more janitors, and wondered what they did. One room had a meeting in progress, and Max asked Rosa about it. "That's not ours," she assured him. "They're just using the room." They passed through a language laboratory with ancient, broken tape recorders, and moved on to the Academic Department.

"Mr. Braden?" asked Rosa, opening the door to a cluttered office dimly lit by two candles in ashtrays.

"Yeah." A gaunt bearded fellow bent over a desk, writing with a quill. He didn't look up.

"This is Mr. Lacey, the new Director. He just got here."

Braden's head revolved slowly to the right and up until he

was staring at Max. The candlelight, or something, gave a strange glitter to his small hazel eyes.

"So you're the Academic Director," Max noted after an uneasy moment. The Guide stressed the importance of "an active, decisive Academic Director." Max hoped he didn't have a problem.

Braden finally answered in a slow, hollow voice, "Yeah. They wanted a native speaker. I was a native speaker."

"I see. And when was that?"

"That was..." Braden's gaze fixed on the candle.

"You don't remember?"

"About four years ago," offered Rosa.

"That right, Bertram?"

After a moment Braden sighed. "Time..." He said it as if the word meant nothing.

"Braden? Are you all right?"

"Just leave him," Rosa advised in a low voice. "He gets like that sometimes."

The two of them backed out, shutting the door. Wondering what drugs the guy was on, Max feared that he did indeed have a problem. *Well*, he thought, *we'll see. Give him a chance.*

The third floor, all classrooms, looked the worst. The walls were solid with slogans, initials, phone numbers and messages. Some of the doors hung by only one hinge. Cigarette butts were everywhere. "I tell them to clean it up," explained an embarrassed Rosa, "but you have to remind them all the time and anyway they don't want to do what I tell them."

Ah, the old machismo.

"It wasn't like this when Mariana was here," she added grimly.

A few classes were in session, none with more than eight students. Through the open or broken doors, Max saw some teachers scribbling furiously at blackboards or leading chant-like drills: *Good morning, how are you? I am fine, and you?* In other rooms, teachers sat on the edge of their desks smoking or drinking coffee, chatting with the students in Spanish or reading the newspaper while their charges studied.

31

"How many students do we have?" Max asked.

"I'm not sure. We can't get the numbers right. One hundred forty-six have paid tuition, but the teachers claim more. And when we go to the classes to count them, there are always less. There used to be a lot more."

A bell rang somewhere, and the students scrambled out of the rooms and down the stairs. Max met the teachers in the hall. After expressing their happiness at receiving him, they began to list their complaints: when would they get a raise? When would the books arrive? Shouldn't they be paid overtime for grading exams? Max, being polite, missed Rosa's warning look as he acknowledged the merit of their requests, and agreed to consider them. As they went to the top floor to see the auditorium, Rosa spoke up: "It would be wise to be careful what you say when there are five teachers or more."

"Why?"

"It's something about the law, about the union. I don't know, but there were problems before. But maybe it's all right. You didn't know."

No, he hadn't known. Nor did he know how they could use the huge auditorium for anything at all when few of the lights worked, half the curtains were missing from the stage, and most of the folding chairs had pieces missing. "How did so many get broken?" he asked.

"Sometimes people get mad during concerts."

Max tried and failed to make sense of that.

Rosa shouted up to the projection room, and Max soon met Samuél and Hector, the elderly projectionist and his assistant. Samuél, who said he went by "Sam" because it sounded better for an American Center, looked sleepy, but he and Hector greeted him with respect.

"How many films do you show per month?" Max asked.

Sam shrugged. "When they send something from San Genesio, once or twice a month. But we don't decide that. We just run the projector."

"And the lights," added Hector, "when there's a concert or something, like when Mr. Harvey comes and plays with other musicians."

"Mr. Harvey?"

"Mr. Tyrone," Rosa said. "He's from the Embassy and sometimes he comes here and everyone has such a good time–he's so much fun and plays the balalaika so beautifully!" Hector and Sam nodded agreement.

A balalaika player from the Embassy? Max remembered a Harvey Tyrone identified as the Embassy's Cultural Officer in the information packet he'd received. The guy sounded interesting and he looked forward to meeting him.

As they returned to the ground floor, Juan and Manuel were duct-taping plywood to the broken door. "Will that tape hold?" asked Max.

"If we use screws, it will unhappily damage the aluminum frame," explained Manuel.

"I understand. However, this is not the first thing people should see of our Center. Please see about getting it replaced," he told Rosa and Manuel. "And give the bill to me." They all looked at him as if it were a strange order. He himself wondered if he'd regret the noble gesture when he saw the bill.

Manuel and Juan opened the other door to admit a group of people carrying paintings and sculptures. The newcomers nodded and smiled as they entered and headed for the stairway. Max looked at Rosa questioningly.

"Oh, they're using the exhibition hall tomorrow. They're from the *Colegio de Artes,* a high school that sort of specializes in art. We've always let them use the room for their exhibits."

"That's generous of us."

"They don't pay, but it doesn't cost us anything except for the lights. If they want drinks or anything, they bring them."

"I see." He liked the idea of the Center helping local students, at very little cost to itself. If he had no reason to feel proud of what wasn't his doing, he'd nonetheless share in the civic merit of it all.

"But of course you have to be there."

"I do?"

"The Director is always there! You're sort of the host, even if you're not, and it would be insulting not to go."

"Yes, I can see that." *My second day in Nueva Alcalá I'll host an art show. Talk about hitting the ground running!* He was also cheered by the photos that hung on walls everywhere. Most were group photos of young or old people smiling, almost always including one or more apparent Americans. In some of them, costumes or musical instruments or diplomas suggested the occasion for the photo, but all of them exuded goodwill. *Good stuff,* he thought. *Happy Americans and Engañadans sharing good times. Mutual understanding and friendship. Art shows for local students. Who wouldn't want to be part of it?*

Max heard noises of drawers and doors closing. "It's almost eight o'clock," Rosa noted.

"Right. Time to go home." Which reminded him that he had no home, hadn't even thought about where to stay. He asked.

"I'd try the *Hotel Alcalá.* It is about eight blocks away. It's the best one, except for the really expensive *Pensión de Engañada.* I'll call a taxi for you. Really, you can walk, but you have those suitcases."

While he waited for the cab, Max took a better look around his office. The paintings seemed a bit amateurish, but nice. The desk was large with spacious drawers, and his office even had a private bathroom. He went in to splash some water on his face and straighten his tie, noticing a small closet with a few coat hangers dangling from a bar. *Not sure why I need a closet, but probably there's a reason. Nothing like a private bathroom with closet to affirm your importance.*

Chapter Five: Everything's *Fine!*

Max's surprisingly expensive fourth-floor room at the Hotel Alcalá offered a view of tin roofs, an occasional church spire, and part of a narrow street where sand and gravel spread out in front of a building under construction. The dripping, noisy air conditioner kept him awake much of the night, despite his weariness after the long day. He had written a dutiful letter to his parents, assuring them he had arrived and all was well. He fell asleep in the fifth chapter of *For Whom the Bell Tolls*, awakened now and then by noises from cars, the kitchen, loud guests, or strange clunks from the air conditioner.

By morning he was determined to find an apartment soon, but in the meantime the dreary hotel was a short walk to work. The white *guayabera* he had bought the day before was more comfortable in the humid climate. It made perfect sense, hanging down outside the pants to let air circulate across one's back. With four large pockets, it served well year round. Descriptions of Engañada agreed that its proximity to the Equator meant little climate change throughout the year, though there was a rainy season in December and January.

The intrepid agent acclimated quickly, adopting native garb the better to throw off suspicion. He'd imagine the rest of the story later.

The lobby was a bit cleaner this morning than it had been yesterday. Max found Manuel, who was the custodial foreman by seniority, and asked him for a full walk-through of the building. He found most of the classrooms of decent size but depressing due to neglect. They could be fixed. All it took was money. Similarly, the auditorium was very large with a well-designed stage and fairly new equipment in the projection booth. It shouldn't cost too much to put the place in shape. The only frightening thing he saw was the fire escape that ran down the center of the building next to the elevator and was being used for storage. The stairways were cluttered with boxes, broken fans, and other things Max could not see clearly because most of the security lights were burned out. Imagining people falling down the stairs to be trapped in a fire he ordered the stuff cleared away at once and the light bulbs replaced. Manuel complimented him on his wise decision. Elsewhere, the dust and cigarette butts were far less evident than yesterday, and the air conditioner was working. As soon as Rosa arrived, Max asked her to get Jethro Jackson on the phone, then sat down to review the BNC *Guide* and its lists of reports he would have to send to San Genesio and Washington.

The most important reports dealt with 'contacts,' the local VIPs like the University Rector, who constituted his 'target audience.' The Guide encouraged him to cultivate these with visits and small gifts, in the hope of improving their understanding of the U.S. *If they understand us,* the Guide seemed confident, *they will approve of our policies. To know us is to love us.*

Max worked for about an hour sorting mail and learning about reports; then the interruptions began. First, people stepped in to say *Buenos días;* then they returned for *consultas,* asking him questions he could not answer except where the answer was so obvious that he wondered why they had asked. (*Yes, Manuel, check the valves to see if they are causing the leak in the third-floor bathroom. What am I going to say? "No, ignore the damn leak"?*) The librarian wanted to consult about the book orders from the Embassy. Luis Verde came in with a notary public and bank forms for Max to sign. Rosa tried not to bother him with petty things, but kept him informed of her inability to get through to San Genesio, and brought him dozens of letters to sign. For example: a regretful 'no' to a rural school principal requesting band instruments and/or free English classes for all his students. "Everyone thinks the American government supports us," Rosa explained, "and that we have rooms full of dollars." Mariana had taught her how to write polite refusals.

Then came a steady stream of people from within and without the Center. Parents stopped by to complain that their children's teachers were lazy, rude, incompetent, or simply absent. One little old man walked in claiming to have worked in Chicago forty years before and demanded his Social Security check. Max gave him the phone number of the Embassy Consular Section, which probably didn't handle such things, but would know who did. Nonetheless, Max managed to work his way through important and fascinating government circulars such as the *BNC Guide: Change in Section VIII, Para. 7, Library Procurement.*

Still, he wondered if he'd ever get through the mail. There were kilograms of advertisements for English teaching materials. *Are you still using outdated ESL methods? Give your students the modern electronic system developed by Dr. Harriet Feely and already in use at leading universities everywhere!* Ads from publishers and insurance companies and furniture dealers. The letters from creditors were more alarming. But it was all paper, and Max knew how to handle paper: route it to the appropriate office, to the Academic Department or the accountant or wherever. Yet he was tempted to answer some letters himself, if only for the fun of it:

San José (California)
US of A
March 6
Centro Engañada of American Culture
Casilla B-3459
Alcalá, South America

Dear Sir or madame whom it May Concern:

I am 22 and just got my BA in Spanish with a TOEFL (Teaching English as a foreign language) miner from Calstate and would like some practicle experience teaching native spanish speakers as I hope to into teaching in California. I am interested in teaching at the Alcalá center as I feel this would give me real life teaching situations which would be very useful and also because I am very interested in increasing mutual understanding and really seeing other cultures as I feel when people really know each other as persons they don't start wars and I personally feel that peace is very important.

If there are any position at your instition please let me know as I will send my curruclum viti and my transcripts. I speak fluent Spanish and am a native speaker of English. Also please tell me how much my salary will be as I don't have much money. Also if you could provide information about housing and the health situation like the water I would really appreciate it as I feel this is very important when a person is trying to teach professionally.

Sincerely yours,
Cheryl Fletcher

P.S. I hope you can pay my airfare down, I don't have much money.

Why, certainly, Miss Fletcher. Just brush up on your English spelling and come on down. Our last native speaker just died of typhus.

Just then Rosa announced a call from San Genesio. "Maybe the lines work better when you call from there," she shrugged. Max scribbled "Thanks no thanks" in the margin, and without further consideration, marked it for Braden's action. Surely the guy knew how to write a letter.

He was only a little nervous at speaking for the first time to his new boss, the head of Embassy Press and Cultural Affairs and the man who would write his efficiency reports. Yet his sense of relief was far stronger than his nervousness. *Now I can find out just what I'm supposed to do and how to report it. The* Guide *can say what it will, but it won't write any reports.*

The line crackled, then a clear voice came through. "Hello?

This Lacey? Max Lacey? You there?"

"Right. Lacey here. Good to talk to you, Mr. Jackson."

"Then why inna hell you didn't call? That's first thing you shoulda done, boy! They told me you arriving yesterday and I was waiting."

"I know. I tried as soon as I got here and we've been trying all morning, but the phones..."

"That's what I figured. Only thing surprises me about the phone system here is when it works. When you in this country long as me, you won't be surprised at nothin'. Say, how things down there?"

"Well, mostly all right, but–"

"They damn well better be. You know old Grimaldi, he left that Center in good shape, real good shape. Got all his reports in on time, just did one hell of a job down there. Had a bunch of exhibits and concerts and stuff. I ain't sure how much good they do but centers are supposed to have 'em, and he sure did. Don't want you messing it up, hear? Don't want that Center turn into no hangout for a bunch of hippies and weirdoes and radicals like some I seen, looking like a damn circus."

"No, I sure don't want to—"

"Good. Well, we real glad have you there and anything I can do for you, you just let me know, hear?"

"Fine. As a matter of fact, I found some problems. Like the air-conditioning. I don't know yet what it will cost, but—"

"Hold on just damn minute. Now that's one thing I don't want to hear about, Center need money for this and somethin' else. Ain't got no money for that. No way in the world, you understand? I mean like if they ain't sending your mail or if your Mamma die or something–your Mamma alive?"

"Yes, just fine—"

"Well, something like that, get you a ticket real fast. Got funds for that. You know we have a string quartet from somewhere coming next month? Going to your place first then up here. Want everything arranged right. Make sure you set up straight-backed chairs! You give these people the wrong chair, they raise a fuss. Anyway, them damn centers got to pay their own way. This ain't the Johnson Administration, you know! You just got to raise prices or whatever else you have to do, maybe fire some of them people there, got too many anyhow. But don't come cryin' to me about no center money problems which you shouldn't have anyhow 'cause Grimaldi tole me he left that place in real A-1 first-class shape and even Harvey Tyrone, for whatever that's worth, tells me the place is just great so I don't want to hear about no problems, you got that?"

"I think I do." *Well, if a balalaika player says it's just great, it must be so.*

"All right. Now when you coming up here to say hello to the Ambassador like you're supposed to?"

"Well, just as soon as—"

"All right. Don't screw around about it too long. Gotta place to live?"

"Right. No, not yet. And it'd be real pleasure have you come on down here, Mr. Jackson." *Why am I picking up his accent? What the hell's wrong with me?*

"Uh-uh. No sirree. No way! I been to that god-forsaken stinkhole twice, and I ain't going again if I can help it. Catch a damn disease getting off the plane. You watch yourself, hear?"

As Max promised to watch himself, the line went dead. Rosa advised him it was unlikely they could get through again. *Fine,* he thought. *I've had enough of Jackson for today.* But he had only two clear orders: don't bother the Embassy about money problems, and keep doing reports and exhibits. Even after one day he knew there was more to it than that. He wished he knew just what.

Before he could worry too much, Manuel came in to ask for an employee loan to cover costs for a child "to whom a fever had fallen, my little Angelita who is so brave and never cries, she has the same fever that took my poor godson Hector to be with the angels." It wasn't much, just a few hundred *honores*, and the idea made him feel good as he signed the request form that Manuel presented. Then the door burst open anew to admit a tall slim young woman with brown hair flying in all directions, wearing paint-splattered jeans and a denim work shirt. He stood as she entered, but she waved them both to the sofa.

"Meester Lacey! You're Meester Lacey! I'm Gloria the Cultural Assistant and I'm so sorry I wasn't here when you came but I was so busy in my studio that you don't believe it there's the *Exposición de los arboles* next month I've still got two pictures I haven't finished them yet and I don't know how I can get them done but I will somehow one of them it's an oil is all right I guess but I can't get the balance just how I want it on top. But it's so good you're here in time for the exhibit that it's the most important one of the whole year and you can meet all the artists and everybody and we have to set up the exhibit–our own, I mean, not the *Arboles* one–here, that we haven't had one for months and we're lucky though because guess who's agreed to have an exhibit here? Luis Delgado! And it would be all arranged but that stupid Lucho—Lucho Verde the accountant?–he said no but he always says that and anyway it will only cost with drinks and transporting the things—you have to rent a truck—and some little canapés to eat that we've got to have or everyone always says why is the American Center so cheap that they spend billions on bombs but they don't even give you a drink? Anyway I've got it all figured out and all I need is your okay and I'm so glad you like the idea and it will be the best—but, do you have a place to live yet?"

Stunned by the silence, he delayed a moment. "No. No, I don't. And you're the Cultural Assis—"

"That's right I was hired by Mr. Bell he was here before Mr. Grimaldi such a nice man and he knew everybody in Alcalá but oh *que cosa!* You know Elena Gutiérrez? She's moving out of her apartment, it's the nicest in the city right over the river, to move in—¡*que escándalo!*–with Bernardo Juárez that he was and he really still is married to her best friend Silvia Montero and they almost got into a fight last week in the market! Anyway in a week or two we can see it and I know it will be perfect but first could you initial these? They're estimates for the moving and the drinks– we get it cheaper this way–for the exhibit and then I'll arrange everything with Lucho. Really the Center will get so much prestige from this exhibit–oh! Here's one more to initial. Do you like poetry? Thank you. Anyway there's a wonderful poet here,

Simón Bolívar Blanco Gonzales, who'd love to give a reading at the exhibit shall I tell him or maybe you'd like to meet him?"

"A poet?"

Gloria babbled on, but Max wasn't listening to her so much as to his own reactions. *Okay. What my office needs is a push-button mechanism that would either lower a soundproof glass bell over the woman or dump her through a trap door. She's pretty; nice lively gray eyes. Not as attractive as Rosa, though.*

Max wanted to be fair, and admitted that at least she had energy and ideas. She'd just arranged an art show. Jackson wanted them, so Max was right to approve those expenses. She seemed to know the artists and in fact was one of them. She might find him an apartment.

Listening now and again, he learned that Washington Maldonado was "the Activities Director you know that we coordinate everything because he has to get the rooms ready but sometimes he forgets and makes me so mad!" Maldonado was presently on vacation, but expected back shortly. The local Archbishop was a nice old man whom Lacey would have to meet, but very conservative and troubled by the young liberal priests, whom some said were Communists, but it wasn't true; "they just want to give the money to poor who need it or something." The artists were divided into camps loyal to Moscow, Peking, or Havana, and fought among themselves, especially since the last elections at the university, which the Maoists had won. There had been gunfights. "And one of them almost died that he was shot right in the Medical School!"

Even Gloria had to stop for breath sometimes. Max observed, "We have an exhibit tonight, or the Art School has one."

"Oh yes but they're not really artists just students but some of them will be artists and so many have had exhibits here and they're so grateful even when they become Maoists or something and denounce us and oh did I say you've got to call on the Rector of the University soon?"

The University of the OK Corral? "Please pick a day when there are no gunfights."

"Oh, that almost never happens!" After mentioning

something about a string quartet that was coming soon, Gloria finally fluttered off to contract a truck, or add some orange, or something. Then Max shut his eyes for a few moments until Rosa came through the door connecting their two offices.

"You met Gloria," she observed.

"Yes," he smiled. "I think that was her."

"It was. Now Lucho Verde wants to see you. Should I say you're busy?"

He didn't feel much like having another interview but if there were financial problems, he needed to know. And if there were no problems, it would put his mind at ease. "No, I'll see him."

Luis Verde came in carrying several file folders, nodded to Lacey and sat down without invitation. He looked pretty much as Max expected an accountant to look–balding, thin nose, beady eyes, wire glasses and a pale careful face. Only a pot belly differed from the stereotype. Max thought his countenance ratlike, then banished the uncharitable thought.

"Mr. Lacey, there are some things we should review."

"Yes," Max agreed. "I wanted to see you about the financial picture. I understand we're short of cash at the moment, that we have no money to fix the air conditioner, for instance?"

Verde chuckled. "No, not at the moment and not in the foreseeable future."

"Oh." *So much for putting my mind at ease.* "What seems to be the problem?"

The accountant held up a memo. "You want to loan San Martín five hundred *honores?*"

Max recognized his initials on the form and remembered Manuel's sad face. "Yes," he told Verde. "We really had no choice. You see, his little girl is sick and they don't have medicine–or clothes, either. The same disease already killed his godson Hector. We can hardly just turn him down for something like that, can we?"

Verde sighed. "Mr. Lacey, San Martín's godson Hector is nineteen years old and works here as an assistant projectionist."

"Ah," Max said, staring at Verde. *I met a Hector.* "Ahh."

"But you are not the first to loan money for poor little

Martita."

"I thought it was Angelita?"

"Manuel must be getting old. He borrowed money to bury Angelita two directors ago. She's married to one of our teachers now."

"I see. Well, I guess we'll just forget about that loan, then." *Should I feel more amazed at Manuel's nerve, or angry at his lying to play on the new guy?* "Are you sure?"

"Yes. And anyway, we don't have the money to loan him."

Max rubbed his chin. "We don't have the money to loan him," he repeated, "and we don't have the money to fix the air conditioner. Do we have money for anything?"

"We have," answered Verde, pushing his glasses up on his nose and opening one of his files, "enough to pay salaries for this month, and the light bill, the water, and probably the telephone."

"All right. I suppose there are other bills?"

Verde grinned maliciously. "Yes, there are. For example, the Social Security contribution of forty-five thousand *honores*, more or less. For example, the donation to the firemen of twenty thousand *honores*. For—"

"We make donations?"

"Required donations. In Engañada, fire and police protection and other services are regarded as civic rights for which people cannot be taxed. So a system of donations has been developed. We have also to pay the Birthday Bonus, a month's salary on the employee's birthday. This month we have only two, and fortunately one is only partial since young San Martín is under twenty-three and has been with us only a year."

"Birthday Bonus?"

"Formerly," Verde explained, "and still in some parts of the country, it was the custom for the *patrón* to give his *obreros* a gift on their saints' days, but after the unions were formed they said this was a patronizing custom, and that rather than receive such payments as gifts from the exploiting *patrón,* the workers should have them as a legal right. The details were worked out in, I think, Espejo's seventh term. Also, they decided that saints' days were a vestige of clerical domination, and changed it to birthdays. The

Church opposed this, naturally."

"Naturally. Anyway, we don't have much money?"

"No, we don't." He gave a dizzying recitation of bills due and soon to be due. There were mortgage payments, "we mortgaged the entire property in order to pay for the new addition," and a required bonus called the 'thirteenth salary' due at the beginning of the school year, of insurance premiums and bills for cleaning supplies, of provision for contributions to policemen and garbage men and for the obligatory fourteenth salary payable at Christmas. Max indicated that he had the idea, but Verde went remorselessly on: payments on various loans taken out for various purposes, such as repair of the air conditioning system, payments on the furniture in Lacey's office, and a two-thousand-dollar debt to the U.S. publisher of the English textbooks. Until that was paid, the Center couldn't order any more textbooks. "I don't blame them," Verde allowed. "It's been pending for more than a year."

"Right," Max agreed. "Seems fair. But look, I understood the Center was in good shape. In fact, Mr. Jackson said so just today when I talked to him. He said Harvey Tyrone, the Cultural Officer, confirmed it."

"Mr. Jackson doesn't keep the books, and knows only what he has been told. And Mr. Tyrone—" Verde sighed, "has never shown any interest in financial matters. There are, of course, ways of making things look better than they are." Verde described the overdraft privilege at the bank–in effect, short-term loans–which they had used to cover deficits caused by, among other things, an increasing number of payments on long-term loans. "These and a few other maneuvers have allowed us to keep the doors open."

Max leaned back in the armchair on which money was owed, thinking it was as well to know the hard reality. More importantly, he needed to get it on the record: it all happened before his time.

But how can I get it on the record when Jackson insists the record says everything is fine? To go back and correct the record, to show that the place had been a disaster, would make Jackson look incompetent. At best I'd take him down with me. A polite cough from Verde interrupted his meditations.

"Excuse me," Max said. "So tell me now, how much do we

need?"

"You mean short or long-term?"

"Both."

"Short term...a million *honores,* say. Long-term: if someone gave us ten million we'd be all right. Unless, of course, enrollment kept declining. If that happened, ten million wouldn't be sufficient."

"Are you going to tell me about another problem?" Max asked with a sad smile.

"No, I'm merely going to explain the cause. Our expenses haven't gone up so much as income has gone down. We have maybe twenty percent of the students we had ten years ago."

"Why did it go down? And what can we do to get it back up?" Max knew the question was pointless: if Verde knew, Grimaldi probably would have known too, and the problem wouldn't exist.

Sure enough, Verde only shrugged before pointing out another problem. "We also lose money on the cafeteria."

"Oh? Well, it did seem there were more employees than students when I stopped by there yesterday."

"That's not always the case." Verde said, in a tone of generous concession. "But since it closes for lunch, they don't sell much except coffee and soft drinks and pastries."

"What do you mean, they close for lunch?"

"Raymundo Martínez prefers to eat lunch at home. He says students go home as well, so there'd be no point in staying open."

"Then why do we have a cafeteria at all?"

Another shrug. "It's always been there. It didn't always lose money. When there were more students, they sold enough to at least pay the salaries."

"Looks sort of hopeless, then," Max observed.

Verde nodded his assent. "From a strictly logical point of view, the most plausible course would be to sell the building."

"And what becomes of the Center?"

Verde's voice took on eagerness. "These figures suggest that the best hope for the Center is to declare bankruptcy and dissolve. That way you can dismiss employees–possibly–and then begin anew with a slight name change on a smaller scale."

Max frowned. He didn't become Director to preside over the dissolution of the Center. "Can't we do something else? I mean, do you have to go bankrupt to dismiss people? I don't want to fire anyone, but it's obvious we have too many people here. The cafeteria is the perfect example. If otherwise we'll go broke, and everyone loses his job—or hers..."

Verde laughed. "Very true, and I believe you do things that way in the United States. But here, Mr. Lacey, it is very difficult to fire anyone and very expensive even to try except under very special circumstances. And no, imminent bankruptcy is not one of them. After three months, the worker acquires a proprietorship in his employment, and you cannot take it from him without paying a large compensation. It's far cheaper to keep them."

O.K. I wouldn't enjoy firing anyone. "But why are you and I the only ones to know all this about the bills and the rest? How did Jackson get the idea everything was fine?"

Verde shrugged again. "You'll have to talk to Mr. Gandig, Mr. Henry Gandig. He's the Board Treasurer and prepares the annual statement. The accounting company that prepares the audit belongs to his brother-in-law. I just give them my figures."

"Well, doesn't he know, for the love of God? With these figures?"

"Mr. Gandig and I interpret figures differently. He has shown no interest in discussing the matter with me." Verde turned his face away, but it didn't hide his wounded pride.

"Oh. Well, Mr. Verde, I would be grateful if you would send me copies of these various statements. Thank you for coming to see me. Even," he smiled, "with bad news.

After Verde left, Max stepped into Rosa's office to ask that she make an appointment with Gandig.

"Is next Friday all right?" she called through the door in a few minutes. "That's the earliest he can see you."

"I guess it will have to be, then." With luck, no disaster would happen in the meantime. Still, sooner would be better: Mariana Guzmán of all the answers was gone, Jethro Jackson didn't know or want to know the questions, and Verde offered

47

only gloom. Surely Gandig was the man. Rosa said he was a big businessman, very rich. He'd have the answers. Wouldn't he?

At noon, Max took Rosa's suggestion to try the small restaurant two blocks away. After a fine lunch of chicken and rice, he returned to his study of the Center's financial problems based on Verde's material. At five o'clock Rosa told him he should get ready.

"Get ready?"

"For the art exhibit. You really should wear a suit. They sort of expect it from the *Señor Director.*"

That meant a long walk to and from the hotel. Now he knew why the bathroom had a closet.

When Max returned properly dressed, he found the Center exhibit room already crowded with high-school students and parents, plus Gloria. They seemed happy to see him. Inexperienced as he was, Max understood he shouldn't take it personally: they were happy to have a U.S. representative lend dignity and importance to the kids' artwork. "Max Lacey" was just the guy in the role. Still, he was happy to play that role.

When the room was well crowded, he got up on the little riser and delivered the careful bland speech he had prepared, welcoming one and all to the Center and congratulating the students on their wonderful paintings. The attendees seemed pleased. The art was typical high school-level stuff, drawings and clay statues, but children and parents and teachers seemed enthusiastic. Even so, he welcomed Gloria's assurance that he could leave after an hour. "After all, it's their exhibit and you're really just a guest even though you're the host."

Perfect description of my whole assignment.

Chapter Six: Square Meters and the Human Spirit

Ten days later, on the morning of his appointment with Gandig, Max felt a bit better about things. His daily walks through the Center had apparently inspired Manuel and others to keep the place in better order. He had finally cleared out all the junk mail that had waited for him in his office. By questioning Rosa or Verde or Gloria, he had gotten a clearer sense of just what had been going on at the Center–the exhibits, the English program, and the eternal problems or plumbing and air conditioning. The arrival from the Embassy of *The Good, the Bad, and the Ugly* had let him see what movie nights looked like, and to appreciate Sam's skill (or Hector's) in changing reels quickly on the one projector. The auditorium was nearly full, even for a film a few years old. Probably the studios didn't license embassies and centers to show free films in competition with local distributors. No matter: it was still a good movie. The dubbing was impressive with some Mexican sounding more like Clint Eastwood than did Eastwood himself.

And now that I sort of know what we do, what should we change? How can we attract more students? Cut tuition and hope to come out ahead on volume? Surely businessman Gandig will have more suggestions.

Wearing a suit, he arrived early at the waiting room of Gandig Consolidated. The office was on the sixteenth and top story of a new building. Max wondered if this were Alcalá's highest building; he saw none taller. The atmosphere brought to mind a Manhattan skyscraper's office waiting area, with its sumptuous furnishings and decor. Sitting on the rich leather couch, glancing at a copy of *Fortune* and watching the pretty secretary at her IBM typewriter, he almost forgot he was in Engañada.

Gandig's office was even larger and more luxurious than the waiting room, with a conference table and bar at one end. The sun smiled benignly through tinted sealed windows. Max looked out at the city as he waited for Gandig to get off the phone.

"Sorry to keep you waiting. Sit down." The tall, gaunt, balding man shook hands and smiled briefly with perfectly capped teeth. His starched white shirt showed how comfortable life could be when the air conditioning worked consistently. "So, welcome to Alcalá. Guess we'll have to have a board meeting soon. What can I do for you?"

"Thank you. Well, I was talking to Luis Verde, the accountant, and it seems we have money problems–"

"Oh, crap! That old woman is always–excuse me." Something had buzzed. Gandig picked up the phone, pushed a button, said "all right" and pushed another button. "Hi, Harry. How's the weather up there?"

Max tried not to listen to the discussion of units and deliveries. He scanned the paintings on the wall, noting a particularly large one with bright and dull colors alternating in no order that he could understand. It was signed *Gloria.* Of the other paintings, about half were Latin American scenes: villages, churches, burros, *campesinos.* The rest looked American, mostly sailing ships. He heard Gandig hang up.

"Nice pictures you've got here. Is that *Gloria* our Gloria Córdova in the Center?"

"Which?"

"The big one there."

"I guess so. My secretary picked them out. Anyway, Luis Verde is worrying you about money, right? Don't pay any attention to him: he knows next to nothing about business. But then, I suppose you don't either?"

"Well, no. I had a course once–"

"The important things are net worth, liquidity, and debt. At least for a non-profit place like the Center, all that matters is whether you're worth more this year than last, and that's where inflation helps you."

"Ah," Max said as if he understood. "Inflation."

The door opened and the secretary brought in a pile of papers for Gandig's attention. As he signed or initialed them, he continued Max's education. "That building has about tripled in value since the new wing was built, and even though the mortgage payments are indexed, the inflation on property is higher than the index. The building is worth more than the Center's debts, so anytime you wanted to sell out, you could pay off all debts and come out ahead. You'd want to go through bankruptcy to reduce the staff, which is way too big. Maybe you should think about that. Of course, the Board would decide, but it would make it easier if the idea came from you, which would mean the Embassy agrees. Probably make you look good," he added, giving Max a sort of conspiratorial look. "The Embassy would be glad to have done with all the headaches."

If Gandig's cynical recommendation surprised Max, so too did his own hurt reaction. "I didn't come here to undo all the work people have done for the Center over the years. In any case, we need a big space for the exhibits and everything."

Gandig stared at Max for a few seconds and then shrugged. "I have as much sentiment for the Center as anyone, but if the community won't support it, why break your neck? Meanwhile, you have to keep borrowing on the increased value of the place, pay off the older mortgages and service the new one. We've done it twice and just did it again. You'll have another million *honores* next week."

"I will? Oh. Good. I see," Max fibbed, glad that the Board Treasurer seemed confident, and that a million honores were on their way.

"So," Gandig asked, signing the last paper and gathering up the whole bundle, then bouncing them into order on the desk, "what's the problem?"

"Well, Verde says–maybe he exaggerates, but this is what he says–that we have all these bills coming due, and we don't have enough money because enrollment keeps dropping. But then, he didn't know about the million."

Gandig nodded impatiently. "Of course, if the market collapses–that's what I meant by the community not supporting you–then you've got a problem servicing the debt, and you're not viable. I've told the Board that. Maybe they'll listen to you.

51

You've got to get revenue above operating expenses over the long haul. So you can try to get your share of the market back from all those new English academies or do something else."

"Like what?"

"Well," Gandig went on, as if Max weren't getting it, "like I say, that building is a resource. You've got to optimize resources."

The phone buzzed again. Gandig leaned back in his chair and spoke to "Bernardo" about write-offs and foreign tax credits. Max thought about marketing, and how to optimize his resources. Gandig finally put down the phone, stood up, and began stuffing papers into a briefcase. "So, everything clear?"

"I guess so. The million takes care of the immediate problem, and we should get busy with those resources. Do you have any ideas?"

Gandig walked over to a wall and pushed. A door popped open revealing a small closet. He took out an expensive-looking gray jacket and put it on. "You've got two basic resources there: people and space. You've got to use that space. Get enrollment up so your teachers produce. If that's impossible, and you want to keep on with cultural stuff, then you should think about selling out and getting something smaller."

"Space?" asked Max, his mind running in a new direction as he followed the executive into the outer office.

"Right. Simple square meters." Gandig stopped at his secretary's desk to say he'd be at the Union Club, then rejoined Max. "Every square meter costs you so much and should produce so much."

A young Engañadan in a gray suit much like Gandig's joined them, shifting a briefcase to take Max's hand as Gandig introduced them: "Max Lacey, Jorge Pinzón, Marketing Manager. Max is the new Director of the Center."

There was no time for pleasantries as Gandig at once got into an intense discussion of "moving things" as they took the elevator down. On the sidewalk, Gandig turned from Pinzón for just a moment. "Good luck. I'm always ready to help." Max barely heard him over the street noise, and shouted his thanks, but the two businessmen had already turned away.

Max loosened his tie and took off his coat as he walked back to the Center, wondering what stupidity kept these businessmen wearing the damn things when the airy *guayabera* made such fundamental sense.

How many students could he put in a square meter? Where to get them? TV ads? *'English is the language of business and travel, and it's fun to learn at the modern* Centro!*'* No. Boring. He could imagine ten thousand potential students changing channels. Maybe a busy international airport with a guy asking directions in Spanish of a ravishing French or Polynesian girl. *She turns away. A taller, better-dressed fellow approaches and asks directions in English, whereupon she smilingly offers to show him to Gate 24. They walk off arm-in-arm, while the first guy mutters that he too should have studied English at the* Centro Engañado-Americano.

Max himself could appear in these ads. Maybe with Rosa. She wouldn't have to speak much English. It might work. But what does television advertising cost? *And why am I even wondering about TV advertising? That isn't what the Foreign Service is supposed to be about!*

And yet, he thought as he dodged around a dozen housewives bargaining simultaneously with a fruit stand vendor, *maybe it is*. The Foreign Service makes all sorts of demands on people; that's why it's such an elite service. Maybe that meant he had to become an aggressive businessman and a creative advertising director. Hard-nosed and energetic, immersed in the real world. And with another million *honores* to work with, there was no reason he couldn't bring it off. Max arrived at the Center in an upbeat mood.

Manuel opened the unbroken door as Max came up the steps. Workers he'd never seen were replacing the glass in the other. "Many people await the Señor Director," he warned.

Max smiled his way through a hall full of grinning old men and one fat scowling woman. The latter followed him into his office where Rosa, entering from the other door, looked as if the worst had happened.

"I yam *Doctora* Esperanza Romero Ycaza," the woman began suddenly in loud English. "You haf 'eard of me." Her shrill voice filled the room, just as her two hundred sagging pounds in a bright floral print dress dominated the office. She glared at Max through thick glasses in a pink frame.

"Ahh," said Max, looking an interrogatory to Rosa, who replied in Spanish.

"The same one you asked about the other day, Mr. Lacey. The Regional Secretary of the Department of Child Development."

"*Por supuesto.*" Back in English he said, "Well, a pleasure to meet you, *Señora.*"

"Señorita!" she corrected, as if he were to blame. "I sit down." And she did.

"Yes, please. Have a seat. Now then, what can–"

"You know that I am Doctora Esperanza Romero Ycaza, *doctorada* in development of the child in University of Edaho, United Estates, *altamente calificada* in *profesión!*" She waved a finger at him.

"I'm sure you are," Max agreed. "Very highly qualified. Yes. Well, and I hope things are well with the Department of Children. It must keep you very busy."

"The work it go terrible! Idiots around me! I don't haf a car. I don't haf enough secretary. I don't haf money and my salary a disgrace to someone like me *doctorada* in United Estates! So child development terrible–the people know nothing!"

Max made sympathetic noises.

"So I gif lectures here. I gif first lecture what the child think. Also I talk about the psychology of the child when he repressed. Also the environment of the house so important in the oral stage. For this I get five thousand *honores* the lecture. I use the lecture hall."

"Well..." Max began.

"The lecture hall you will clean it first. It filthy."

She settled back and continued to glare at him as he explained, first, that the lecture hall was not filthy; he himself had seen that it was cleaned. Secondly, the condition of the Center would not permit him to make any promises right now, though of course he understood the importance of such lectures. Her eyebrows arched, pulling one of her chins up after them.

"This is a North American center, no?"

"Well, it's an Engañadan-American Center. But surely a hospital or a school would be more appropriate?"

"Ha! You think those people understand about the child psychology? I go there. Nobody do it. You do it here: this is American technology I bring from United Estates. How you not do it in the American Center?"

Max wished he'd put on his tie and coat instead of draping them over the back of the sofa: after this ambush, he needed all the dignity he could muster. Nor did he know with whom he was dealing—a frustrated minor bureaucrat, or someone with pull? *When in doubt, stall.*

"I see your point," he said, flipping through a calendar on his desk, imagining appointments for the blank pages. "Next month we're full. Possibly June...no, we have something in from the States on the twenty-fifth. Suppose I let you know?"

"June twenty-fif you say?" She had taken out a notebook and pen.

"No, no. That date is already taken. I'll let you know."

"*Bueno,* June twenty-fif. I make lecture."

"No!" *Either she's dense as lead, or she's pretending to misunderstand.* "I said *not* the twenty-fifth. I can't give you any date! I'll let you..."

As he spoke, *Doctora* Esperanza Romero Ycaza left the office in triumph, if not satisfaction.

Well, at least the unpleasant scene can wait until June.

"I wanted to tell you," Rosa said when the door had closed, "she also writes in *La Voz del Pueblo* and is something, sort of a local reporter, for Associated Press."

"I'm sure she's highly qualified," Max grinned. It struck him that lately his conversations in English had mostly been unpleasant, while those in Spanish were courteous even when difficult, as with Verde. He was happy to stick with the local language now.

"Oh yes," Rosa giggled. "But there are other people waiting, the men from the Alcalá Patriotic Historical Society and also the poet, Simón Bolívar Blanco. I think you can see them all at once.

They probably just want to say hello."

"Hmm. Okay, I guess. But tell me something: does everyone just drop in like this? Doesn't anyone call for an appointment?"

"Not usually. But you must see the men from the Society! The Center has always been open to everyone. If you refused to see them on their visit to welcome you, it would insult them terribly!"

"Right. Just let me put on my dignity here." His shirt collar was clammy with sweat, and the tie didn't want to stay centered. Rosa straightened it for him and went to open the door.

The old men filed in, shaking Max's hand warmly. He didn't retain any of the names, which seemed to leapfrog over each other. They formed a semicircle in front of the sofa. None could have been less than sixty years old; the most distinguished, a patriarchal figure with flowing white hair, stepped forward as spokesman.

"We, Mr. Lacey, are the Directorate of the *Sociedad Historica Patriotica Alcaleña,* come to welcome you to Alcalá both on our own initiative and at the suggestion of our mutual friend and fellow member, Luis Gonzales Carvallo. We find, by happy chance, that we are joined today by a man you will have been very eager to meet, the finest poet of Alcalá and indeed of all Engañada, the most worthy Simón Bolívar Blanco!"

They applauded while Max smiled, and inferred that the sad-faced little guy at the end, who wasn't applauding, must be the poet, surely the same one Gloria had mentioned.

"Thank you very much, Mr..."

"Caballero. Jorge Caballero Pristino."

"Bueno, Mr. Caballero. Thank you. This is very good of you. Really. Won't you please sit down, all of you?"

"In a moment. First permit me, in the name of the Directorate, to request that our *vocal,* Dr. Jaime Alfonso Espejo San Martín, read the Society's official resolution of welcome." He nodded to one of the others, who went to the door and snapped his fingers. The man returned with a photographer who began taking photos from various angles. Then the portliest of the group, evidently the *vocal,* pushed his few stringy white hairs back on his head, put on a pair of half-frame reading glasses, stepped forward and unrolled a scroll from which he began to read with deep gravity:

"*Considering:* that the Alcalá Patriotic Historical Society has as its most sacred object the encouragement of patriotism among all Engañadans and a deeper appreciation of the glorious culture with which Engañadan history is replete, and

"*Considering:* that the *Centro Engañado-Americano*, notable representative of the great sister Republic of the North, has always and in every way lent assistance to the Society in furtherance of its aims, and

"*Considering:* that it is the will of the Society that this cooperation continue and grow to even more notable successes, and

"*Considering:* that the esteemed and honorable Señor Max Lacey has assumed the noble office of Director of said Centro, be it therefore

"*Resolved:* that the Directorate of the Alcalá Patriotic Historical Society call upon the said Señor Lacey and extend to him and to his esteemed spouse, the estimable and chaste Señora...Mr. Lacey, your wife's name? We couldn't find it, unfortunately."

"I'm not married."

"Oh. Well then...call upon him–no, extend to him, the most cordial and warm fraternal embrace of welcome to our beloved city, and be it further

"*Resolved:* that the Directorate of the said Society cordially invite Mr. Lacey to join us as Honorary President, as did his several illustrious predecessors in his esteemed office.

"Given this Twenty-first Day of April in the City of Nueva Alcalá.

"*Certified:*

"Jorge Caballero Pristino, President
"Manuel Angel Suárez Caballero, Vice President
"Dr. Jaime Alfonso Espejo San Martín, Vocal

57

"Guillermo Pristino Espejo, Treasurer
"Arquitecto José San Martín Suárez, Secretary

"I have spoken."

They all applauded, then each embraced Lacey and shook his hand again. The *Vocal* grandly presented him with the corrected scroll. Manuel appeared with a tray of drinks, inspiring Caballero to propose a toast:

"That our esteemed friend and colleague Max Lacey may have every success in his tenure as Director of the *Centro Engañado-Americano*, and that the laces of amity and understanding which have long joined our two sister republics may be strengthened and enlarged through our joint efforts!"

They all drank to that hope. Max smiled broadly, laughing inwardly at his role but also touched by their friendliness. There was a sudden silence and everyone looked at him. Rosa, behind the others, pointed at him and silently mouthed, *your turn.*

"Ahem," he began, wondering what level of absurdity would show the proper respect. "Esteemed Mr...." he glanced at the scroll they had given him. "Mr. Caballero, admirable Mr. Angel–no, Suárez. Dr. Espejo, *Vocal.* Mr. Treasurer Pristino and *Arquitecto* José San Martín Suárez. Gentlemen: it is with a, ah, profound sense of...obligation and deep pleasure that I, uh, receive this distinguished delegation of the distinguished *Sociedad Patriotica Historica de Alcalá,* which has so distinguished itself in its distinguish–in its extraordinary work of promoting so many good things." He felt himself blushing, but the group seemed pleased and attentive.

"I have long heard of the excellent work of the distinguished society," he went on, wondering at once why he had invented this lie, but happy that they beamed. "So it is with a profound sense of humility that I find myself here, in the company of gentlemen and patriots who have distinguished themselves not only here in Alcalá but throughout Engañada and even..."

Max had the curious sensation that he was outside all this, watching some little-known and dangerous aspect of his personality taking control.

"And even," the aspect continued, "throughout the Americas. And so, gentlemen, it is therefore for me today a high honor and a low–excuse me, a deep pleasure to accept your invitation to join in your patriotic and historic labors, and I pray only that, with the help of the Highest, I may be worthy of this honor that you upon me today so graciously bestow. Thank you."

Their enthusiastic applause joined with the pride, shame, cynicism and cheer roiling inside him to strive for his attention.

More Scotch appeared. They toasted Max, who toasted them in return. All toasted the Republic of Engañada, the United States, and the friendship between the two countries. Architect Suárez suggested a toast to past Center Directors and "to our old friend and supporter Harvey Tyrone," when Max found his glass empty. Another bottle of Scotch appeared at once, brought not by Manuel but by a slim worldly-looking young guy wearing a green *guayabera* and sunglasses. As he deftly filled Lacey's glass he smiled and said, "Hi! Washington Maldonado."

"A very great honor surely," Max smiled back.

Then Guillermo Pristino offered a toast in which he noted that the honorable representative of the dynamic and democratic Colossus of the North was in a unique position to implement his well-known and selfless dedication to the sacred ends which they all held so dear. All drank heartily to this proposition. Max answered in turn that on this, one of the truly great, truly ineffable occasions, words failed adequately to express his deep sense of gratitude or the totality of his devotion to the ends so nobly described by the honorable Treasurer. He realized he'd drunk too much when he found himself sitting down, about to hear a poem by Simón Bolívar Blanco, without remembering how this had come about.

The quiet little man stood with his back to the door. His voice was surprisingly powerful as he boomed out:

"Where?" he cried, "Where are the beetles of my childhood,
Those that through the long nights of infancy and innocence
Chirped to me legends of the world before war,

Of an age of peace and love?
And where are the crickets of youth's hot blood
That shared with her and me the garden grove
There, beyond the outhouse and the orange tree,
When in Desire's throes we tasted the primal nectar of life and love?
And oh where are the little ants, that my little son and I
Sent marching in their ranks with sugared bait,
Pretending we were kings and they our subjects
All dutiful, as he, in innocence and love?
Where, or where, my little friends, O whither are you fled?
Where? Say not where! I know that you are dead.
I mourn for you in this my humble rhyme,
You little dears, killed by fatal fate,
Insecticide most pitiless
The mighty hunter Time!'"

All applauded. Max was pleased that he had understood almost every word and even sort of enjoyed it. Blanco enunciated very clearly in a purer Spanish than the truncated local dialect. When another poem was proposed, Max joined in urging Blanco to hold forth once again.

"My *Hymn to Alcalá*," announced Blanco shyly. "It is also my homage to a fellow poet, and a statement of my poetic creed." He smiled weakly. "I hope that I haven't overburdened the little poem–or you. Ahem."

Shifting vocal gears once more, Blanco read his poem in a bold, passionate voice that moved the hearer quite apart from the meaning of the words:

Body of Alcalá, green hills, green skies,
Where are you now? Oh where?
Show yourself, and my surrender
Will breed poems like bats, flying through your streets!
Exiled from you I was rock, a barren tree,
A rusted Ford immobile in a quarry.
I towed myself anew to your moist clime;
Your love renewed the motor of my soul.

I shall return again, enchained by love
Of the warm and muddy Cholo, of the song
Eternal of crickets and bees and flies,
Entomologic Symphony, my first and only Muse!
Body of Alcalá, odorous city, stay:
My poet's hunger has no food but thee,
No voice my soul denied your warming rain.
In your grace only, am I an Endless Noise.

A moist-eyed silence followed, succeeded by applause and embraces of the poet, delighted praise of the reading, and another round of drinks. Everyone spoke at once, mostly to Max, who understood less and less but who smiled and nodded and said *excelente* several times, genuinely pleased with all this and increasingly oblivious to the cynical George voice in his head. It felt as if his old colleague were sending him psychic sneers from Mexico. *Damn it, George. Aren't I here to improve U.S.-Engañadan relations? What could serve that purpose better than this?*

The second bottle empty, the delegation began to file out, embracing Max as they went. All except Blanco, who asked for a moment to settle a small matter. Once they were alone he sat next to Max on the sofa and presented a dirty, wrinkled business card:

Simón Bolívar Blanco Gonzales
Declamador Profesor Traductor
Redactor Agente de Libros
Av. Naciones Unidas 415
Alcalá

"As you can see," he began in his quiet, sad, non-recital voice, "I pursue various activities but all, you will observe, of artistic and educational merit. I am among other things the exclusive agent in Engañada for the American publishers Invisible Voices."

"Invisible Voices?"

"Of New York. You have of course heard of them? They are

the exclusive publishers of the works of Woodrow Lively."

"Oh, *that* one..."

"Yes. As it happens I have in my office a few unsold copies of Lively's major works, translated by myself. You would perhaps find it interesting to compare them with your copy of the original? I would suggest you begin with *Home Had Two Doors*, my personal favorite, which I translated as *Donde ya el Hogar?*"

"I'd enjoy that very much." *And I hope that's all you want. I'm drunk, I'm tired, and the longer this goes on, the more likely I'll say something stupid.*

"I'll send it over. But to the purpose: I spoke with your assistant, Gloria Córdova Medellín, about a poetry reading next month as part of an art exhibit. On a Thursday, I believe, the best day for such things."

"A Thursday? Well, yes, I suppose so. Gloria keeps the schedule, so if she thinks it will fit, very well." *What the hell, poetry readings come with the territory. We're all about culture here in the Center.*

"Fine. Then she and I can work out the program, the poems, etc. But there is one matter, which Gloria indicated she was not prepared, or perhaps I should say authorized, to undertake. I refer to the honorarium."

"Right." *Here it comes.*

"Yes. You understand that my interests are most certainly not pecuniary and for myself I would simply forego it. But in our society I fear things are valued rather by their price than by their worth, and uncompensated art is not taken with the proper seriousness."

"I think I can understand that," Max answered. He was disappointed, but not too much. Six old guys came to welcome him, and other than the whisky, wanted nothing. Besides, a poetry reading couldn't cost much.

"Moreover," Blanco went on, "my fellow artists, and I must sadly admit that some have less than the proper attitude themselves, would resent a free performance as a threat to their own livelihoods."

"I see. How much?"

Now disappointment flickered on Blanco's face at the blunt, vulgar question. "As I say, the figure is of little importance in itself, but takes on symbolic significance regarding the value, not the price!" Blanco sat up straight and waved his right index finger vaguely at the ceiling. "The value, I say, which we place upon art, upon the magic words of poetry, upon the lyric song of the human spirit!"

The rolling Spanish syllables made it seem like a warning from an oracle. "Right. And that would be?"

Blanco smiled and shrugged. "Mr. Lacey, what price shall we put on the human spirit?"

"What price indeed?"

"But we must, finally, arrive at a figure. Let us proceed logically: my maid recently demanded a raise in her salary to 2300 *honores* per month. I am told the city's garbage men earn now a minimum of twenty-five hundred per month. My nephew, who sells trucks, last month earned commissions of twelve thousand *honores.* Shall we value art with the collection of garbage or the sale of trucks?"

"Well, no," Max answered reasonably, remembering his younger days changing the trash bags at a McDonald's. "I don't think we can compare a poetry reading to a month's work at anything."

"Precisely. And so, not to take any more of your valuable time, let us agree to twenty thousand *honores.*"

"No, no! My time's not *that* valuable," Max smiled. Blanco started to return the smile, then turned somber and sad and proud.

"Mr. Director, I am not a rich man. In fact, one might even say that I have serious financial embarrassments at the moment. Indeed, that my life as an artist has been, from a material point of view, very ill rewarded. Please! No sympathy! I do not complain. I do not regret the comforts that would, at my age, be so welcome. When I devoted my life to art, I understood that the rewards would be not material but spiritual, and I have been satisfied. My wife shares my decision, and perhaps an operation would not help her anyway. For myself, I do not complain. No. But in this instance, Mr. Director, I represent not my poor self, but Art. And on the part of Art, I cannot permit that the poetic Muse be insulted by a pauper's fee."

"God forbid we should insult the Muse." Max suppressed a smile as he reflected that this eloquent shakedown was worth 20,000 honores. About $200. But not to the struggling Center. And he wondered about that operation.

"Twenty thousand, then?"

"Really, Señor Blanco, I quite agree with you that twenty thousand is a more or less adequate symbol of the esteem in which we hold poetry. Too low, if anything. However, we have the mundane practical problem that the Center doesn't have that kind of money."

"I could accept monthly installments."

"Very good of you, but I'm afraid that doesn't solve the problem. We too are passing through a period of financial embarrassment. We could let people think you are getting twenty thousand so that the name of poetry is honored, but in fact settle on something the Center can afford?"

"Such as?"

Wishing he had that famous Mariana Guzmán to help, Max tried, "Three thousand?"

"Really, Mr. Director, don't you think it rather unworthy of Art for us to proceed in this conniving way? Does Art need subtleties and even deceptions to uphold her name? Would it not be a violation of the highest and noblest aspirations of poetry for us to make the Muse a party to this...this fraud, however well intended?"

The plywood had begun to bang against the window, as it always did when the afternoon breeze came up. *Now the fraud is objecting to fraud. Or maybe not. Maybe this is the Muse inspiring the old man to watch her back. I doubt it, but ...* Max had figured out something about beggars in Mexico: whether their stories are true or false wasn't his problem. He was fortunate beyond all deserving, and able to give them a little something. Maybe Blanco was really hard up. Nonetheless. *This is ridiculous, trying to persuade him to accept three thousand honores to read a few poems. And it's not my money, but the Center's. Verde would*

64

faint.

Max shifted in his chair as if to arise and usher the poet out. "Well, Mr. Blanco, I'm sorry we couldn't work this out. It would have been fine to have you read here."

"Let me think," the poet responded quickly, then stared at the floor for a moment. "Euterpe is not vain, but lyric. She might approve and even enjoy the transformation, or let us say the transfiguration, of commercial terms into a sort of elegy. Agreed, we will publicize the higher figure but, so as not to divorce word and deed too completely, let us say five thousand, just between you and me."

Center Director Lacey turned thoughtful. Maybe the man really did need it. He looked pretty seedy. *And it's like the poor bastard is trying to hang onto some dignity.* Moreover, even bargaining at the vegetable market had its courtesies. If Max insisted on his first price, he'd feel like a jerk somehow. And he could pay it himself rather than deal with Verde's disgust and dismay.

"Four thousand," he said, and they shook on it.

The door had hardly shut behind Blanco when it opened again. In walked the worldly fellow in sunglasses who had come in before. He sat down in the easy chair with one leg over the arm and asked, "What'd he touch you for?"

"What did who touch me for?"

"Blanco, for the poetry reading. Whatever, don't feel bad. The last Director gave him two thousand *honores* once."

"Oh. But, excuse me, you're..."

"Washington Maldonado, your Activities Director. Just back from vacation."

So this is Maldonado. Max wasn't enamored of his sitting down as if it were his office, and suspected that here was one of the types Gonzales warned him about. Maldonado seemed at once young and old, with thick black hair but also lines beside his eyes and in his cheeks. He had flopped into the chair gracefully, yet his voice had a slight wheeze that reminded Max of his grandfather back in Annandale.

"So tell me, Washington, just what is it you do here? No one seems really to know."

"I arrange things," said Maldonado, a bit lewdly.

"What things?"

"Anything. Art shows, lectures, conferences. Even repairs and contracts. Stuff like that."

"I thought Gloria handled art shows."

"That witch! She drags all her weird friends in here, but I'm the one that gets the pictures hung, the place cleaned up, and sees that chairs are arranged. There's a lot more to it than inviting in some phony with a paint brush."

"Hmm. You arrange string quartets? We have one coming May 19th. You know about straight-back chairs?"

"For the musicians? Yeah. No problem, and we'll only need most of the regular chairs for half the concert. Lots of people come to hear whatever, but most the kids skip out halfway through that classical stuff. Anyway, I'm here to help you arrange that or whatever needs arranging, though right now the best thing I could arrange for you is a good lawyer."

"Why do I need a lawyer?"

"The new contract the teachers presented to the Labor Ministry."

"What? Just a second. Rosa!"

She came in carrying a letter. "Did you leave this on my desk?" she asked.

"No. What do you know about a teachers' contract with the Labor Ministry?"

"That's what the letter's about," she said, handing it to him.

"Didn't you open it?"

"No." He stared at Washington, who shrugged and said someone had to open the mail between directors. Max forgot his irritation as he read, then looked up. "This seems to say that the Labor Ministry has recognized a new contract for our teachers, one that gives them a fifty percent raise plus, let's see–"

"Plus an hour's pay for every four exams they correct," helped Washington, "and the Center agrees to provide four cups of coffee per day plus two sandwiches for each teacher."

"What in the hell is going on here?" Max shouted in English.

Their puzzled looks brought him back to Spanish. "I remember the teachers saying something about a raise, but when did the Center agree to all this?"

"Right here," pointed out Rosa, "it says 'agreement reached with tacit approval of the Employer or Authorized Agent of same.' I think that's because you said they were right. You remember?"

"I don't remember about the sandwiches. And anyway, what kind of damned way is that to write contracts?"

"That's the law," shrugged Washington. "I wish I'd been here to advise you. *Mala suerte.* Maybe it can be fixed up, but we'd have to see what the lawyers and the judge would cost compared to the new contract."

"Oh, Christ," Max moaned, wishing he could agree that it was just his *mala suerte,* his bad luck and not his stupidity, that had put him in this mess. He saw his million *honores* disappearing by the end of the day.

"That's all right," soothed Rosa. "You didn't know."

That would be a fair assessment of my career here, along with "you're really just a guest even though you're the host."

"Besides," offered Washington, "pretty soon there won't be any students anyway so we won't have to pay any teachers!"

"We have to pay them anyway," corrected Rosa, "if they have a contract for a certain number of hours."

"Yeah, and a lot of them do," Maldonado admitted.

"I can see you're going to be a big help, Washington. Maybe you can find a way to pay the bills when there are no students."

"No problem. Lots of ways. I told the last two directors we'd be better off without English classes."

"Oh yes–flee pairs!" exclaimed Rosa.

"Flee pairs? What are flee pairs?"

"Pinball machines. Video games," explained Washington. "You know: *ding-ding-ding!* And there are the new ones where you shoot down UFOs or sink ships. Those places are full all day. Kids can't stay away, and at seven *honores* a shot we'd make a fortune."

"Ah. *Flippers.* Come on, be serious, But, Washington, that does remind me of something: space. We have square meters here.

You know, there's something you might arrange for us. Maybe there's something we can do with all this space? Like renting it out, maybe?"

"That's what I've been trying to tell you!" Washington exclaimed. "You don't like flippers, okay. But we've got a prime location here for lots of things: a shoe store, a branch office of a bank, a lawyer's office. You could use that."

"I'm not here to run a shoe store," Max answered. "That's not what the Center is about."

"You don't run it, just rent the space like you said. But okay, no shoe stores. Why don't we at least charge all these schools, writers' groups, and garden clubs that use the place?"

"It's a thought." Max had more or less understood why they hosted the high school art exhibit, but wondered about some literary meeting a few days before, and a band practice in the auditorium. Rosa had assured him: "They're just using the room like they always have. I don't quite understand why, either, since we have to clean up after them. But it is what they have always done, and it was not my place to object." Max had shrugged, considering it a goodwill practice.

"But we've never charged schools," Rosa reminded Washington. "And they don't have any money anyway."

"Neither do we." Max's voice turned grim. *Yes, we're onto something. No wonder the Center is going broke, providing free housing to all comers. If they're going to use my square meters, then they can damn well help pay for them, for their cleaning and cooling and lighting and all the rest. There's a resource we'll start using all right.* And that reminded him of something else. "Television advertising," he said aloud. "Why don't we arrange some good television advertising to get our students back?"

Rosa shook her head. "There's only one station in town and most people watch the national station from San Genesio. But the station here won't give us any more advertising until we pay for what we had two years ago. I remember, because we got a letter from them just a few weeks ago reminding us that we owe them 95,000 *honores.*"

"And the advertising didn't work," added Washington. "It

was pretty bad."

"Let's jazz it up!" insisted Max. "Get some pretty girls and stuff and sell English courses just like they sell beer or shampoo! And we'll use the national station if we have to."

"Right, right!" agreed Washington in an indulgent voice. "That's what I said: make it sexy. And that's what Xavier Muñoz said; he's a friend of mine who works in advertising. But the Board shot it down. Said it wasn't dignified enough for the Center. So they went with some boring thing that put people to sleep."

"Oh."

"And we couldn't afford it now anyway," cautioned Rosa. "Do you know what it costs? Just to make the ad, even?"

Max sighed. "Never mind. Let's go back to square meters."

"What?" Rosa looked at him quizzically.

"Space. Rentals."

"Right," Washington agreed. "Look, there are a lot of other people we could rent to, like the evangelicals. They wanted to use the place once but it was against policy. How about them?"

Max thought about it. "That requires some finesse. The Center can't lend itself to religious or political activities, of course, but a discreet meeting of, say, theologians? Maybe."

"And businesses, for business meetings?" Washington was growing almost cheerful. "You could charge them plenty for sales conferences or stockholders' meetings. And wedding receptions?"

"Hey, not bad, Washington!"

"They'd get drunk and break everything," objected Rosa.

Washington smiled a naughty smile. "So we get a big damage deposit and keep it all. They'll be too drunk to remember if they broke the door or not."

"By God, we just may have something here," Max beamed.

"And kids' birthday parties and confirmations or baptisms or First Communions, and *quinceañeras* for rich girls? I can keep the place full, okay?"

"As long as they pay," declared Max. "And are...respectable."

"Yes, please keep it respectable," laughed Rosa, also warming to the idea.

Max felt absurdly optimistic, as it just naming a solution

brought it about. "Right," he laughed. "Respectable, but with money. Especially with money!"

"Okay," Washington agreed. "Respectable. No gypsies, drug runners or lawyers. Anything else?"

Max thought a moment. "No circuses."

Chapter Seven: Human Resources

Max spent part of his weekend in his office with a calculator and financial statements, projecting a budget based on rental income estimates. After another two hours on Monday morning, he thought he had the picture. It wasn't pretty: even the most optimistic reasonable rental estimates simply could not compensate for the damned mortgage payments. An increase in enrollment would be a much better story. After playing with various figures, he reached his conclusion as he circled the digits '300' as the magic number. With that many students plus the rental income, the Center would be solvent. And there had more students than that in the past. Max went up to the Academic Department.

Braden wasn't there. One of the teachers sat working at another desk, an attractive middle-aged woman in dark slacks and a white blouse. Max couldn't remember her name and his embarrassment showed. She smiled.

"I'm Pilar San Martín. Bertram will be here soon. Probably."

"It's eleven o'clock," Max noted.

She shrugged. "I know. But at least these exams are ready. We need them for this afternoon."

"Did you live in the U.S.?" Max asked. She had almost no accent.

"Yes, in Oregon. I studied there and when I got back they made me the Assistant Academic Director, which means I get to make up the tests!" Her smile denied bitterness. "But I suppose you want to talk about the contract."

"No, I didn't come for that. But now that you mention it, it was sort of a surprise. I mean, someone might have told me what was going on."

"If we had, then you'd have asked someone on the Board who would have fixed it up with the Ministry, and we would have gone another five years without a raise. It was sort of a rotten thing to do to a new Director, and I know it will make the Center's problems worse, but we were all so tired of promises. Besides, we really couldn't live on that salary, you know?"

"Yeah, but who said fifty percent? And I never heard anything about sandwiches."

"We had to say something. Fifty percent was the least we needed. You're right about the sandwiches, though. The others outvoted me. I don't like the pay for grading exams either. That's part of the job. But anyway, it all comes to a raise, and four students' tuition will pay the teacher."

She was about right; Max had just calculated 4.4 students to cover teacher cost in a class. And even with their fifty percent raise, they still weren't making much money. He didn't see how anyone could live on seventy-five honores per hour, especially those who didn't get very many hours because there were so few students. Except, of course, for those teachers whose contracts pay them for a minimum number of hours, classes or not. He wondered how they got those contracts.

But, he reflected further, people do live. As in Mexico, life here is about half again as expensive as in the U.S. if one aspires to U.S. standards for housing and food and TV sets or books. Since most Mexicans and Engañadans make far less than Americans, they crowd into ill-built houses, eat little meat, and share things or do without. Even if that was just the way it was, as George had shrugged, Max couldn't help feeling some guilt. He had more, not because of his own personal merit, but solely because he had been born to it.

What was more, the poorly paid teachers generated the Center's operating income so that it could remain open to promote things that the United States wanted promoted. The problem was that the average class had only about seven students, and the Center needed more than 2.6 of them for other expenses.

"Well," he said, "we'll have to live with the contract. And we could, if we had more students. You know we have only about seven per class?"

"That's the problem," she acknowledged, just as Braden came in.

"You always arrive at this time?" Max asked, politely.

"I've been working," Braden answered in his slow hollow voice. "I work better at home. I worked on my advanced class. See?" He held out a manila folder crammed with papers. "They're poems."

"Poems?"

"Poems. This is an advanced class. A special class. A special advanced class." Completely deadpan. "They write poems in Spanish, then translate them into English. Want to hear some?"

"No, not now. We need—"

"This is by our best student:

The Cholo will run red when Yankees know
The People's rage, when we take up the gun!
United peasants will put on a show!
Gringos will be dead or on the run!"

"What do you think?" He asked it the way most people did when showing Max photos of their children.

"So much for mutual understanding," Max answered. "I got to wonder: the guy hates the Yankees so much, why's he studying here?"

"*She* doesn't hate you!" Braden's voice came to life. "An Engañadan writing poetry has to write in the Latin American tradition, and that's all about opposing U.S. imperialism. It's their destiny."

"So when my blood's running into the Cholo River I shouldn't take it personally?"

"Of course not."

"That's a relief. How many students are in the class?"

Braden sat down and thought. "There's Pablo," he said at last. "And Javier. And Mariana of course." He thought some more. "Three students."

"Right."

"You think the class is too small. Three students don't pay the teacher. I know. Pilar tells me that. But I don't get paid by the hour. Besides, two of them have scholarships."

What the hell, let it go for now. "Okay. So how can we increase enrollment? We have to do something about that."

Braden looked both bored and offended. "I'm not a businessman," he said, as if denying that he were a pimp.

Max snapped, "Neither am I! But I'm damned well trying to become one to keep this place going. And you'd better too if you want to get paid!"

Braden smirked and announced proudly, "I don't do getting and spending." Before Max could formulate a properly outraged response, the intercom buzzed to announce a call for him from San Genesio. Max glared at Braden, told Pilar with restrained calm that he would be talking to her again, and left the office thinking about Engañadan labor laws and the loopholes that must exist.

And damn it, I had wanted to ask Braden about something. What was it? At the bottom of the stairs he remembered the letter from the girl who wanted to teach here. *I'll check on it later. I suppose it's probably sitting on his desk, gloriously ignored.* As Max approached his office, Washington came up behind him, grabbed his arm and waved two crisp thousand-*honore* bills at him. "We've got a wedding reception for next weekend!" he said. "Friend of mine I saw this morning in a café, said his cousin's getting married and they hadn't been able to find a place! He jumped at the idea of having it here and his uncle was over half an hour ago to make a down payment. We get another three thousand the day before the wedding!"

"Way to go, Washington!" Max pumped his Activity Director's hand gleefully.

"My only mistake," Washington went on, "was I put the price too low. I hadn't checked what they get in other places, and I had to say something. But I checked later. You know what the hotels get? Fifteen, twenty thousand, even more! We can get ten or fifteen for the next one easy!"

"No harm done," Max observed. "Once we have one reception, all the people who come will know about it and that's the best advertising. We've got to have everything in shape, right? Make these people really happy!"

Rosa stepped out of her office to say that 'Hetro' was on the phone. Max shook Washington's hand again, held the two thousand *honores* over his head in triumph and handed them to Rosa with a smile on his way to his desk.

"Hi there, Jethro! How you today?"

"Lacey? That you?"

"Sure is!"

"What you sound so damn happy about?"

"Things are looking up, Jethro, definitely looking up!"

"Lookin' up? How things gonna look up when I *tole* you that place in A-Number One shape when you got there? But I didn't call to talk about your Center, and I'll tell you what you can look up about. You can look *up* to the mountains and get yourself *up* here next Tuesday, like you should have done before this, because we got us a Country Plan meeting and I want everybody here, you understand?"

Max certainly did. Of all the papers an embassy's Public Affairs Section sent to Washington, none was holier than the clumsily-named *Country Plan,* the document which set forth the cultural and press projects for the coming fiscal year, justifying each in precise relation to worldwide goals established by Washington. Of course, the plan was never fulfilled, or even remembered, but that did nothing to diminish its importance. The reputation of the post and its officers was made or marred by the reception of their *Plan* in Washington.

"I'll be there, Jethro."

"You'd best. Get some real work done instead of having your picture taken with a bunch of old guys look like they were hauled out of a crypt."

"You mean the *Sociedad Historica* gentlemen, who had such

kind words for the United States and the Center during their visit?" *How can this jerk just write off good relations with local groups? Isn't that what we're here for?*

"Yeah, that's them. Right there in that rag you got there—what's it called?"

"*La Voz del Pueblo?*" Max hoped that was the one. Press and cultural officers were expected to read the local papers, and Max hadn't got to them today. There was no need for Jethro to know that.

"Yeah. Anyway, we're trying to reach young people, the ones the communists are always trying to sign up. These old guys ain't our target audience!"

Max almost asked him if he'd prefer a photo with some of the many Che Guevara clones in Alcalá. Before he could do so, Jethro reminded him again to be at the Country Plan meeting on the 2nd. He then hung up.

Not that Max would have dreamed of missing it. Even if meeting Jethro promised to be dentally unpleasant, here was a familiar and understandable task. It did not depend upon beatnik academic directors, reluctant students, or strangers' wedding plans. Max got out his copy of Washington's *World-Wide Goals* and set to work jotting down various formulations of Year Projects for Alcalá. After a number of the usual distractions about schedules or student complaints and the rest, Max set the formulations aside and turned to the local papers that had been waiting for him all day. *La Voz del Pueblo* hardly cheered him up: an article by Dra. Esperanza Romero announced "a very important lecture on the development of the child" to be held in the Engañadan-American Center on June 25th. Max wondered if there was any way to derail it and keep the obnoxious woman from invading his Center, and to avoid the expenses involved.

On the next page, there he was with the smiling board of the Patriotic Historical Society gathered in his office, promoting Engañadan friendship. Of course they looked like they were recruited from a crypt. They were important *because* they were older, had been around forever and knew a lot of people. If they were no longer themselves great movers and shakers, they influence those who are. Somehow. *So I'll just have to do the Embassy's work despite the Embassy.*

Chapter Eight: In High Places

Alcalá Airport was crowded and chaotic and the airline claimed not to have his reservation, just as Rosa had predicted. In accordance with her advice, Max tenaciously held his place in the crowd of shrieking women and cursing men until, slipping a hundred-*honore* bill to the clerk, he got his ticket. Then he wandered around the airport that was as Alcalán as the seaport: disorganized and shabby, but suggesting excitement and mystery, as if the heavy air were full of possibilities.

Such air was especially thick in the international section, where happy family groups received sons or sisters arriving on the Air Engañada flight from Los Angeles. In front of the desk, an obviously American young woman carrying a guitar had attracted everyone's attention. She wore shorts, a work shirt, a backpack, sandals and a floppy hat, and was arguing with the clerk in Spanish so bad it hurt even Lacey's ears.

"Es una 'hippy'!" smiled a fat little man as he walked past Max with his wife.

"Es una puta!" corrected the scowling matron.

Hippie or whore? Max thought they might both be right.

The American looked around until she saw Max, who had been too late in trying to hide his American-ness behind a corpulent mother of at least four. "Do you speak English?" she shouted across the fifty feet that separated them, moving in his direction. His own Spanish wasn't good enough to deny it amidst so many natives, so he resigned himself to hearing her problem.

"They don't have my luggage, or they have it and won't give it to me. I thought I saw it but the man keeps pointing at my ticket and, like, I don't know what he wants, you know?" She swung her head slowly to the left and let her long blonde hair fall behind her, then looked at Max with vapid blue eyes.

Max asked the clerk what the problem was. The *señorita*

norteamericana, it seemed, had arrived with an unpaid ticket. They could not release the luggage until payment was received. Max explained this to her in English.

"But I don't have any money. Like, the place I'm going to work said they'd pay for it, and I just showed them the telegram at the airport in L.A. and came, and I don't see what all the hassle is." She might have been discussing an argument between preschoolers whose mothers would soon arrive.

Max suggested she call her employer. She didn't know the number.

"Well then, what's the name of the company? I'll look it up."

"It's the Centro Engañado-Americano. Of Alcalá, like."

Max stared at her for a moment. "Could you please repeat that?"

"The Centro Engañado-Americano. I'm going to teach there."

"It must be a mistake."

"No way, man." She pulled a crumpled piece of paper from the huge bag that hung from her shoulder. "Like, I have the telegram right here." Max read it:

CHERYL FLETCHER 3611
HONEYSUCKLE SAN JOSE CALIF USA
SURE COME ON DOWN. WE PICK UP
AIRFARE. WATER OK.
BRADEN, CENTRO ENGANADO
AMERICANO

"I know the number," Max sighed. "How much is the airfare, anyway?"

"Lemme see. It's nine hundred and eighty-three dollars and forty-seven cents. Hey, are you Braden?"

"No—what? Almost a thousand bucks?"

"Yeah, but that includes the extra baggage I brought. I plan to stay a long time."

"Don't count on it," he muttered. "Look, that telegram should never have been sent. And the water is lousy, really. Lots of dysentery. Maybe you should just fly back the way you came, and you can pick up your luggage in Los Angeles?"

She smiled dreamily. "Hey, where you coming from? Like, I just got here, and I don't have the money in Los Angeles either." She shook the hair out of her face.

"Maybe your father?"

"Hey, really! I haven't seen him for a year. All he cares about is getting reelected."

Max closed his eyes. Images of Congressional investigations took shape, Jethro Jackson waving an official letter at him. He tore a page from his pocket notebook and wrote the Center phone number for her, then thought of a simpler solution. "Here's forty *honores*. Take a taxi—make sure the guy understands you won't pay more than forty–and go to the Center. Braden's there. But be sure you talk to Rosa and Washington. We'll worry about your luggage later. I'll be back tomorrow."

"Hey, thanks, but who are you anyway?"

"Lacey. Tell them Lacey sent you. And wait a minute." He took back the page with the phone number and scribbled a note to Rosa, asking that she or someone help Ms. Fletcher find a place to stay for a while. "Give this to Rosa at the Center," he said. "Now excuse me, I have to catch a plane."

"Okay. See you tomorrow," she said, brightly and as if by right.

The flight lasted one interminable hour as the ancient DC-3 rocked and swayed through clouds that parted occasionally to reveal mountain peaks not fifty feet from the wing; some of the peaks soared far above the plane itself. Max prayed that the sudden violent turns were precise, and prayed again in thanksgiving when the sky suddenly cleared to reveal their destination. Below them, so close that he could see details of colonial churches, nestled San Genesio in its mountain valley.

An Embassy driver met him, and as they drove through the cobbled streets, Max began to wish he had been assigned here. This city had a past. In Alcalá, the termites and humidity consumed most wooden structures in fifty years, whereas some of San Genesio's stone and brick churches had endured since the sixteenth century, damaged now and again by earthquakes but on the whole surviving to see their Counter-Reformation splendor illuminated, Max supposed, by the same gaudy neon lights he had seen in Mexican and Alcalá churches.

The air was delicious. *And if I was here, I wouldn't have to worry about providing sandwiches to teachers. On the other hand... darned if Alcalá doesn't seem sort of like home.*

It seemed like another kind of homecoming when they arrived at the Embassy: the Marine guards with their metal detectors, the busy secretaries hunched over IBM Selectric typewriters, and American voices mixed with the low clatter of coffee cups. All the sights and sounds were familiar. It might have been Mexico or, without the Marines, the General Services Administration.

Jethro Jackson was disappointingly like Max had imagined him, a tall, fat, pinstriped Colonel Sanders, but friendlier than his phone persona in a backslapping way. He dragged Max from one office to another, introducing him to Political Officer Terry Gaines and Econ Head Walt Jones and Security Officer Dave Guarini and Admin Officer Charlie Brown ("Yep, that's really his name!") and many others whom Max couldn't keep straight. Nonetheless, he thought it nice of Jethro to do it at all, even as his appreciation mixed with a strange reaction: these offices began to seem to him like prison cells.

They had an appointment with Ambassador Webster at eleven. Arriving a few minutes early, Jackson took him first to the connected office of the Deputy Chief of Mission, Harold Delaney, who looked up impatiently from a mountain of paperwork and said "Good to meet you now if you'll excuse me I'm very busy here." Jackson and Lacey stepped right back out.

"Don't take it personal," Jackson advised. "DCM got worst job in the embassy, got to answer for everything. Now this Ambassador," he went on as they made their way back across the large office where two secretaries had desks, "don't like to hear about no problems, and I don't want him to hear about none neither. He get track of something, he be sniffin' around for months. Gets into too much stuff ain't none of his business, this one does."

The tall man with silver-flecked hair looked the part of an Ambassador, and was gracious enough even if he had little interest in Max or his Center. So far so good. But he had the sort of pale blue eyes that stared right into one's mind and seemed to say, *We both know you're a twerp, don't we, Lacey?* Of course, what Ambassador Webster said was "Welcome aboard" and "Hope you enjoy your tour" before he glanced at his watch and stood up. "I have an appointment at the Foreign Ministry."

"Yessir, Mr. Ambassador, sir, we'll just move on along then. Sure was good of you to see Max here. Wasn't it, Max?"

"It certainly was, yes. Thank you, Mr. Ambassador." Embassies are the last remnants of monarchy in the American system. But Max knew how to act here. *On the other hand, in the Center I have to guard against flattery rather than practice it. 'Better to rule in hell than serve in heaven'?*

The Ambassador held out his hand. "My pleasure."

As they left the Ambassadorial suite Jackson asked Lacey in a low voice, "You know the most important thing about handling ambassadors, don't you?"

"Take a lot of pictures," Max answered in the same low voice.

"That's right. You learn that in Mexico?"

"Uh-huh." George had run a good school.

The meeting to discuss the Country Plan was held after lunch, with all members of the public relations staff attending except the Cultural Attaché, Harvey Tyrone.

"Don't know where he is," grumbled Jackson. "Ain't seen him for a week. All time off on 'cultural projects.' That's what he says, anyhow. Anybody know where Harvey is?"

No one did, but Assistant Cultural Attaché Barbara Deedy, who looked like Cheryl Fletcher in formal dress, said he had mentioned something about checking in with some academics upcountry, and that she would fill in for him.

"Let's get going," said Jackson. "We got just one month to get this thing A-1 perfect and send it in."

They started with Press Goal I: Private Ownership of the

Press. How to achieve that in Engañada? Mike Black, the Press Attaché who even looked like George the Press Officer in Mexico, right down to the cigar, outlined his first Activity: a film to be requested from Washington and shown to the owners of the local papers. The film would urge them to support private as opposed to state ownership of their newspapers. The hard work was writing up the specifics of the project: to whom exactly would it be shown? (List names.) When? Where? Who would be influenced beyond the immediate audience? (The public, which would read the editorials inspired by the film.) How would it be supported locally? (Specify that the Embassy had a movie projector.) Did the requested content of the film overlap with other Activities? If so, cross-references would have to be included.

"And look here," cautioned Jackson, holding up a copy of the forms to be used, "see that line there on the margins and at the bottom? Don't write outside that line! Says right here, 'Do Not Go Outside Line,' and I'll tell you right now, we send these up there with words slopping over the line they gonna come back so fast we all have to duck!"

"Noted, Jethro," Black mumbled as he relit his cigar. "Don't go outside the lines. You hear that, Barb?" he asked the Assistant Cultural Attaché. Nudging her with his elbow. "Don't go out of bounds. Except with me."

"Señora Martita told me it's not worth it," answered the girl primly. The dozen people present—five Americans, seven Engañadans—laughed heartily. All except Max, until one of the locals leaned over and told him Señora Martita was the ancient cook in the Embassy cafeteria.

The discussion continued. Max's contribution wasn't due until they reached the next section (Provincial Press Activity I: Presentation to Local Editor of Copies of Representative U.S. Newspapers), giving his mind rein to wander to subjects like enrollment and Bertram Braden. *I'd better fire him as soon as I get back. How? "Braden, you're not the man for the job?" Or "Braden, you turkey, you're canned?" The gentle approach: "Bertram, I'm afraid we'll have to make some changes?"*

Jackson's bellow brought him back to the meeting. "Lacey!

What you thinkin' about, boy?"

"Sorry." He made his presentation well enough to please Jethro, though Max himself derived little satisfaction from it. By the time the meeting was considering Cultural Contributions Activity II: Steps in Ballet, Max's mind had returned again to Alcalá. He was calculating how much they might make by having the cafeteria cater the wedding receptions in the auditorium when Jackson shouted his name again. The others looked at him strangely.

"Something botherin' you, boy?" asked Jackson when the meeting ended.

"No, no. Just tired. Maybe the altitude."

"Oh, yeah! That'll do it sometimes. Old Grimaldi got sick as a dog first time he came up here," said Jackson, leaving it at that.

There was a dinner that night at Jackson's house. Max had always enjoyed those sorts of events in Mexico, and this one was pleasant, with the fireplace providing a welcome warmth against the nighttime chill. Mrs. Jackson was a perfect hostess in the best Foreign Service spouse tradition and Max would have enjoyed it greatly except for his preoccupation with Center business matters. They so distracted him that, when Jackson asked him how he liked everything down there, Max forgot himself so far as to answer honestly. "More or less, but I'd like it a lot better if the Center wasn't in such a mess. I think maybe we can solve them, but the place really has problems, Jethro."

Jackson was both surprised and offended. "What the hell you talkin' about? I told you Grimaldi left it in A-Number One shape!"

Max plunged onward like a drunk driver racing a train to the crossing. "I don't know how he arrived at that. Enrollment has been going down for years, the place has a huge debt, the building is falling apart, and nothing has been done about any of these problems for a long time." Then he caught himself. *Oh. Holy. Crap. That was rude, dumb, out of place. But all of it is true. Jethro's a good ol' boy. Maybe he'll understand.*

"I can show you the damn reports!" breathed Jackson, his face pale.

Max twisted the glass in his hand and stared at the fire. "Then the reports may be outdated. Or something."

Jackson's voice grew cold and even. "I signed off on those reports."

"Oh."

They sat in embarrassed and hostile silence until Jerry, a guy from the Consular Section, came over and asked how business was down in Alcalá.

"If we had as many students as you have visa applicants," Max answered, "we'd be in great shape." *Damn it. What the hell is wrong with me?*

"And if we gave visas to all the applicants," Jerry answered cheerfully, "there'd be no one left to study English."

"Sure is right," Jethro agreed, evidently trying to forget Lacey's *faux pas* and return to a party mood. "Every one of 'em would be in Miami!"

Max laughed, tacit acceptance of the smoothover, and accepted Jerry's invitation to join the game of Charades they were getting up at the other end of the room.

After the fifth and definitive session, which Max's team won by identifying President Ford, Barbara Deedy told Max he'd have to find a way to visit San Genesio for a week or so. "There's a lot to see here, colonial churches and the street fairs where you can buy anything."

"And bullfights," noted Jerry of the Consular Section. "You don't have those in Alcalá."

"Wonder why here, but not there," Max mused.

"Maybe they're more civilized on the coast," offered Barbara in a stern voice. "I saw one here for a while, until I couldn't take it anymore. Torture an animal for half an hour and then kill it."

Max was going to ask about the poetry of it, all that business about courage and fate and whatnot that he'd read in *The Sun Also Rises,* but a look at Barbara's face told him that would be another *faux pas*—as if he needed any more of those tonight. He saw her point. From what he knew of bullfights, they didn't seem very poetic. Maybe you have to be Spanish or something to see past the cruelty and find the profound mythic significance that redeems it. *If so, I'll probably never really understand Engañada. On the other hand, if the people in Alcalá don't like bullfights either, maybe I'm right where I belong.*

"Which is the oldest church here?" He spend the rest of the evening in proper small talk, far from the clutches of candor.

Chapter Nine: University Education

The Center employees, especially Rosa and Manuel, seemed pleased to have Max back from his short trip. Yet Rosa seemed a bit cool as she told him that Pilar San Martín had agreed to host "that Flaycher girl" temporarily. Max had no time to wonder about it. He felt some satisfaction that at the least, he was needed: accumulated housekeeping problems awaited him, like the newly broken handrail on the stairs. More complex problems were pending.

"Rosa," he announced, "we've got to have a Board meeting."

"I'll try, but it's so hard to get them together. They're always traveling or busy or something. Anyway, they never seem to do much. Why do you want one?"

"There are some things the Board should discuss."

He didn't want any more surprises like that teachers' contract. Braden had to go, but it had to be done right, without any monstrous *desahucio* payment. And what were their legal obligations to that hippie girl? For that matter, where was she?

Before he could ask, Gloria Córdova bounced in full of good news about the Delgado art show. All was in order, and "especially it's so wonderful that you want Simón Bolívar Blanco to read he's such a nice man and so many people will come!"

Max welcomed the reminder of upcoming goodwill and friendship. These, after all, were the Center's reason for being. He looked forward to hosting the exhibit, glad he wasn't one of those poor sods locked in an Embassy office.

"Oh and how could I forget," she continued, "you can move into the apartment next week now that Eleana is out and you haven't forgotten about the Arboles art show?"

He had, but was more interested in the apartment. In San Genesio he'd learned that his furniture (if not his car) had arrived, and could be delivered whenever he wished. But he thought he should look at the apartment first, despite Gloria's assurances that no one could fail to love it. She agreed to take him there on Monday afternoon: "It's right on our way to the university."

"We're going to the university?"

"Didn't I tell you?"

"No."

"Oh, I'm so stupid! I called the day we talked about it you remember? But it's so hard to get an appointment there and today they said today then called to change it to Monday and what else was there about that? He told me something very important when we got there." She thought for a moment. "Oh yes, we have to go in the back door."

Max didn't ask why, lest she explain, but spent the rest of that morning and week with Washington Maldonado, Pilar San Martín, and a calculator. Washington first told him proudly that a *colegio*, a private high school, had called to reserve the auditorium. "When I told them that they would have to pay, they screamed in agony, but eventually we worked out a fair price. I anticipated that, so I started high."

"Well done, Washington."

"I also talked to a friend who works for a Sony distributor. He thought they might rent space for a demonstration concert."

"You have some idea in mind of the damage deposit we'd need?" Max was thinking of broken chairs.

Maldonado assured him that he did.

Next, Max talked to Pilar about the academic program, but without mentioning that he had already decided to sack Braden and give her his job. "I can see a lot of changes that need to be made," she warned, leaving much unsaid.

"That's the point," Max answered.

The fundamental problem, said Pilar, was discipline. Some teachers arrived late or not at all, wasted time in class, were either arrogant or too familiar with the students, and corrected exams late and badly. Not all of them, of course, "and the rest would mostly be all right if they thought someone cared. Until the teachers shape up, we have little hope of attracting more students. Part of it has been morale, as most were really unhappy with their salaries."

"I think I've taken care of that," said Max dryly.

"And there are other problems too," she went on. "I don't know how much they spent on the new wing of the building, but none of it went to the classrooms for the students. They resent the dirty walls and bad light. I don't blame them."

Max sighed. "I wish we had that money again, to spend it differently. We'll see what we can do." He thanked her for hosting Cheryl Fletcher for the moment, until they could find a room for rent.

"I hope it's only for a moment." Pilar's rolling eyes said a lot.

The next week, in deference to academic propriety or pomp, Max changed into the suit he now kept in the bathroom closet. Before leaving to see the apartment and visit the university, he set Manuel and Juan to work on Classroom Five with some leftover paint they found in a dusty storeroom. The same storage room had earlier yielded a length of stairway railing.

The apartment turned out not to be too bad: a somewhat charming, older third-story two-bedroom unit with a view down the Cholo River toward the estuary, and three blocks from the cathedral. Its main drawback was being downwind from the pungent market. And while there was a phone, it wasn't working. The owner, Señor Morales, said one need only call the phone company to have it connected, though it might take a while.

"Like at least six months!" Gloria clarified. "My cousin Federico has been waiting almost a year!"

Max decided there was nothing he could do about that, but Morales wanted an exorbitant rent about ten thousand *honores* beyond the Embassy's housing allowance. Max wasn't surprised – surely Morales asked more from Americans – but there *was* something he could do about it and soon talked the rent down to near the Embassy limit. After getting the landlord's promise to paint it and do something about the various electric wires hanging from the ceiling and walls, he agreed to take it. They'd just shaken hands on the deal when a clatter and a yelp came from the kitchen where Gloria had gone to check the cupboards. A dozen large insects skittered through the living room. "We have trouble with roaches this time of year," explained Morales, kicking a couple of them through the door.

"I thought they were the neighbors."

"No..." answered Morales, unsure what Max meant. "A spray gun comes with the apartment."

As they went back downstairs, Gloria introduced him to a couple of his human neighbors. Pablo and Pedro, who seemed not to use surnames, were artists and students (sometimes), as well as apparent clones of Che Guevara. "Pablo's a Maoist," explained Gloria as they got into her car, "and Pedro is the Fidelista. They have the most terrible fights sometimes!"

"About which end of the egg to nationalize first, I suppose."

"¿Cómo?"

As they drove to the *Universidad Alcalá* two miles outside of town, Gloria did her chaotic best to inform Max. They were going to the 'new' university on a campus built only fifteen years before, hence not yet finished. The old university in the center of town had become far too crowded after the students had demanded "with a strike the lasted the longest time!" that it be made democratic through the elimination of entrance exams and tuition fees. It became even more crowded after the university buildings were opened to the homeless at night, "but in the morning they wouldn't leave and if anyone tried to make them then they'd beat them up and say the people had a right to the people's university and sometimes they'd have class with people there eating and cooking and everything." She shook her head. "And then students all over the country went on strike until they agreed to build a new campus so they built it here where there were just some slums before and then the old place burned down when a stove fell over or something."

"Did they rebuild anything," Max asked, "or what did they do with the property?"

"They finally sold it to help pay for the new campus. You know where that huge Bank of America building is? That's where it was."

Dr. Carlos Ibarra Gonzales had been elected Rector a few months before, she explained, as the Maoist candidate.

"I'm surprised he'll see me at all."

"Oh but he's not anti-American or anything and in fact he isn't even a Communist, but he didn't get along with the Moscow-line people, *los rusos* as they call them, because one of them said Ibarra stole part of his book and there was some kind of family fight with the *Fidelista* people. Dr. Ibarra's sister used to be married to one of them."

"He's not a Communist?"

"Of course not! The Masons and the Archbishop support him. But you have to run as something!"

A six-foot adobe wall marked the university boundary as far as the eye could see. As Gloria's little blue Fiat entered the campus, Max imagined that he had stumbled across the set for a *Planet of the Apes* film. They had driven past green fields on their way here, even past what Max supposed to be the jungle's edge, and down palm-lined streets. Within the adobe walls, bulldozers had vanquished every green thing. They had left behind a huge, dusty plain broken only by a dozen or more buildings, none more than four stories high. It could have been the cover of a science fiction novel. It looked to Max exactly like a time after the Catastrophe in an *Apes* film: dirty, neglected buildings, broken windows, wires dangling from the walls.

But while it was desolate, it wasn't deserted; a large group of students bearing placards clustered in front of one building. Most of the place consisted of dusty stretches of empty ground with wind devils blowing across them.

Max wondered how they did it. Everywhere else, even in the busiest streets of Alcalá, the jungle fought back. There was always grass coming up through any crack in the pavement. Little palm trees sprang up everywhere. *What'd they do, hit it with some surplus Agent Orange?*

Gloria hid the car in the shadow of a garbage truck resting partly on large rocks, its rear axle missing. "It's safer here," she said, glancing nervously at the demonstrators. "That's the Administration Building, where we have to go." Max caught only a few words of the students' chanting, notably *derechos* and *imperialismo*. Max assumed they were in favor of rights and against imperialism, but allowed he might have got this wrong as he had so many things since he arrived.

As they walked around to the back, Max studied the multi-colored slogans painted on every wall or hung as tattered banners between buildings and light posts:

EL FUTURO PERTENECE POR
COMPLETO AL SOCIALISMO!
CIA AFUERA!
SOLIDARIDAD CON LAS MASAS
REVOLUCIONARIAS DE UGANDA!
RECUERDE EL 26 DE JUNIO
Y MIGUEL QUINTANA!

"I understand the future belongs completely to socialism, that the CIA should get out and we should all show solidarity with the revolutionary masses of Uganda, but what happened on the twenty-sixth of June?"

"Gee, I'm not sure," Gloria frowned. "Was that when the students declared Engañada a Marxist-Leninist Republic? No... that was May 1st." She looked around and saw the banner. "Oh, Miguel Quintana! That's when they made everyone get out of one of these buildings—I think it was the Science Building—then set off a bomb and wrecked a whole floor. Miguel Quintana was the leader."

"And was he sent to prison? Or killed by the police, or the bomb?"

"Oh no! The police aren't allowed on the campus, never! But the University canceled his registration for a year and he had to repeat all his courses."

They found a back door closed with a heavy chain and padlock, and continued until they reached an open side door. They worked their way through grimy hallways solid with posters, slogans, and pictures of Mao and Che Guevara, then climbed to the third floor via the back stairway. "Stay here," Gloria whispered.

Max tried to look inconspicuous as he stood by the stairs

glancing through *Art Treasures of the Smithsonian*, the presentation book he had brought for the Rector, but passing students only stared the more. He wished he hadn't worn a coat and tie, especially such an American-looking outfit. He stood out like Jethro would. It was the book, too, with its bold English title. He put *Art Treasures* under his arm.

Gloria came around a corner from his left and beckoned, just as another young woman came around a corner at the right and shouted, "There he is!" to someone behind her, signaling whomever it was to follow. Before Max could reach Gloria, the woman who had shouted was joined by three angry-looking young men with beards and/or berets. One yelled, "Stop the spy!"

Max grabbed Gloria's wrist and began running, wondering how far it was to the Rector's office. "There!" Gloria said, pointing to a slightly ajar door with *Rectorado* in large faded letters. From behind it peeped someone in heavy-rimmed glasses. Then the door slammed shut. Max heard a bolt shoved home just as he tried the handle.

They resumed running, the footsteps behind them growing louder. Max saw a landing, which should surely lead to an exit door at the bottom. Before they could start down, they heard activity downstairs, and more shouts from behind them: "Get ready! They're going down!" Max veered left, almost yanking poor Gloria's arm from its socket, and ran down a corridor that led to another staircase. With luck, it would be unguarded. *Better be*, Max thought grimly as he took the steps two and three at a time, not so much dragging Gloria as guiding her flight. On the second floor landing, Max saw students beginning to ascend from the ground floor. One had what seemed to be a machete.

Probably just a slide rule, Max thought, dashing down yet another corridor and around a corner. *What do I do when we're caught? Fight? Bad odds. Pretend not to be American? Not with my accent. And who knows what Gloria will say or do?*

His tactical planning ended as they slowed for a corner and a door opened. Someone reached out and pulled Max in, which of necessity brought Gloria with him. He tripped on something and sprawled belly up on the floor, Gloria tumbling over on top of him. A familiar voice came through the semi-darkness:

"Ah, I'm sorry, Mr. Lacey, Gloria! I hope you're not hurt?"

Max looked up and made out Luis Gonzales smiling softly and motioning him not to speak. Someone else in the room walked quietly to the door and locked it as footsteps hurried past. All in the room remained frozen while angry voices and footsteps passed and re-passed. The process took long enough for Max to notice that Gloria was heavier than she looked. Gonzales whispered something Max couldn't quite understand to someone, and Max began to laugh softly.

"Max! What are you doing?" she whispered urgently.

"I'm having an adventure in a foreign language!"

She crawled quietly away.

The footsteps passed once more and someone wiggled the locked doorknob. Then all was silent save for the chants that had serenaded their entire visit. He could hear them better now: "DOWN WITH FASCISM AND IMPERIALISM! WE DEMAND WORKER RIGHTS! YANKEES OUT!"

Gonzales helped Gloria up and said in a low voice, "I think they'll give up now. You stay here for a while and then slip out."

Max got up, dusted himself off, and looked out the window. The demonstration was petering out a bit as students sauntered off in small groups, some joining soccer games in progress on the dusty quad. Then he turned to shake hands: "*Señor* Gonzales, what a surprise! But I am, truly, glad to see you."

"My pleasure, Mr. Lacey. Permit me to present my colleagues Jorge Pinzón and Raúl Rojas." The two young men stepped out of the deeper shadows and shook Lacey's hand. Pinzón wore a business suit and looked familiar. Rojas wore army fatigues, and did not. Gloria turned out to know them both, and each kissed her on the cheek, then all sat down on chairs or the small dusty sofa.

"Well, well, Mr. Lacey," began Gonzales, pulling his chair close to Max. "We meet again under unexpected circumstances. Tell me, how do you find Alcalá?"

Max hesitated just a second. "Interesting," he smiled at last.

"Interesting! Very good. And something more, I should think.

I hear that Mariana has left the Center. But—you have Gloria to listen to. You do advise Mr. Lacey, don't you, Gloria?"

"Oh but of course!" She began to describe the artistic questions on which she advised Max, but Gonzales smoothly cut her off.

"And I should have mentioned this before. Your colleague Harvey Tyrone has a great deal of experience that could help you. But tell me, how was your visit with the Rector?" He reached over and turned on a small lamp. Max saw he was dressed in the same white outfit he had worn on the ship, and that it was as immaculate as ever.

That's what I really need to know: how does he do that? By the time I get to the office, my suits look like I slept in them.

"Brief. A brief visit. I waved to him as we ran past his door."

Gonzales chuckled. "It was rash of him to schedule it with his known pro-Americanism. You do know he was a Fulbright student twenty years ago? But I suppose that's just why he did it. He's still very grateful, you see, and he'd like to renew some sort of exchange. I suppose he'll forget that for a while."

"Yes," said Gloria, rearranging her hair. "The poor man can't even come to the Center anymore, but you know he still uses all those books on—what is it?"

"Economics," helped Gonzales.

"That's right, and Carmen Jaramillo the Librarian she has to wrap the books up in plain paper and send them with Manuel or someone to his house and he sends notes back to say what he wants next and it's like they were spies or smugglers."

Raúl Rojas murmured something, causing Gonzales to reach over and pat his arm. "Poor Raúl, he should have been chasing you too, Max! You know he's very active in the student movement, and not at all pro-American."

"No, I'm not," the youth confirmed grimly. "But," he cheered up, "What could I do? A professor's office is sort of a sanctuary, like a church, so if I'd told them you were here it would have complicated things. And it wouldn't have been fair to catch you that way."

"I'm glad there are rules," Max said. "I guess I'd better learn the rest of them if I'm to be 'effective' as we like to say."

"The Rector would agree with you," Gonzales nodded, "had you talked to him. He would have expounded his 'game theory' of university and Engañadan politics—how students and everyone pretend to be something, or hate something, or love something. Always the Revolution, of course, though the rules don't require you to define it very closely. And while you don't have to believe in it any more than a soccer player believes in the offside rule, you have to observe the conventions."

"That's how he became Rector," added Pinzón, "pretending to believe in Mao Zedung. And he played the game well, even memorizing quotations from the *Little Red Book* he carried with him during the campaign."

"Is that the object of the game," Max asked, "to win elections?"

"To win or do anything!" Gonzales clarified. "Or to *be* anything. Because it's not entirely a game. But if you think of that aspect too much, you turn into a bore, as I'm afraid poor Ibarra does at times. You see, he's afraid that the real Communists will just seize the moment when these games produce enough chaos, and then all games will cease."

"Only if they betray the Revolution!"

"Raúl, Raúl," Gonzales said painfully. "We've been through this so many times! The real revolutionaries always betray the Revolution; that's how you know they're real."

Raúl grunted.

"Well," Max asked, "excuse me, but what are you doing here? I mean, you teach here, I take it?"

"For the last forty years, on and off," Gonzales confirmed. "I'm also a Maoist, by the way. This time." He winked at Raúl. "But I don't teach much just now, with the strikes and, recently, the occupation of the Law Faculty by the people opposed to the Espejo Party. Raúl is one of the occupiers in fact, but came in for some help on his thesis."

"Then I suppose you're identified with the Espejo Party, even if you are a Maoist for the moment?"

"On the contrary, Max, I'm one of their most bitter

opponents. It's a bit ironic that my classes are suspended by this occupation."

"I see."

"Do you? Well, good. But I wonder if we can get some coffee while we wait."

Pinzón slipped out the door and Max looked around the office. Among the diplomas and awards hung a photograph of a younger Gonzales with a tall, gaunt, patriarchal figure taken in a luxurious office with flags behind a desk. There was handwriting on it: "To my faithful Lucho, with best wishes from the Rio Plata. Juan."

"That was taken in 1948," Gonzales explained. "It was during his eighth? No, seventh term. And just two days before the coup. He sent it from Argentina."

Pinzón slipped in with five small cups of coffee and a large sugar bowl. *I swear, if two Latins were about to fight a duel, they would first share an* espresso. Accepting one, Max glanced at Pinzón, trying to figure out why he looked familiar. To buy time, he asked Raúl how his law studies went when he wasn't on strike.

"All right, but they are not important. The important thing is to build..." He looked at Gonzales with a conspiratorial smile and concluded, "...the country."

Pinzón set his coffee cup down, looking serious. "To build the country, you should study engineering, Raúl. Or business."

"You're with Gandig!" Max blurted, his memory jogged.

"I knew you'd remember sooner or later, but don't be embarrassed. I sometimes forget it myself in these circumstances."

Max turned again to Gonzales, indicating the picture. "If it isn't impolite to ask, did you and Espejo part company over some political question?"

"Ah, you think that because of the picture, though now I oppose the Espejo Party? But no, there was no disagreement, no falling out. If he returns, as today's news suggests he might, I may support him again."

"What news?"

"The government today published a Resolution of Provisional Return which says that all exiles, including former presidents, can return so long as their presence does not conflict with the democratic institutions of the country and the patriotic duty of the military establishment."

"So he'll return, and you'll support him?"

"Well, first we have to see if he does return. The *junta* said they would issue the implementing decree, which allows the Resolution of Return to take effect, 'at the appropriate point in the evolution of the political maturation of the populace.' That usually means 'within a month,' though it could be more, and the decree itself may specify later dates for various things. But yes, I suppose I might support him."

Raúl interrupted to excuse himself; he had a political meeting to attend. He shook hands with Max and Pinzón and kissed Gloria on the cheek. Gonzales put his arm over his shoulders and led him to the door where Raúl whispered urgently for a moment. Gonzales sighed and patted Raúl on the back. As Raúl left, Gonzales advised him to see if the Muñoz book didn't help with precedents.

Gonzales shook his head as he returned to the group. "A good boy, Raúl. He warned me about you, Max. I can call you Max? He asked me how I could be sure you're not a CIA agent. Are you?"

"Dr. Gonzales—"

"Please! Call me Lucho!"

"Thanks. Well, Lucho, you know that either way the answer will always be 'no,' but what difference does it make? I serve the capitalist fascist running dog Wall Street imperialists who are draining the blood of Engañada's workers, peasants, and intellectuals, so what difference does it make which branch of the Empire I'm with?"

Gonzales laughed along. "Of course, but I wouldn't point that out if I were you: good boys just might follow it to its logical conclusion. Never give the Raúls of the world too many ideas at once; it only confuses them."

Gloria then jumped in with something like panic in her voice. "Oh excuse me Max, Lucho, but I just remembered I don't want to forget and you too Jorge—to tell you to be sure to come to the Luis Delgado art show on the fifteenth that we're so excited about it!"

"Of course, Gloria, if I can. I'll have to consult some people first. You know how these things are."

"Oh I know but Luis Delgado never fought with anybody and everybody likes his work even the *Fidelistas* who complain about everything!"

"Yes, I'm sure, but we'll see. Being out of the country, one loses touch with the finer shadings."

"Excuse me," interrupted Max, "but did you start teaching here right away? I mean, if you've been out of the country all these years?"

"I never left, Max. Not the University. I was doing 'professional investigation' as we call it. When I got back I just picked up a few new students from colleagues—mostly, I direct theses—and some of my old ones. Many of whom, I'm afraid, have made little enough progress in my absence. Raúl, for instance, or your Washington Maldonado."

"Washington? I didn't know he was a student."

"I sometimes wonder if he remembers it himself. But, we were speaking of Espejo."

"Oh, I hope he does come back," said Gloria. "His campaigns are always so much fun and he always supported art so much like he built the museum when he was President three times ago and maybe if he's elected again he can finish it!"

"Well, if he's the best man for the job," shrugged Max. He realized that he was shrugging a lot recently, though not yet as well as a native or even Braden. *I don't think Jethro has picked it up. Might be a coastal thing.*

"I wouldn't say he's the best," Gonzales responded, "but rather the only one. You must understand in our politics, the welfare of the country is not its object, and only in part its subject. It's a drama, rather as your Shakespeare said."

"Not ours, but I see where you're going."

"It's the notion that all the world's a stage. But here it's especially true. We use politics to dramatize what we would wish to be, or what we would wish to imagine ourselves to be. It's not simply that we deceive ourselves into thinking that we are innocent enough to be deceived by them. Do you see?"

"Excuse me," broke in Gloria, "but it's getting late and I think we could leave now. It's almost dark."

She was right, but Max needed to hear more. This was how one really learned about the country, which is what Foreign Service officers are supposed to do. What did Gonzales mean about deception and imagination and innocence? "In a while," he said to Gloria, and to Gonzales, "I don't think I see. Not yet."

"Ibarra's game theory," picked up the old man. "All right as far as it goes, but it concerns only students—at least insofar as it's dangerous. Anyway, being innocent enough to imagine oneself a knight is the first and necessary step to becoming a knight. Don Quixote is the model. We know we can't be knights and can't have one for President, but with a man like Espejo we can reach the point that we believe that we believe in it, and can consequently feel betrayed by the oligarchy, who especially want to believe—old aristocratic families, you know, authentic or not— or the military, who almost do believe, or by the *yanquis*. They're the best ones to blame, for they alternately approximate and mock the belief, producing great Presidents like Washington and Lincoln as well as miserable ones like Polk and Johnson–either one, Andrew or Lyndon. And then again, insisting the law applies to everyone, even to President Nixon. Amazing! Then Nixon gets a pardon! So we nurse our sense of betrayal. That's our real genius. That's why Kennedy was so popular here–Camelot and all that– and his murder both expected and mourned. And we mourned him for another reason too: unlike most Americans, he managed to hide his contempt for Latin America, allowing us to believe he even respected us."

Before Max could issue a shocked denial, Gonzales intervened: "Please, Max, don't hurt yourself!" His smile was just slightly bitter. "I don't even blame you so much; after all, one can't deny the terrible telephone service, contaminated water, constant political turmoil, *etcetera*."

"What did I ever say about that?" asked Max.

"Nothing, Max, not a word. Few Americans say it openly. But it's in your face and in the margins of your encyclopedias. No, please! I said I don't blame you, or at least that I understand it. But that's another reason we need an Espejo, to let us believe the whole thing is not just contemptible politics and incompetent plumbing. With him, we can believe in romance and a sense of innocence. Without Espejo, there's only cynicism—your contempt, in our terms—and despite the fact that we're a cynical race, we're unwilling to accept the notion that no other attitude is possible. In that, maybe we really are innocents! Anyway, Sancho Panza loved Don Quixote for a reason. But that's enough political education for one day. I'm sure it's safe to leave now."

Still confused, Max said goodbye, leaving the heavy *Art Treasures of the Smithsonian* with Gonzales, who promised to get it to the Rector. Their escape was merely a nervous evening walk across a quiet campus. On the way back to town Max tried to construct arguments against the charge of contempt for Engañada. It wasn't easy. *What can I do? Their water is contaminated, and I don't see why they couldn't clean it up if they really wanted to. I've already spent a fortune on bottled water.* Resolving nothing, he posed some other questions to Gloria. "So, is Gonzales really with Espejo or not?"

"Well, you have to remember that everyone is an Espejista. It's just that some of them don't think Espejo is."

I am no closer to figuring this out.

Chapter Ten: Legal Counsel

The Board meeting that finally took place ten days later was sparsely attended: of the six members (two positions were vacant), only four said they would attend, and three actually did, leaving the meeting two short of a quorum. Max was relieved that one who did attend was Dr. Carlos Ramírez, the President and legal counsel, a short, plump, pleasant man. He wore a spotless lightweight white suit, brass-buckled brown shoes, polished cufflinks, and fashionable gold-framed glasses. Not a salt-and-pepper hair was out of place, and he smelled of expensive aftershave. Max hoped that such luxury guaranteed competence.

Gandig attended as well, though he kept glancing at his watch. The third member at the conference table in Max's office was a sweet old lady named Harriet Bowman de Carrasco, an American who had arrived with her husband fifty years before. When widowed, she found that she couldn't leave; Alcalá had become her home.

As Mrs. Bowman entered the Center earlier that morning, Max was in the lobby and watched the employees welcome her warmly. Rosa later explained: Mr. Bowman had run the American mill *Molinos de Engañada*. He and his wife were famous for their kindness and generosity. A job at *Molinos* was highly coveted because the mill paid not only all the benefits required by Engañadan law (something many local companies managed to avoid), but added even more. Mrs. Bowman, Rosa said, had celebrated births with employees, and mourned with them at funerals. In this she was like the best of the traditional *patronas* on the large estates, but with none of their aloofness from social inferiors.

The good woman's dress this morning was that of an Engañadan matron, a rather elaborate gray outfit with flowers embroidered on it. She knitted throughout the meeting, following the conversation with a bemused smile that suggested she had seen it all before. She told Max she was very much looking forward to tomorrow's concert by the Genesee State String Quartet, and appreciated the invitation. Max said she was welcome, and silently thanked Gloria for reminding him to send the invitations "which we always do with these State Department tour things that give us so much prestige!"

Ramírez made a brief speech welcoming Max to the Center before they got to business. Since there was no quorum, Max would not see what a regular meeting involved, and any decisions they made would be provisional until approved by the next meeting that was not inquorate. "But don't worry about that," said Ramírez, "It's always been that way." That was fine with Max, who needed legal advice and support more than decisions. If he got it, the meeting would have proven more productive than most, judging from the past minutes he had read. Now he raised the three legal questions.

Dr. Ramírez addressed the first two clearly and briefly: "The new teachers' contract is a fact. Unfortunately, you didn't know the rules, but you could hardly be expected to. Since the contract has been recognized by the Labor Ministry, we would have to get a reversal of that recognition for the purpose of taking away from our teachers benefits that they presently enjoy. Very difficult," he sighed, "and the sort of thing the newspapers love. We'd take a lot of abuse and probably lose anyway. It's not worth it.

"As for the Fletcher girl, we are obligated to pay her airfare and give her a teaching contract for a reasonable time. If she doesn't work out within three months, we can dismiss her, though we'd have to pay her return fare. We invited her to come. The telegram, signed by our representative, constitutes a legal obligation. Also, I'll have to arrange a work visa so she can receive her salary legally. And, has she a place to live? We should find a family for her to live with. I think I know of one, the Pristinos."

"They're lovely people," added Mrs. Bowman.

"But surely we're not obliged to do that?" Max asked, immediately wishing he hadn't. He owed it to Pilar to get the girl out her house as soon as possible.

"No, but it's prudent. The girl will be identified as an American, and as our teacher. For her safety and our reputation, it's better this way. I'll make a call."

He paused, took off his glasses and polished them, then held them up to the light for inspection. "The third point is more complicated and interesting. If or when we fire Braden, we must pay him the legal severance pay of one month's salary for every year he's been with the Center. But I don't think that's a huge amount. And we must send copies of the documents, with the reasons for his discharge, to the Ministry of Labor. The accountant, Luis...?"

"Verde," Max supplied.

"Yes, Verde. He can prepare the form. I'll call him to provide some language about our reasons. But, and here's the nice part of it, we can probably get most of the money back: Braden was not authorized to send that telegram, was he?"

"No. I sent the letter to him with a note, that he should tell her 'no thanks.' I thought that if he answered at all, he'd write a letter saying as much; we don't even have enough students to keep our present teachers busy. But maybe he thought it was just a suggestion and he was authorized to do whatever he thought best?"

"He could try to argue that, but it is not reasonable. Someone in Mr. Braden's position should know that the Center does not let the Academic Director make decisions obligating the Center to pay that much money. So, we charge administrative ineptitude and deduct the cost of the airfare from his severance pay."

"Sounds fair to me," Max agreed.

"He doesn't have any family, does he?" asked Mrs. Bowman.

"No, I believe he has not," Ramírez assured her. "And fairness is not the point, but legality. He could contest it, of course, but I believe we'd win. We're fortunate that he's a supervisor–and an American! You never win with local workers."

Thus far, Gandig had listened to Ramírez' explanation in sullen impatience. Now he surprised them all. "It's a loser!" he said, harshly.

"What do you mean?" asked Ramírez in a cool voice.

"I mean, even if you win, what then? The problems of this Center don't begin and end with Braden. He's just another problem, like Fletcher is just another problem. And when we had the market, it made sense to fight these battles, but the way enrollment is going, you're only putting off the inevitable."

They all stared at him. "What do you mean?" asked Ramírez again.

"I mean, I've looked over our enrollment figures for the past ten years; it's a constant downward trend. Whether it's been the competition or the recession or what, we haven't been able to stem it. I think it's time to face up to it."

"But we have!" smiled Mrs. Bowman. "We've had special prices and Mariana prepared that lovely folder a few years ago."

"That's the point," Gandig insisted. "We haven't just sat on our hands. We've tried—and failed. Basically, we can't compete with all these other schools because they have no overhead, just their teachers and minimal rent, while we have this huge building with a library and a cultural program to maintain."

"What do you suggest, then?" asked Ramírez.

"That we face the fact that the Center has outlived its marketability."

"You mean, sell out?"

"Well, you could do that."

Mrs. Bowman answered with a resentful sigh. Ramírez nodded as if running legal options through his head.

What in the hell? Max's mouth fell half open. In his office, Gandig had been grandly unworried about things, at least in the short term. *What's going on?*

Whatever it was, Max wasn't going to accept this. *No way.* He was sure that they either didn't try hard enough, or didn't try the right way. He and his staff could do better, and the rental thing would help a lot.

Max explained all this to the others as cogently as he could, perhaps over-emphasizing the one wedding reception rental. "Mr. Gandig made an excellent point to me about the need to make square meters productive. I intend to put that into action."

"Parties weren't what I had in mind," said Gandig with a frown.

"If done with dignity, that could be a good source of revenue," Ramírez said.

"I think it's a wonderful idea," offered Mrs. Bowman.

"Well," Ramírez said, "we certainly ought to give these measures a chance before we take any drastic determination."

Gandig frowned but said nothing, and there it lay. The meeting broke up with small talk, in which even Gandig joined a bit. Max had a victory in a battle he hadn't planned for, convincing them not to abandon their own Center.

Rosa took the phone number of the Pristinos, which Ramírez had provided, and promised to talk to Cheryl and then contact the family to confirm the arrangement. "She'll need some money for rent, I think." Max heard something of pity and disgust as well as coolness in her voice. He promised to tell the accountant, and wondered about that coolness. *Jealousy? That could be good.*

Luis Verde sighed in turn. At first he seemed dubious about firing Braden, but asked for time to study the pertinent forms. The next day, Max stopped by to ask if Verde had drawn any conclusions, and got a surprise: "It's a fine idea. The best thing we've done in years. Doctor Ramírez called and provided excellent points which I've included in the documents which we must provide to Braden." He handed Max a fat envelope that contained a long official-looking dismissal form with a cover letter to Braden. "When we deduct the airfare from the severance pay, that will reduce it to almost zero. And a good thing, too, because Mr. Gandig's million *honores* won't last us long. It's these extra things," Verde moaned, "like the advance to Miss Fletcher."

"She has to live somewhere," shrugged Max, "and if she gets a room with a family, that's a lot cheaper than an apartment. Anyway, we'll take it back out of her salary."

As he prepared to go up and tell Braden the news, all the fun went out of it. He'd never fired anyone before. As a career Federal bureaucrat, he regarded 'Termination' as an unthinkable death sentence from a benighted age, like hanging, drawing, and quartering. He didn't want to hurt Braden the man, but only to remove a fatal flaw in the Center. But what if Braden needed the money?

Then he should have cared more about doing his damn job! Thinks he's too good to worry about money. 'I'm no businessman,' he said. So why should it bother me?

Because I'm the one firing him.

Max looked back at the other hand: a lot of jobs depended on the Center, and Braden was endangering them all. But maybe he didn't have to throw the guy completely out of the lifeboat. The man couldn't manage anything but he was, as he had informed Max early on, a native speaker. *So let him teach. That's it.*

Braden was working at his desk. "Class schedule for next term," he said, looking up at Max. "Next trimester starts the fifteenth."

Max sat down. "How many classes will there be?"

"Thirty-four, if I've added them right. Pilar wants three, Luis four, Carlos two..." When he finished adding he had thirty-six.

"And how many students do you think we'll have to fill those classes?"

Braden shrugged. "That's not my business. I set up the courses, and teach."

Thanks, Braden. That makes this easier. "That won't do," he told him. Braden stared. "The Academic Director does have to worry about that. And about other things, like teachers showing up on time, for instance. And the Academic Director has to know he's not authorized to commit the Center to hire a teacher and pay her airfare without consulting or even informing me. Anyone who won't or can't do that shouldn't be Academic Director."

Braden still stared.

"I've had parents complain about teachers. Several times."

"I'm a native speaker," Braden answered at last.

"That's not enough. So, you can stay as a teacher. That's all."

"You're firing me." Neither anger, nor surprise, nor dismay.

"Yes. Here's a letter for your records." He handed over the fat envelope.

Braden picked up the envelope and stared at it for a moment, but didn't open it. Then he got up and walked quickly from the office. Max waited five minutes to see if he would return, then called Pilar San Martín in to discuss her first steps as Acting Academic Director. She seemed upbeat, perhaps because she was being promoted, perhaps because she thought she could make the program better, and in part because, she said, Cheryl had told her she'd be moving in with the Pristinos.

When he left the office, Max noticed that the usual hallway chatter was on low volume. Teachers looked wary as he passed. Ten steps on, Max happened to glance at his watch. Several of the teachers scurried into their classrooms. He felt powerful and optimistic, but something else sunk in. To these teachers, he was now The Man, and could never talk to them as anything else. He was not to blame; nor were they. Yet he had never seen so clearly that this is the way things had to be.

Damn, it's lonely at the top.

The next night, the Center hosted the Genesee State String Quartet concert. Preparations went well. Manuel and company had the auditorium in very good order, including straight-backed chairs; Sam and Hector had arranged the spotlights properly, which was about all they had to do. No amplification would be needed.

Max had overseen some such arrangements as these in Mexico. The routine was to meet the musicians at the airport, take them to a hotel and then to the Center so they could see the stage and practice a bit, make any adjustments in lighting or anything else they needed, then set out bottled water. The group consisted of two men and two women from the Genesee State Music Faculty, who were gracious even as they lamented the impact of Alcalá's humidity on their tuning. Max couldn't hear much difference, but he hadn't much of an ear. He took the group's musical talent as given: they got picked for a State Department tour, didn't they?

Certainly some of the audience that night appreciated The Dvorak American quartet, Samuel Barber's String Quartet in B minor, and other pieces. Perhaps a hundred people stayed to the end–all the Center Board except Gandig, the *Sociedad Historica* people, the inevitable *Doctora* Esperanza Romero Ycaza, and scattered others whom Gloria introduced as prominent citizens or music professionals. Some were too shy to greet the Director. Washington was right about the kids, most of whom disappeared during the intermission.

"We're used to that," smiled John Finnegan, lead violinist, after the concert. "Rock rules the world!"

"We're sort of like missionaries," added the viola player, a middle-aged woman named Elizabeth Downs. "Every soul is priceless, so if we save even one, it's worth the trip!"

By the time he had escorted the tired group back to their hotel, Max felt real satisfaction. *Music, beauty, goodwill, all happening in the Center. Maybe we saved more than one soul.*

Chapter Eleven: Of Fish and Art

The Embassy mail arrived about 10 AM, and included a letter from his parents that had taken two weeks to arrive. They were glad that he was well, but unsure just what his job was. Max was still unsure himself and doubted that he could explain it, even if he knew.

The afternoon brought the local mail, including late cards of welcome from school and museum directors to add to the others accumulated since Lacey's arrival. He would call on all of them sooner or later. Now he suppressed the unkind thought that some might ask for band instruments or scholarships or projectors.

Then there was an envelope from Gandig Consolidated containing a letter of resignation from the Board for motives "beyond possibility of delay." Gandig wished the Center well.

As if he really cares. The bastard! Max didn't know which of Gandig's possible motives was more disgusting: that he was too busy making money to sacrifice an hour a month, or just mad because the Board didn't go along with his idea of selling out. Another possibility was that the Center really was hopeless, and Gandig didn't want to be associated with its failure. "To hell with him," he muttered. "We'll get somebody else." He sent the letter on to Ramírez.

A package from Simón Bolívar Blanco contained his translations of Woodrow Lively's *Home Had Two Doors* and *The Stoned Prophet.* Preferring to read the original, Max went to the library, albeit with scant hope: they had precious little Hawthorne, Melville, or Faulkner, so probably nothing by this unknown writer. Alcalá surprised him again: not only were both books there, but the due-date slips showed that they had been checked out often. Both books had originally been published in the 1930s, and Max read the title poem of *Home Had Two Doors*:

Home had two doors: the one was tall
And stately to the view.
The other low and dark and foul
Was used by very few.
One was Truth, the other Lie,
So what was there to choose?
We used the one with company,
The other with the Muse.
The first was our more common door,
We went out as we were.
The second opened on ourselves
More vile or more pure.
Home had two doors. The first confirmed
A neighborly good fame;
The second was a magic door:
We'd not return the same.

Max had read worse, but doubted Blanco made much money selling this in any language. He then consulted the translation and discovered that Blanco had in fact authored a derivative poem of his own. Rendered back to English, it read:

Where Now the Home?
Where is the house that had two doors
Where I first learned to play?
Where the door of Sunday best?
The door of every day?
Where is the truth, does it lie
Within that old home yet?
Where, O Muse, the company?
Where are they now met?

And so on. *Can't translate poetry*, remembered Max, *and sometimes you shouldn't even try.*

But if *Home* was a strange collection, the later *Stoned Prophet* was stranger yet. Notable in the second volume was "I Sing What I Am Not" in which the poet announced boldly what

111

had been implicit in the earlier volume. "I am Hypocrite," it began, and went on to claim,

I am the great Indispensable.
I am Judas.
Without my Sin, Virtue has no growth,
Nor never will Cruelty's heavy hand be lifted.

A glance at Blanco's version indicated that the translator had grown ever less faithful to his original, with these lines coming out, "Where is the inevitable Judas? / Does he sin where Virtue grows? / And where shall fall the cruel hand of Fate?" Maybe Blanco was too sane to follow Lively's deterioration, or too innocent to share the American's glorification of hypocrisy. Then again, maybe he just didn't understand English very well.

Max was closing the English *Prophet* when he saw something in another poem. He flipped back to it and read, "Her heart as false as smile of Alcalá, / How could I fail to love her?" Another line claimed that "the lying estuary of my sinful soul / Leads on to Cholo's peace." *Damn. At least that tells me he must have been here.*

He took out the name card. Like the due-date slip, it went back only to 1960. Blanco's name appeared several times—*had he never bought his own copies?*—amid an extensive sampling of common Engañadan names—Espejo, Gonzales, Ibarra, and such. But the most frequent name toward the end stood out: Bertram Braden. "No wonder this place is so screwed up," Max mumbled as he slammed the book shut and replaced it on the American Poetry shelf, next to Longfellow.

Max invited Rosa to dinner that evening before the *Arboles* art show, hoping for information on the people he would meet in some form other than Gloria's breathless orations. Rosa had accepted only after he made very clear that the dinner was to discuss the artists, that they would then go directly from the restaurant to the show, and then she would take the bus home. He understood. She had to watch her reputation. *Not that she has anything to fear after what George said; this is was strictly business.*

Washington had suggested Mazzini's: "best Italian restaurant in town." And the only one; but very pleasant, built on an old pier above the river near the park hosting the exhibit. The menu offered all manner of strange seafood in addition to the expected pastas and meat dishes. Rosa tried to explain to him just what *linguado* was, and how it differed from the *corvina* or the indeterminate *pescado* ("fish"). He went with her recommendation of the *linguado.*

When the drinks arrived, Max held his up as if to offer a toast and stared at Rosa in the candlelight. *God, she really is lovely.* As she stared back, he forgot what he'd meant to say until she smiled and looked down. "Here's looking at you, kid," he said clumsily.

"What?" she asked in puzzlement. Max explained about *Casablanca*, which Rosa hadn't seen, and how the line had become a sort of custom.

"Oh," she said, "you've seen so much. You're lucky."

She wanted him to tell her where he'd been and what he'd done. Wishing he had more to tell, he embellished a bit, making his summer ROTC training sound more exciting than it was—"the explosives were the most fun, blowing things up"—but it still didn't last long.

"That's *congrio*," advised Rosa as the waiter walked past with yet another strange fish on a plate.

"*Congrio*? Not to be confused with *linguado* or *corvina* or *pescado,* even though it is some kind of *pescado?*"

"That's right!" she laughed.

"How do you know so much about fish?"

"I've cleaned every kind of fish there is, and eaten so many that some morning I'm going to wake up with gills. That's what we did in San Andrés, mostly; fish. Or, the men fished. We cleaned fish. Father Pedro blessed the fishing boats every year and we had a big party for the blessing."

Max imagined an idyllic seaside village. "Right on the beach?"

"Yes and no. Not on the ocean. San Andrés is on the *Estuario*

San Miguel. About a hundred kilometers north of Alcalá."

Max mentally moved to a riverbank deep in the jungle. "What's it like?"

"I miss it," she began, then stopped and thought. "I miss Father Pedro, even though he was always talking about sin, especially sins of unkindness—nasty gossip or making fun of poor Juancito Morales who wasn't right in the head. But he seemed sad about it more than mad. And he was always...there. If someone died or was sick or had a baby, he was there." She shrugged. "It's strange. The city has so much: running water and stores and movies and high schools and television and buses all the time. Or most of the time, at least. But even so, I miss San Andrés, even though there was nothing to do but clean fish and fry bananas and gossip."

"Don't you gossip here?"

"Of course, and even the gossip is better. But in San Andrés, even though there wasn't much to do just for fun, we spent more time doing it. Here, I spend half my life working, on the bus going to work, or taking my little brothers somewhere. Maybe it's just that all I had to do in San Andrés, besides clean fish, was play. School only had six grades. We came here when I was fourteen."

"What brought your family to Alcalá?"

"A cousin told my father there was a truck for sale. Fishing hadn't ever really supported us, so Papá also built boats, but even that wasn't enough. He decided that even a one-truck transportation business in the city would support the family better. He wanted a better future for us children, too; there's no work in San Andrés, and only the elementary school."

"It seems as if it worked out well, though?"

"Yes, I think so. I took a secretarial course in a commercial *colegio*. I couldn't have done that in San Andrés. It was exciting, I did well, and that's how I came to the Centro. Mariana would only hire the best graduates." Rosa paused, smiled. "So it was one of the happiest days of my life when I got the job. Even if it doesn't pay that much, you learn English for free. With that and the experience, you can get a good job at a bank or with a big company."

114

"And how's your English?" Max asked in English, making room on the table for the plates the waiter now brought.

"I no... no, no: I *don't* speak English well," she laughed. Max thought her accent charming. But she seemed uncomfortable and he switched back to Spanish.

"Have you had these offers, to leave the Center?"

"One," she said, "but I didn't take it. It was with Bernardo Gómez, but I don't like him."

"Who's he?"

"A lawyer. He's the one that has something to do with those empty buildings by the Center. And he got the poor people kicked out that were living there. I don't know where they went. The children used to play in our patio."

The *linguado* was as fine as Rosa had promised. They ate mostly in silence, as people do when unsure how much they want to say to each other. At length Max asked, "So, you've been happy in the Center?"

"Yes, now, again. It was nice when I started, everyone happy, and everyone cared about the Center. Then it changed somehow, maybe because of the money problems. Everyone seemed to blame each other and a lot of people didn't care, especially after Mariana left. But now I think it's going to be better again."

Dinner over, they strolled along the riverbank toward the park and the art show. Occasionally a breeze promised coolness without delivering any, but still it was almost fresh after the oppressive midday heat. At times the trees obscured the city street that ran parallel to the river. Looking across the dark water at the few lights on the other side of the Cholo, Max could almost imagine he was outside the city. "Is this anything like San Andrés?" he asked.

"Hmmm." She stopped and sniffed the air. "If you close your eyes, it could be. But no, you can hear too many cars."

"Must be a quiet place."

"Ask Manuel! You know he's from San Andrés too? His family is one of the few not related to mine. He says it's too quiet, that he would have turned into a stump if he'd stayed longer."

"I'd have thought Manuel would appreciate a place where nothing can go wrong because nothing happens."

"Things can go wrong, believe me! Besides, things do happen sometimes. President Espejo has visited San Andrés in every one of his campaigns. Did you know he's my godfather?"

"No!"

"Yes! My father was always an *Espejista,* like my grandfather, and the President came to our village to campaign before I was born. My father asked him, and he came back for the baptism. So, you see? Of course, half of the country is his godchild."

"Probably Simón Bolívar was, too," said Max. "He's been around long enough."

Rosa laughed. *How can she have such perfect teeth? Surely there's no dentist in San Andrés? Maybe fish and rice and bananas are the secret. Hasn't helped Manuel, though.*

"There's a joke," Rosa said, "that Engañada has two kinds of government, Espejo and the *junta.* But Espejo was first, because the generals didn't arrive until 1492!"

They reached the park where the art show was arranged along the river beneath the squat obscene-looking *Ceibos* trees, their bloated trunks and limbs like organs or monstrous vegetables, out of all proportion to their small flat leaves. Lights had been strung between them. But for the triple-thick clouds of mosquitoes under the lights, the ambience would have been pleasant indeed.

Few of the paintings pleased Max, but here he was a tourist, and not obliged to comment. At the Center, it would be different, or when they joined Gloria and she introduced him to the artists. For now, he could smile at or dismiss the canvas that seemed no more than a stretched cleaning rag, and then enjoy a better one without pretending it was a Picasso. They passed a bright, enigmatic painting depicting a ship docking at port devoid of people. "Makes you wonder what happened, doesn't it?"

"No," Rosa laughed. "That's Alcalá, and the ship arrived at lunchtime!"

They came at last to Gloria's stand. As he had somehow feared, her paintings were the sort of which he could say nothing: compositions of ragged multi-colored squares, mostly dull, with here and there a bright orange or electric blue. Some consisted only of squiggly lines. "Do you like them?" she asked.

Back on Director duty, Max thoughtfully picked out one painting, pointed to the right middle area and said: "I'm puzzled by this: is it a continuation of the basic theme, or intended instead as counterpoint?"

"What do you mean?" asked Gloria.

"I mean, in terms of chromatic alternation."

"Oh. Oh, I think I see. You mean does the green here balance the gray over here between the black and the red?"

"Yes, or I thought, possibly, just the opposite."

That was enough to get her chattering on happily for five minutes. Max seemed to listen intently but kept glancing at Rosa beside him, delighted by her suppressed smile. The occasional tightening of her hand on his arm communicated understanding and solidarity.

Gloria then took them on a tour of the whole exhibit, introducing artist after artist. As she did so, Max remembered that he was supposed to have discussed painters with Rosa at dinner. *Did she forget about it too? What does that mean?*

Max's neighbors Pablo and Pedro were side by side with paintings much alike, except that Pablo favored rural themes while Pedro concentrated on city slums. "Americans are blind to oppression," said Pablo matter-of-factly.

"They don't want to see it," shrugged Pedro.

"That's why we have artists," said Max, "to make us see."

Pedro and Pablo looked at each other uncertainly, and then Pedro brightened: "Would you like to buy one, then?"

"Of course, now that I have a place to hang it."

They came next to a stall in front of which twenty or so young people argued simultaneously with each other. "That's Miguel's stall," said Gloria sadly. "I told him he shouldn't show that one, that picture of Espejo."

Max looked around and saw it, perched defiantly above the other paintings. It showed Espejo on a balcony, arms outstretched, exhorting followers in a plaza. "What's the matter?" he asked. "It looks all right to me." In fact, it was far the best thing he'd seen and he could hardly take his eyes off it: the crowd, the buildings around the plaza, even the noonday sunlight seemed not so much to provide a setting for Espejo as to depend upon him and his gesture for their form and coherence. It explained more about Espejo's relation to Engañadans than did Gonzales' comments about imagination and innocence. Or maybe it brought those comments to life.

"Anytime you hang a picture of Espejo you have fights," Gloria sighed. "The Espejo Party people will say it doesn't show the proper respect, and the *Espejistas* will say the Party people are trying to bury Espejo, and the *Fidelistas* say the painting is a bourgeois attempt to take over an authentic hero of the People, and, oh, I don't know but they talk and talk and make me so tired!"

Max looked at Rosa. "Is that right? Is your godfather so controversial?"

"Of course he is," she answered proudly. "He's the only one who makes anything happen in this country."

Max would have liked to meet this Miguel who had gone off somewhere, but Gloria urged them on to the Luis Delgado exhibit to see the collection that would shortly be moved to the Center. All of Delgado's paintings depicted wide-eyed children. Max could see nothing distinctive about them, no reason for Gloria to have chosen Delgado as the expositor rather than any of a dozen others—over Miguel, for instance, who was clearly the best.

Delgado, a thin, gentle-looking young man with long hair, naturally asked what Max thought of his work. He couldn't very well say that it reminded him of the fuzzy pictures sold in U.S. dime stores to be hung in bathrooms, mostly little girls with huge eyes in pajamas, trailing a blanket. So Max pretended to ponder for a moment, then said thoughtfully: "I can see why Gloria wanted you in the Center. Who can resist children?"

They wandered to a dozen other exhibits. While a few paintings pleased Max, or at least interested or puzzled him, he found most of the work amateurish. But what did he know? He probably would have thought Picasso just weird when he first exhibited those fractured things. In fact, he had never understood the genius that knowledgeable people found in them, so it was better not to think of his artistic ignorance. Doing so made him feel like a fraud in his role as cultural attaché.

It was nearly midnight when they said goodbye to the last artist, and to Gloria. The streets were almost deserted as waiters carried chairs and tables in from the sidewalk cafés. "I didn't realize it was so late," Rosa said.

"Too late for the bus?" Max tried to keep the hope out of his voice.

"They still run," she answered, and he walked the four blocks with her to her bus stop. A small group of people were gathered there, gesturing to each other in irritation. They weren't arguing, but agreeing that it was deplorable that the bus drivers didn't maintain their vehicles better. Someone said the driver of the last bus that did stop had said the buses for two routes, including Rosa's, were out of service.

"Maldito!" Rosa muttered. She very rarely swore. Max flagged down a taxi. "I've got to make sure you get home all right," he said. "My fault you got stuck here."

"But I live way out, and you'll have to pay to come back, too."

Seeing the driver's leer, Max wished again that his own car had arrived. "As Director it's my job to see that employees get home safely," he said lightly.

"You don't want to go there." She blushed a little.

"Why not? It can't be that far." *Oh, damn. It might be a slum, and maybe she's embarrassed.* Then she straightened up and looked him in the eye, just as when she'd told him the door was still broken. "All right," she said.

As they drove through the city, Rosa identified various things: the stadium, the much-rebuilt Church of San Francisco, the unfinished Convention Center begun in preparation for an OAS meeting in 1966 (moved to Caracas after the Engañadan coup of that year), and the 'new' railroad station. This had been built in 1919, replacing an older one in the center of town, but retained its 'new' designation in a city loyal to its institutions and memories. The districts grew more humble once they passed the station, and the paved streets turned to dirt. Rosa grew quiet. They passed rows of huge gloomy apartment houses emitting pale light, then drove past several blocks of single houses crowded together. Farther on, the road got worse and the houses more separated, though Max could see little of them as the streetlights became sparser.

Max knew they were headed north. As the road grew worse yet, bouncing them to the roof of the car, he wondered whether she lived as far as those thatched huts he had seen in the estuary. He hoped she did. The taxi driver began to complain, slowing down and stopping completely at times to navigate ditches, potholes, broken-down trucks and buses, even the odd drunk. The headlights outlined palm trees for brief moments. Sometimes they'd hear a baby cry or people arguing in the low houses.

Max could sense Rosa's tension but said nothing. *If the barrio were less depressing and squalid, I might, but if I say anything now it would come off as willful blindness. To acknowledge the squalor would be stupid at best, even cruel.* The tension proved contagious.

Finally Rosa spoke. "I think you're the first American, the first Director, to come here. Most Americans think Alcalá is just the pretty downtown part."

Max wouldn't describe downtown Alcalá that way. That she did made him somehow resentful. Rosa had been cheated.

"What do you think of it?" she asked.

"It's sad."

"You don't have places like this in the United States, do you?" Her voice combined challenge, shame, apology, and resentment.

"Some," he answered, "and maybe worse. There are places with a lot of violence too. But still, we're lucky." *I'm not sure she would believe me if I went into detail about Watts or Appalachia.* If Engañadans have real reasons to envy America, he mused, how much greater must be their envy and resentment of that America of their imaginations, where all were handsome and rich and powerful?

They rode in silence until the driver stopped in front of a wide ditch, saying he could go no farther. "The buses pass!" protested Rosa, but to no avail. "All right," she said, opening the door. "I can walk now. It's only a little way."

Max got out and took her arm. "Looks slippery. I'll go with you." The taxi driver demanded money before agreeing to wait. As Max and Rosa disappeared into the darkness, the driver turned off the engine and sat back with a cynical smile.

He looked surprised when Max returned in five minutes.

Chapter Twelve: *In Loco Parentis*

Max pushed aside the calculator and the sheets of paper on which he had jotted hundreds of figures, with sums and differences and products circled in apparent chaos. He smiled as he leaned back in his chair and stretched his legs under the desk. Not out of the woods yet, but things had gone pretty well in the past few weeks, at least where rentals were concerned. And Rosa said today a letter had arrived from an electronics store asking about renting space for that 'demonstration concert' Washington had mentioned. He asked her to bring it in.

A religious group was renting the auditorium on Sundays, and if they prayed amidst the rubble of Saturday night wedding receptions now profitably catered by the Center itself, they were too enthusiastic to complain or even notice. Max even saw hope that enrollment might increase, as two students had recently signed up to join a class mid-course. There was a sense of discipline and seriousness about most of the classes now; maybe the word was getting around. *We just might reach that magic 300-student number.* Cheryl's students would surely return for the next term: she seemed to leave hand-in-hand with a different boy each night. Max chose to believe they went for coffee. He swiveled around in his chair and reached for the newspapers. *That's enough worrying about figures for one morning, including Cheryl's.*

It felt strange how everything had become so familiar so soon, and that it almost seemed he'd read *La Voz del Pueblo* every morning of his life. Well, a lot had happened, for better or worse. The Center had improved, even if the minor fixes in the building served mainly to highlight the extensive work still needed. Most notably, the atmosphere of confusion had changed to purpose: not only to save the Center, but to make it again everything it should be.

Max felt he had now completely settled in to Alcalá and his

place in it or, better, among *them*. It was about people more than place. Washington and Gloria and all the staff were part of his day, some of them fast becoming more than colleagues even if, for most, Max must remain The Man. Rosa had gained confidence, urging that they should advertise on Radio Alcalá. A few calls to advertising agencies had confirmed her own impression that it was the most popular station among young people. Washington and Gloria took it from there, and it seemed to work, judging from the inquiries they'd received. *Maybe we'll get the old TV station debt paid off and we can try television again.*

What else? He had now visited the editors of the local papers, presenting "representative newspapers" or books and agreeing with the journalists on the vital role of the press. Few of the school directors – he'd met about a third of them -- had asked for anything, while seeming grateful for the little gifts Max brought. And he had his private space.

The apartment was comfortable enough, and he had reached an implicit agreement with the roaches: he would slam the door when he returned and stand in the living room for a moment. They would go into hiding from the kitchen table and sink. His neighbors Pablo and Pedro proved friendlier than he'd expected, inviting him for coffee and trying to denounce imperialism politely enough not to hurt his feelings too much. For his part, after they surveyed his bare walls and suggested good spots, Max had kept his promise to buy a painting from each of them. They'd given him a good price, if Gloria could be believed. Max even grew to like the urgent bright scenes, especially Pablo's oil of a village square in the jungle where peasants bartered over vegetables and cheap aluminum kitchenware while a fat policeman stood disdainfully by. The only overtly political note was a slogan painted on the base of the statue of Bolívar, "Down with Imperialism." The painting comforted him in a rather obscure way. *Maybe I can give locals another perspective on 'imperialism.' Maybe that's impossible because it's so much part of their own narrative. So I'm helpful, or blameless. I can live with either one.*

He began to think of the blocks around the apartment as his

neighborhood. He was on nodding or even small chat terms with various people he saw each Sunday at the 11 a.m. Cathedral Mass, and on one of those Sundays had even met the Archbishop. He felt embarrassed that he had not yet made a formal visit to the Chancery and corrected the omission within a week, presenting the pleasant old cleric with a Presentation Book on John Carroll, the first U.S. bishop. Moreover, both Dr. Ramírez and Mrs. Bowman had invited him to dinner where he had met their families, and come to know the two board members as more than Center fixtures.

His weekend walks had made the city familiar to him. If the Alcalá Museum smelled of mold, the smell fit the history it displayed: paintings of Spaniards standing proud as they surveyed jungle and river, sepia photographs of men in dark suits standing on a platform or in a train station, ancient and horrifying surgical instruments from the first hospital, and even more ancient weapons from the war for independence. The neighborhoods he traversed were generally very humble, though crossing a street could suddenly place him in front of huge houses surrounded by high walls with glass shards embedded on the top and a guard in front of the gate.

He even got in some tennis. Guest fees at the Cholo Tennis and Bridge Club were not exorbitant. Lacking a partner on his first visit he'd taken a lesson from the tennis pro who had introduced him to a few players of similar ability. He won or lost against Guillermo Méndez and Jaime Maldonado and Lincoln Sanchez and then chatted with them over beer or lunch. They inevitably had acquaintances in common in this town – Gandig and Ramírez and the board of the *Sociedad Historica* – and he saw others he knew, including Jorge Pinzón, and his own landlord Morales. So he felt he was making a life here.

On the negative side, the rats were harder to deal with, sometimes slinking back onto the kitchen drain board before he could even change his clothes. What should have mattered more: Max's relationship with Jethro Jackson had deteriorated to one in which Max sent formal reports on 'program progress,' receiving career-slayingly tepid responses from San Genesio. *And there's*

124

still...

As if answering his thought, Cheryl Fletcher appeared at the door, just come from class in her shorts and sandals with a guitar in her hand, appearing, in one of her favorite phrases, "like I really am." *If the students and parents don't complain, why should I?* Still, something about her bothered him. She was like a large child far from home, who couldn't care for herself but was too stubborn to listen to anyone else. Especially Max. She'd eat her guitar before she'd take his advice. Yet he felt responsible for her—if only for her being here. *How could I have relied on Braden?*

"Hey," she began brightly, perching on the couch with her legs folded under her, "I hear you have a really great apartment by the river, right? Well you know that Pristinos family I'm with is nice I guess but really too straight. I mean, they pray before dinner!"

"That's the way nice families are here," Max shrugged.

"Yeah but I've got a better idea. Why don't we share your place? I mean I'll pay for the food or something and we can just share everything?" She said it as though she were asking to borrow a guitar string.

"Well," Max began. Rosa interrupted, bringing in the letter from Coastal Electronics. He thought he felt a chill, as if the air-conditioning had suddenly decided to work. Then he looked at Rosa, who was staring at Cheryl as she handed Max the letter. She gave him a stare as well before leaving.

"I don't know, Cheryl. I think there'd be some... Hey, look: it's much better for you to live with the Pristinos, a real Engañadan family. That's the way to learn a language and a culture."

"Oh, you mean your thing with Rosa? Just because we live together doesn't mean we have to sleep together."

"She wouldn't see it that way!" Max blurted. "I mean, what thing, anyway? Besides, I only have one bed. And this isn't California. They still talk about scandals here."

Cheryl nodded tolerant understanding. "If you're gay or something I can deal with that. I mean I respect everybody's, you know, sexual preference."

"I don't *have* a..." Max caught himself in time.

"If you're really hung up," she helped, "there are two bedrooms, aren't there?"

Max closed his eyes. "One is my shrine room," he explained. "I practice *Hatcha-togi.*"

"Oh. That's heavy," she breathed. "I can understand that."

"I thought you would." He sighed and looked at her. *What a pity. She'd be really attractive if she'd dress up a little and fix her hair or something. How do I go about asking her if she uses drugs? Shouldn't be too personal a question for someone who'd just suggested she should move in.* "Are you, eh, using anything, Cheryl?"

"Like, that's what the pill is for, right?" she said with a wink.

Max shut his eyes and sighed. "I meant...controlled substances."

"Oh. Just a little grass, mostly. Coke is hard to get here, believe it or not, and I don't like the hard stuff."

"Look, you be careful, okay? You shouldn't fool around with that..." He stopped as she began to smirk. "I mean, the stuff you get here, you never know, you know?"

"Okay," she agreed perkily, "I'll be careful. I can hardly be anything else living with the Pristinos who are nice and all that but so... Catholic or something."

"But not like in the States," Max assured her. "No Irish priests here, and there are all kinds in Alcalá. You want evangelicals? Got 'em right here every Sunday. Agnostics, too. We can probably find any kind of family you want."

"I really don't like any of those religions," she pouted momentarily, then brightened again. "But hey, don't worry about it! I can take care of myself and anyway, the Pristinos aren't *that* bad. For now, anyway."

"Good."

"Besides," she added in a taunting voice as she bounced up and headed for the door, "Miguel thinks he'll have a place of his own pretty soon."

Max didn't know whether to worry about her or the Center's image or his own missed opportunity, so he resolutely sent Cheryl and all her domestic affairs to hell and turned to his neglected newspaper.

ESPEJO RETURN SUPPORTED BY DISSIDENT ESPEJISTAS

San Genesio, June 11. The return of former President Juan Francisco Espejo Suárez has been welcomed by a dissident faction of the *Espejista* Party that broke ranks with the party leadership at a heated meeting last night in San Genesio. The dissidents, led by Alcalá lawyer Luis Gonzales Carvallo, condemned the leadership for rejecting "the greatest man in Engañadan history and the founder of our party," and announced they would form a new group, to be called the *Partido Espejista Leal*, with headquarters in Alcalá, in defiance of Decree 138-B which requires that all political parties be based in the capital.

Espejo, whose return is expected as soon as the government issues the implementing decree of the Resolution of Return, could not be reached for comment in Panamá, but it is expected he will ally himself with the Gonzales faction

Dr. Ramiro Gómez Gómez, President of the Partido Espejista, characterized the dissidents as a "motley collection of opportunists who have turned their back on the principles of the Party." Further, in breaking party unity the Gonzales group "serves only the ends of the oligarchs, the Marxists, and the United States." He reiterated his firm opposition to Espejo's return on the basis that the presence in the country of the former President would only undermine the efforts of the Party to realize the goals towards which it has always worked.

Asked how the Espejo Party could oppose the return of its founder and namesake, he answered:

"The sacred historic work of President Juan Francisco Espejo Suárez is finished. It is perfected. In founding the Party he imparted to Engañadan society the stimulus of the noble ideas of justice, of the common welfare, of the equality of the worker and of national sovereignty in the face of foreign influences from whatever source. The noble work of achieving these ends has fallen to us, his successors, and the presence of the great old man, who is in any case not the Espejo who inspired us so nobly, could only create division. In short, it would be a contradiction."

Dr. Gómez characterized as a "cruel hoax" the attempt of Dr. Gonzales to bring back a "shadow" in an obvious ploy to wrest control of the party from its rightful leaders. Referring to the fact that the dissident faction is composed almost entirely of members from President Espejo's birthplace, he commented that this was "just another typical Alcalá trick."

As Dr. Gonzales Carvallo and his followers left the meeting they vowed to start anew in Nueva Alcalá and to reject the "pretensions of the Genesiaños."

Well, that old liar, Max thought, remembering Gonzales' words, *"Yes, I suppose I might support him." Now I wonder how long Gonzales was working on this, and if his homecoming ever had any other purpose. To hell with them, too,* he thought, happy that he need not worry about these labyrinthine disputes in addition to enrollment and free-love hippie teachers and cracked plaster.

Rosa came in with a worried look on her face. "This just came by messenger," she said, handing him a heavy envelope covered with stamps and seals. Max hesitated, then opened it to find a letter equally decorated with revenue stamps and signatures. Written in an ornate and complicated style, it informed the Señor Director that the undersigned attorney, Guillermo Paz, had the honor to represent Señor Bertram Braden in his suit against the Center for five million *honores.* There was more, but Max found the lines blurring. He asked Rosa to call Dr. Ramírez.

The letter puzzled the Board's lawyer as much as it did Max. "I will call Guillermo Paz, or better yet, I'll talk to Bernardo

Gómez. I think Paz still works for him. In the meantime, please don't worry. Even if they won, they'd get nothing like five million." Max said he'd try not to worry. He didn't think he'd succeed.

He went to Verde's office to make sure the forms recording Braden's dismissal were correct. "Of course," said the accountant. "Here are copies, and you can send them to Dr. Ramírez if you wish, but I'm sure they're correct."

"Probably they are, but Dr. Ramírez will need them anyway, so I'll do that."

"I understand." Verde said. "I am very sorry that this lawsuit comes up now, just as I was going to say goodbye. As you know, this is my last day with the Center."

"What are you talking about? You can't quit just like that!" A question had been forming itself in Max's head, but Verde's surprise announcement banished it.

"But I sent you the letter two weeks ago, as the law stipulates."

"What letter? I didn't get any letter!" Max tried to keep his voice down.

"Strange. But here, I have a copy."

Sure enough, the letter dated two weeks before expressed in the best Engañadan prose Verde's sorrow at leaving the Center to which he had "so many sentimental as well as professional ties." But he was sure the Señor Director, "with that sense of justice which characterized him," would recognize the force of the motives that had compelled Verde to take this decision. He recommended Hernan Magaña as his replacement.

"Somebody offered you more money," said Max dryly.

"Considerably more."

"And who's going to oversee the books? Who's Hernan Magaña?"

"A young fellow I know well and can recommend highly. Indeed, he's been in here for a few hours a week to familiarize himself with our system. Since you said nothing, I assumed you approved my recommendation. He's to start tomorrow."

"Oh, he is? Well, we'll see. What's his maternal name?"

"Verde. He's my nephew, but I wouldn't recommend him if he weren't completely competent, especially since the Center has so many and such unique problems."

"Well," Max glowered, torn between suspicion of Verde and the humiliating prospect of having missed a letter and screwed up yet again, "let me see his application and then I'll talk to him."

"But there's no need!" insisted Verde. "I know who he is and his experience and qualifications. Of course, if you wish. But I couldn't approve, or rather agree, or feel comfortable with anyone else. Really. Not with this Braden problem now. And time is so short."

The man looks nervous. Something is rotten in the books of Alcalá. "Nothing has been signed, has it? I hope we don't have another hire like that of Cheryl Fletcher, done without my knowledge or approval."

"No, no. Of course not."

"If he wants the job," Max said coldly, "tell him to apply in the proper way and I'll think about it." He scooped up the Braden termination papers and stalked out.

Rosa angrily swore she had received no letter from Verde. "As for a new accountant," she asked, "why not get someone completely new? Someone who has nothing to do with the Center or with Lucho? There are plenty of them around."

"Surely there are, but where should we look?"

"We don't even have to hire one. In fact, we shouldn't! The bookkeepers do most of the work anyway. Lucho just went over their figures and checked them and transferred them to the books he kept. Or something. I never did think he did much. But we can have a contract with an accounting office for them to come in and check the books. That's how Papá does it. An accountant comes once or twice a year to fill out tax forms and things for him. Mariana talked about this once. It would be a lot cheaper than hiring somebody!" Rosa finished almost breathlessly, excited by her enthusiasm and still offended by Lucho's implication indicting her competence, as if she'd lost the letter.

"Good," Max agreed, "good idea. Look up some accountants in the phone book, would you?"

"It would be better to go to the Bishop." Seeing his puzzlement, she added, "The Archdiocese has an employment office where they help people find work. They have lists of all kinds of people."

"Can we trust the Bishop not to send a relative?" Max smiled.

"I think so. He's not from here." As she got up to leave, Max finally identified what had been bothering him.

"Did you tell Verde about Braden's lawsuit?"

"No. And the letter just arrived."

Max was sure he hadn't mentioned it when he asked the accountant about the dismissal forms. He sat down feeling suspicious about Verde, and upbeat, for a moment, about the prospect of saving money on accounting services. He reached for his calculator and tried to figure out how many new students they would need to handle a five-million *honore* judgment.

The Center didn't have enough square meters to hold them.

Chapter Thirteen: The Mentor on the Motorcycle

On the day of the Luis Delgado exhibit, Gloria was in a world of her own, excited by the art and by her own presentation of it. Max himself could look at only so many paintings titled *Child on the Street*, or *Peasant Child on a Bus*, and the like, but he respected Gloria's enthusiasm the more. She was, in her unique way, a serious woman.

Pulling the whole thing off had been a challenge, even though the Center routinely hosted art shows. Before coming to Alcalá, Max had not realized to what degree the physical/social world was the product of will and organization. Always before, lights and air conditioning systems worked because they worked, and chairs were in place because where else would they be? He wished he had been blessed with more common sense. In its place, experience had taught him that things did not happen unless someone made sure they happened. If Manuel didn't make sure, or Gloria or Washington, the buck stopped with Max. If he failed, the function might open to dirty or missing chairs, poor lighting, or some other embarrassment. This reality was hardly unique to Engañada. Nor was the problem of employee forgetfulness, though Manuel's conviction that ornate explanation could substitute for performance had more adherents here than in, say, New York.

So Max had confirmed that lights worked and the paintings hung properly and that refreshments were prepared. But not all problems were mundane, or solvable.

Early in the afternoon Dr. Ramírez phoned about the Braden lawsuit. "Bernardo's been out of town, or so his secretary says, and Paz didn't return my calls. But I ran into him at the courthouse today."

"And?"

"The problem is more serious than I thought."

"But we checked the forms. What went wrong?"

"Nothing. He was fired in the correct way and they don't deny it. The problem has to do with his hiring. It seems he never got a work visa. And probably because he didn't have the visa, a copy of his contract was never sent to the Labor Ministry. So his firing becomes improper as a result: you can't fire someone you've never hired."

"What idiot hired him, then? But anyway, if he was never hired, then he was never fired, right?"

"Not quite. Anytime you pay someone regularly for more than three months you establish an implicit contract, but by not having the contract certified by the Ministry you injured the worker, depriving him of the basis for the protection of his rights."

"But," asked Max, struggling to control himself, "if his rights aren't protected, by what right does he sue us?"

"The law was written so that the rights of workers are protected anyway," answered Ramírez calmly, as if lecturing in the university. "Otherwise employers would have a motive for not registering contracts. Anyway, that's one problem. The other is that we had an illegal alien worker, for which the Center can be fined. That might be more serious than Braden's outrageous sum."

"Oh." Max didn't ask why they required contracts at all, then, or why the government hadn't deported Braden if he didn't have a proper visa. He didn't want to hear it.

"Anyway," Ramírez continued in a maddeningly calm voice, "I'll be talking to some people to see what can be done. There's nothing to worry about right now; these things take months and even years. But I thought you'd like to know."

You got that wrong, Max snarled inwardly as he hung up. He went back to his work, but it wasn't the same. Could he even trust Ramirez? Was the man competent, or just well-dressed? Why wasn't that contract done right when Braden was hired?

Who can I ask about Ramírez? Any Engañadan I ask might be

a relative. Maybe Washington? He's cynical enough, but he's also a sometime law student, probably reluctant to give Ramirez a grudge that would long outlive my tour here. Anyway, it'd be bad form to ask a subordinate for dirty laundry on a board member.

If only I had someone I could rely on, someone who really knew his way around and wouldn't be in anyone else's pocket. That was supposed to be Mariana's job but she's not here. Or 'Hetro's' job. Forget him. After a while Max got up and wandered around aimlessly, coming to a stop in the lobby.

"What's the matter? You look sad." Rosa joined Max as he stared vacantly through the front door two hours before the exhibit opened. At least the door had been fixed. It had cost him the equivalent of $223 out of his own pocket, but it was worth it. Not only was the door presentable, but he had paid for his own mistake. He knew the staff was aware of this. Maybe they were impressed with his integrity. Or maybe they thought him an idiot.

"I do?" He hadn't told her about Ramírez' call, and didn't want to talk about it now. "It's that fountain," he lied, indicating the patio. "I don't know when we'll ever be able to finish it and it looks so sad like that, half-done." He let his eyes rest on her curves, a welcome distraction. Today she had on the green and blue dress. He'd figured out she had only about five dresses in all, though she mixed them up with different scarves and things.

"People are used to it," she answered, looking at him closely.

Then a roar interrupted their conversation. A Harley-Davidson motorcycle thundered across the patio, its engine racing louder as it came up the steps toward the new glass door. Max quickly opened it, and the long-haired old motorcyclist shouted *¡Gracias!* as he flew past, front wheel in the air. In the lobby, the big Harley motor shut down, giving way to the biker's laughter and the women's shrieks as they congregated, calling "Harvee! Harvee!" Rosa didn't shriek, but she too ran to kiss the fellow.

"Whoa, chicas," the old man laughed. "One at a time! There's enough for all!" He got off his motorcycle, pushed down the kickstand, and unslung a balalaika from his back.

"Harvee, play!" cried the girls.

"Wait! Can't play on a dry throat! Where's Manuel? Ah,

there he is. Manuel, my man, how's it going? And the wife, and little Angelita?"

"Very well, Señor Harvee, very well. What honor to have you here again! You will want the Coca-Cola?" Manuel was smiling and bowing with delight.

"I will want the Coca-Cola! And some glasses and ice, and I'll see if we don't have something in the old saddlebag here." He reached deep, chortled again, and came up with a large bottle of rum.

Harvee? Max made the connection as he walked toward the group.

"You've gotta be Max Lacey!" announced the man, holding out a strong suntanned hand. "Good to meet you. Harvey Tyrone here, just in from San Genesio via Tunagua and San Luchito and Santa Rosita and a few other places!"

"Harvey goes everywhere," said Rosa admiringly to Max. *Indeed, Harvey Tyrone, Cultural Attaché. Not likely to confuse him with Jethro Jackson.* He mumbled a welcome, but Harvey cut him off.

"Welcome to *you,* Max! Welcome to Engañada! You're gonna love the place. I mean, jeez!" He shook his head in amazement. "I don't know of another country in South America where you could have the kind of operation you've got here. This Center is one of the finest bi-national centers I've seen in twenty-eight years in the Foreign Service. And the people! The people? My God, you've got people here like, well, like you just don't believe. The finest, friendliest, warmest...look: do you want to know what your Engañadan is?"

His Spanish was fluent and colloquial, as if he'd lived in Engañada forever. *No wonder they love him; he loves them. Sounds like he believes every word. And maybe he'll tell me something useful. Lunatic or not, he'd be the first one from the Embassy who's even bothered to try.*

Of course Max wanted to learn about his Engañadan.

"Your Engañadan is a guy—ho! The Coke!"

Glasses were passed and filled while Harvey embraced a steady procession of arriving employees. Most sat on the floor while Harvey arranged himself casually on his bike and waved his glass as he talked, drinking between sentences. Manuel kept the glass full. Max assumed a dignified posture near the wall.

"Your Engañadan is a guy named Ramiro Ramírez Jaramillo who lives in a town called Llaguahua, up past San Martín, a town you can only get to by driving for eight hours on the roughest, rockiest, narrowest road that I, personally, have ever seen or cared to drive on. You miss a turn on that one and you fall down five thousand feet. I mean, *five thousand feet!"* Harvey's eyes were alight. His audience listened breathlessly.

"So you get to Llaguahua at ten o'clock at night," he continued after a quick deep drink of rum and Coke, wiping his chin with the sleeve of his dungaree shirt, "and the place is shut down. I mean, it is *shut down.* You look for a light? Then you look for a candle or a lantern, because in Llaguahua electricity is just a city rumor! So there you are, you're cold and you're hungry and you can't stand the very idea of getting on that bike again, and you're looking around for someplace, anyplace, to throw down your old down-filled sleeping bag, a bag you've carried with you halfway around the world and I mean through the Himalayas too, and it's the kind of bag you need at Llaguahua where you're at fourteen thousand feet in the Andes and I mean to tell you the wind is *blowing*!

"So you look around, and the only one you see is a little old guy leading a donkey up the road carrying a load of firewood. I mean, it's ten o'clock at night and this guy is bringing home firewood. Then you realize that at fourteen thousand feet in Llaguahua, there are no trees. This guy has been on the road since five o'clock in the morning to go down to tree-line and get some wood, so you ask the guy where, just where in the name of God, you can get out of the wind a little bit and throw your sleeping bag and get some sleep, that you've been riding that damned Harley Davidson 1500 D for twelve hours and you're ready to collapse right there in the road."

Harvey wiped his brow with his sleeve and looked weary, took another drink, and rearranged himself on the Harley. His faded jeans carried a dozen different shades of mud and clay.

"So now you see what your Engañadan is," he resumed in a low slow voice. "What does this guy do? This guy takes you home with him, insists—and he will not hear 'no' as an answer—that you have dinner with him and his wife Maria Inés and their eight kids. And do you think there is any way he is going to let you sleep anywhere but right in front of the fire, the fire he's made with wood he worked all day to get? You think he will? Or that Maria Inés would let you go out there to the shed that you said would be just fine? No way. No way, because you're in the home of Ramiro Ramírez Jaramillo and his wife Maria Inés Sánchez de Ramírez. You're in Engañada and that's the kind of people you have here."

Harvey drank again while the rest applauded and Max wondered how this guy could possibly work with Jackson.

A violent tug on his arm barged into his thoughts. He turned to see Esperanza Romero, looking even angrier than on her first visit. Her English was as quaint and outraged as ever.

"Meester Lacey we haf to talk! I haf my lectures ready almost on the development of the child and I find out you cheat me!"

Max mumbled something, aware that all eyes had shifted. *Might be the first time anyone's ever interrupted Harvey.* Tyrone himself stepped carefully through his admirers, looking puzzled. He gave Max a quick wink before addressing Esperanza.

"Excuse me," he said, "are you... can you be...?"

"I am," she said, drawing herself up to her full four-feet-ten, "Esperanza Romero Ycaza, *Doctora* Esperanza Romero Ycaza, Regional Secretary of the Department of the Child!"

Harvey beamed like a child at Christmas. "You are! It's really you! What a privilege for all of us! Allow me to introduce myself, please, *Señorita Doctora*. I am Harvey Tyrone, Cultural Attaché of the U.S. Embassy. Believe me, I've looked forward to meeting you for a long time."

"You haf?"

"Of course! Haven't I, Max?"

"Absolutely!" Max answered at once. "First thing he said, Dra. Romero, when he got here today, was 'How can I meet Dra. Esperanza Romero?'"

"Good," said Romero. "So maybe we get this right that I willing give lectures here on development of child which is so important and this Lacey he offer me five thousand *honores* the lecture when he going to give that communist so-called poet Simón Bolívar Blanco twenty thousand to read his poem one time! For him! And to me, *doctorada* in United Estates University of Eedaho, that he think I take five thousand for this American technology I bring! Ha!" She crossed her arms and scowled.

"Well," began Max, hoping to herd her into his office and thinking of ways to tell her that those twenty thousand *honores* for Blanco were fictitious. Few of the onlookers understood the English conversation, but they could see that this loudmouth was browbeating their Director. Harvey cut in.

"Goodness, no!" he groaned, putting a hand over his face. "That was not it at all! When Max talked to me about this, we certainly didn't have five thousand *honores* in mind for Dra.—say, do you remember a Dr. Robert Wenchberg?"

"Wencheberg? No..."

"Well, that's not surprising since he's in a different department. But he passed through San Genesio a few months ago—he could only stay one day—and asked about you. He was so sorry he couldn't get to Alcalá and back in time. Anyway, he said he had friends in your department there, and that they still spoke of you as one of the really fine, truly brilliant students they have had, the kind of student that gives far, far more to a university than she receives."

"He did?" She blushed through her layers of makeup. "Well, I have of course very brilliant career there, learn so much about the development of—"

"Yes! So when Max told me he actually was going to have *Doctora* Esperanza Romero Ycaza lecturing in his Center, well, you can imagine how proud I was. Of course we, meaning the Embassy, will want to collaborate on this with, of course, your permission?"

"Oh, that all right I—"

"You can't imagine how pleased we are! But about the honorarium, surely there was some misunderstanding, a problem of language, perhaps?"

"I spik English."

"Precisely! And beautifully, too, and that's where the confusion came from!" Harvey smiled and shook his head in dismay at having missed the obvious. "Anyway, you just leave it to me: we'll bring in some support material from Washington. Films, slides, a book exhibit, that sort of thing. And of course we hope you'll accept these materials for your professional use after the lectures are over. Of course, unfortunately, there are always delays in getting everything in place. You know how the bureaucracy is, and believe me, ours is a swamp of paper! But as soon as we have it, we'll ship it right down and start those lectures, and not at five thousand *honores* per lecture, but at something much more suitable to your professional caliber!"

"Yes," Esperanza agreed, eager to get a word in. "You don't pay a professional like you would pay a... a secretary!"

Max looked over at Rosa, who understood enough English to glare hatred at Romero.

"So we're all set," Harvey smiled, rubbing his hands together. "Max here can handle the details with you, and I'll certainly see you again before the first lecture in . . ?"

"This month! The twenty-five!"

"Oh." Harvey looked downcast. "I'm afraid it's impossible to get the materials that fast, but I'm sure you'll agree a short delay is a small price to pay for the benefits of a properly supported event."

Esperanza scowled but finally agreed that it was.

"Very good," Harvey smiled. "I so much appreciate and admire your comprehension. And it has, believe me, been a tremendous pleasure and honor to meet you."

"Yes. Good," she said, as Harvey smoothly walked her out the door. "It is so nice to meet a gentleman." She glared at Max as she left.

Harvey slapped Max on the back and picked up his drink with a flourish as his fans demanded that he play for them. So he set down his glass, took up his balalaika, re-settled edgewise on the bike and played their favorites: *Mariella de la Selva, Theme from*

Dr. Zhivago, El Grillo and *La Cucaracha,* repeating the last by popular demand. "Mexican cultural imperialism!" he charged, and they all laughed.

By this time the lobby was packed with students as well as employees. Cheryl had appeared with her guitar, and Harvey gestured for her to sit in. She began playing chords to accompany his balalaika melody as Manuel served coke and beer to anyone who asked. Max retreated unnoticed to his office.

Costing us a bundle, but what can I say? He settled down to wait for Harvey to come in and talk business—if that was even why he came. *This is one of my supervisors? Well, he looks to be one of the good guys. Now we can put* la Doctora *off forever and blame it on Washington bureaucrats. Not sure I can bullshit her later at Harvey's level. First I'd have to wrestle the conversation away from her. That's the hard part.* Max also realized that Harvey had upped the stakes a lot with Romero's lecture fee but that seemed unimportant at this point, with Braden's five million-honore lawsuit hanging over them, and maybe an even larger fine.

Laughter from the hall announced Harvey's entry with Washington, Gloria, and Luis Delgado the artist. The door burst open.

"Can you believe this?" Harvey asked Max, arms outstretched with the balalaika in his right hand. "Can you believe that after two weeks on that bike out there, traveling all over this country without even a map and with no idea what day it was, that I pull up here, right here in the *Centro Engañado-Americano de Alcalá,* on the day, the very day, that Luchito is having an exhibit here? I can't..." He looked at the floor, sighed, smiled wanly and shook his head. "I - can - not - believe - this!"

"Believe it," smiled Max. "And have a drink." He supposed Harvey didn't read the reports and plans sent to the Embassy, or he'd have known about the exhibit. Or maybe he had known, but wanted to make his arrival seem like fate, or a blessing.

"Well, Max," said Harvey, sitting on the couch and taking another rum and Coke from the tray which Manuel passed around, "quite a day for you: an exhibit by Luis *and* a visit by *Doctora* Esperanza Romero..."

"Ycaza," helped Luis Delgado.

"*Doctora* Esperanza Romero *Ycaza,* right!" he shouted, and then fell back laughing and lifted his feet onto the coffee table. The whole room joined in the mirth. Then Harvey sat up again, raised one finger high in the air and repeated, "Doctora Esperanza Romero Ycaza of the Ministry of what? Kids?"

"Of Child Development," said Max. "And she's also *altamente calificada.* She forgot to tell you that; can't imagine how."

"Let's bring her back and ask her just how highly qualified she is," suggested Harvey. "But where in the name of God did you find that woman?"

Max shrugged. "She found me. Just came in one day. I didn't even know who she was."

"He didn't know who she was! Do you mean to tell me..." and so on, bringing the rest to tears with his amazement that Max should not recognize the brilliant *Doctora,* etcetera. He did it so well that Max and the others were laughing too hard even to drink. Washington took off his sunglasses to wipe the tears away, letting Max see for the first time that his eyes were crossed. He told Harvey that the Center needed someone like him to handle the Esperanzas: "You don't know how many people we have like that."

"I don't?" Harvey's face was total amazement. "I don't know how many people like that walk into a center? No, I wouldn't know anything about that, since I've only spent about twenty years in bi-national centers beginning in 1943 in Klangeen—of course, you wouldn't have heard of that, and it's part of Bangladesh now anyway. No, in the five years I spent running the center in Vladivostok I never had anyone like that, never had a certain Pyotr Kuznetsov come in and demand that we give him a permanent studio since he was the premier exponent of Socialist Realism east of Moscow. No, I never had a problem like that!" Harvey shook his head while his face became a mask of false innocence.

"I did have a small problem once in Havana," he allowed, "when one of Fidel's lieutenants came in with the mud of the Sierra Madre still on his boots to tell me the Center had been liberated! I got out of that one when Major Jesús Carreón recognized me as his and Fidel's old English teacher, *and* as the catcher he'd pitched to for three years in the semi-pro leagues. Oh, no, I wouldn't know about these people!" He shook his head again.

"Harvee! Play *Cieleto Lindo!*" pleaded Gloria.

"No, no. Look, *chiquititos,* I've got business with Max here, so you all just run on and get that exhibit ready. Washington, I wouldn't trust anyone but you and Manuel to see the lights are adjusted and the drinks are ready—and I'll see you all later. Luchito, you don't know how glad I am to get here today for this. I know it will be one of the outstanding art shows of the year!"

Before they left, Luis the artist greeted Max and thanked him for sponsoring the exhibit, which he was sure would take place without any problems. A few weeks earlier Max would have asked what problems could possibly occur; after his university education on politics and art, he thought he knew, and hoped fervently that Luis was right, that there would be no *Fidelista-Maoista* fistfights.

Before the others left, Harvey remembered something. "Hey, Max and all of you, great job with that Genesee State String Quartet! Elizabeth told me you guys just did one hell of a job setting everything up." Max and Washington and Gloria and the rest smiled appreciatively. Once the room cleared, Harvey stretched out on the sofa with a cushion under his head and seemed to fall half asleep, his voice becoming relaxed and distant. "Man, I am wiped out. Comes from putting in twelve hours on one of those two-poppers bouncing around these roads."

"I can imagine," Max agreed. "Well look, I'll just let you get some sleep."

"Not yet. I guess I'd better ask about the Center. I mean, I'm making this official trip in my capacity as the Cultural Attaché of the U.S. Embassy." He laughed softly. "And Jethro told me to 'see jus' what kinda nonsense that Lacey up to!'" His imitation of Jackson was about perfect.

"The Center? All right, except for money problems and imminent disaster."

"Money problems? Money?" Harvey sat halfway up before

falling back in shock. "I have never seen, or heard of, or met anyone who heard of, a center that did not have money problems." He opened his eyes and stared at the ceiling while Max studied his face, now illuminated directly by the lamp on the end table. He'd never seen skin quite like Harvey's: it was the pink not of an old man but of a child, yet dry and weathered beyond anything Max had ever seen. It was wrinkled and creased, but lightly, as if the wind coming over the handlebars had flattened and smoothed all the marks of age. His full lips seemed permanently chapped.

"These places exist to have money problems," Harvey went on. "If I ever saw a center that was solvent I'd try to get the director fired, because he wouldn't be doing his job."

"Harvey, I promise you I'm doing my job."

"Good," chuckled Tyrone. "How are you supposed to pay for a building, pay the utilities, pay your teachers and your staff and all their social benefits, pay for office supplies, books, repair of typewriters and tape recorders, replace light bulbs, fix the air conditioning if you've got it, keep the elevator going, pay artists' fees, buy advertising, programs, invitations, tickets, drinks, canapés..." He settled deeper into the cushion. "By teaching English to kids who can hardly afford the bus fare to come to class? No way. At least, in my twenty years in these places I never found out how, except to live from week to week. Put off this creditor while you pay half of what you owe to another; sweet-talk the teachers into waiting another three months for their raise, beg free advertising from wherever you can, do what you can yourself and hope the board doesn't screw up whatever you're trying to do. Or the Embassy. I was working with my crew trying to replace the roof of the Santo Domingo center once after a hurricane, and the damned Press Attaché drives up and asks what the hell I'm doing! 'Programs,' he says, 'you're supposed to be working on programs!'" Harvey shook his head in disgust. "That was in the days of 'winning hearts and minds.'"

"Well," Max said, "I'm glad that in my case there's at least one guy in the Embassy who understands the problems."

Harvey nodded sympathetically. "Do you know," he asked, "that I once spent a whole night in Managua with one of the janitors, practically rebuilding the air conditioning system to have it ready for the Ambassador's visit?"

"I know about air conditioning problems."

"Yeah, so the Ambassador comes the next day, goes through the whole place without saying a word until we get to the Snack Bar. He looks at the menu that old Carlos Botarro had posted right there by the cash register. 'Where are the milkshakes?' he asks. Milkshakes? This, in a climate where the only milk you can get is powdered, or watered down, or just putrid. 'You're supposed to project the American Way,' he says. 'In America kids drink milkshakes!'" Harvey shook his head again, all the weariness of his many years in centers appearing in his face. "Right, Mr. Ambassador. Milkshakes. Get right on it. Yessir!"

Max felt some sort of response was in order. "My God, Harvey, you've been around South America enough—I wish I had your Spanish."

There seemed nothing to do but compliment the man.

"You learn to imitate the accent pretty well when you're in the Abraham Lincoln Brigade of the Spanish Republican Army and working behind the Fascist lines passing yourself off as a priest. Different accent, of course."

"You were there?" Max wondered why he asked stupid questions.

"For a year or so, 'till I saw too much. Best thing the Republican side had going was people like old Ernie who wrote good stuff about 'em. Nothing else matters if you have a good story. Anyway, I got there in '36, jumped ship in Barcelona when I found out the old *Shanghai Ayu* was heading right back to China. Didn't want to make that trip up the river again."

Max couldn't help himself. "You were in the Merchant Marine?"

"Started shoveling coal on the old *Herman Harriman* when I was thirteen. Seventy-five cents a day and those were the good times. Later we were glad to get forty. That's why I got into barnstorming for a while."

"Paid better, did it?" *My cue lines are improving.*

"Not too much, once you paid your hospital and baling-wire

144

bills, but it was more fun. Say, you have any more rum here?'"

Max found a bottle that Washington had left on his desk. As he poured he asked, "How about family? You have a wife in San Genesio, kids?"

Harvey sighed. "Had three wives, don't plan on another. The good ones died, Pilar Inés and Teresa. The American just took off one day and I only heard from her lawyer. Seven kids, here and there. All grown up now. Couple doctors, and a journalist and mechanic and three musicians. Eight grandkids," he said with fond pride.

"Say, Harvey, just how old are you anyway?"

"Sixty-seven last March. At least, that's what my papers say. Lost all my birth certificates and stuff in '43, but that's another story. Had some new ones made by a guy in Marseilles."

"They told me that you had to retire from the Foreign Service at sixty-two."

Tyrone smiled. "That's what they say; but when you've put in two years as Congressional aide to the fifth most senior member of the U.S. Senate, well, you get around these things."

If true, that explains a good deal. "Well, you've lived quite a life."

"I'll tell you about it sometime," he yawned. "But unless you have something else, I'd like to catch some Zs before the exhibit. All right if I use your couch?"

"Sure." Max got up and turned off the end-table lamp. "As a matter of fact, I do have something: will you be here to bullshit Romero again when she comes in looking for slides and lots of money and all? I'm not sure I can bring it off."

"Don't worry about it." Tyrone delivered these words with a sort of finality.

"Why not? She won't forget."

"Worrying won't make her forget. And anyway, what makes you think she or you will be alive in a month or six months?"

Max stared. *Odd thing to say.*

Harvey went on. "Those old Greeks or whoever said it first, they got it right. 'All men are mortal.' You remember that, lots of things take care of themselves. Engañadans get it. The worst is going to happen anyway, so don't sweat the small stuff."

Max was thinking this through when Harvey began to snore. He also wondered how far to believe what Harvey said. For one thing, Max much doubted that there was ever a BNC in Vladivostok or anywhere else in the USSR, or that Harvey could really have crammed so many experiences into his 67 years. Yet he decided not to worry about it. *What the hell. It's a good story.*

Max walked quietly into Rosa's office, where he found her preparing to leave. "Going home?" he asked.

"Yes. They're expecting me, and these things can run awfully late, especially when Harvey's here."

"I don't blame you," Max said, imagining the long night ahead. And he was relieved: one couldn't help but feel diminished around Harvey, and he didn't want to feel diminished around her.

Once she'd left, Max sat down at her desk for the reluctant task of reviewing the speech with which he would open the exhibit. "It's a pleasure to welcome you all to the Center," he read. *While we have one, until Braden and his lawyers run us out.* "It is a privilege for us to present the work of one of Alcalá's fine young artists, and one of Engañada's most renowned poets," and so on. It was a dumb speech, and he would feel dumber giving it with Harvey present.

So why not ask Harvey to open the exhibit? Guest speaker, sort of, the visiting Cultural Attaché? Surely he won't refuse. Max stuffed the speech in his inside jacket pocket, just in case, and went up to the large second floor Exhibit Hall.

A dozen guests already milled about, chatting, walking among the paintings. Sure enough, the entire Directorate of the Patriotic Historical Society was there, either attracted by the artist or to hear their friend Blanco. Max was pleased that he could identify most of the faces despite their overlapping names: Suárez, Pristino, Espejo, etc. Of course the President, Jorge Caballero Pristino of the banana Caballeros, was easy to remember: he looked like a painting of Moses without the beard. Max thanked him for coming.

"No! Thank you, Mr. Lacey! This is wonderful. Do you know

that the American Center here has done as much to promote Alcalá art as any place in the city? It's true. No, no, this center is a wonder, a treasure! Ah, but here comes our mutual friend. Lucho! Come over here!"

Luis Gonzales entered with Jorge Pinzón and Raúl Rojas, who looked glum. Gonzales smiled and waved to Caballero, left Raúl with Pinzón, then joined the Directorate and Max.

"You see," he said to Max, "I told you I'd visit you at the Center! How are things going? No, don't tell me. Every time the Center Director answers the question honestly, it means sad stories. The Center always turns out to be as bankrupt as the *Sociedad*, eh, Guillermo?"

Guillermo Pristino Espejo, the Treasurer, laughed and put his hand on Max's shoulder. "If you're as broke as we are, I hope you stocked candles, because they're going to cut off your lights any moment now!"

"They wouldn't dare!" boomed President Caballero. "To turn out the light of culture? Why, that would be to bring back the darkness of barbarism! We'd make a scandal in the papers and Ricardo Pino would have to hide himself in that damned light company he runs!"

"What was that?" asked Dr. Carlos Ramírez, joining them with a smile as impeccable as his grooming. "Light of culture? Darkness of Barbarism? You gave me a scare, Jorge: for a minute there I thought I heard Woodrow Lively again."

"Ah yes," said the ascetic-looking Vice-President, Manuel Angel Suárez Caballero. "The man who made the Center and its Board famous."

"Woodrow Lively," repeated Gonzales, shaking his head. "What a disaster."

"But a gentleman," said Jorge Caballero, "and a great friend of Simón Bolívar."

"Well, they were both poets, or at least they both wrote verse," commented Suárez, by way of clarification that the subject was the poet, not Bolívar the Liberator. But this was too incredible.

"Was he really here?" Max asked. "Woodrow Lively

himself? On the Board?"

"Of course," Jorge Caballero assured him, "of course he was. A fine man, and in my opinion Manuel's suggestion that Lively wrote only 'verse' is very much mistaken. Lively could talk about Beauty and Art and Humanity with anyone. He was a man who took the long view, and who had thought deeply."

"Well, yes," Max allowed, "I suppose. But how did he come here, and when did he leave?"

"How did he come? I don't know..." Caballero frowned.

"He just appeared one day," said Gonzales, "and shortly it seemed like he'd been here forever."

"It certainly did," agreed Suárez dryly. "He showed up everywhere. At the university, the art shows, the Chamber of Commerce, everywhere."

"He was a great admirer of Espejo," remembered Pristino the Treasurer. "So much so that it became an embarrassment to the *Espejistas,* especially after he left."

"Don't remind me!" groaned Gonzales. The others laughed or groaned with him.

"But what happened?" asked Max. "How did he leave?"

"He made a speech which was not well received," answered Suárez with a straight face. The others laughed or groaned anew.

"You may say so," agreed Pristino. "It was at some sort of Center function."

"The annual Assembly of members," Ramírez specified, "and he made the speech as Director. He was Acting Director between Americans. No, wait; he made it not as director but as President, in place of Augusto Morales."

"God rest his soul. A fine man, very fine." Everyone observed a few seconds of silence in memory of Augusto Morales. Max wondered if he had been any relation to Morales the landlord. Probably. Ramírez proceeded:

"Morales was supposed to make the main speech at the Assembly, but he was out of the country—or was he already sick?"

"He was sick already; I attended him." Dr. Jaime Alfonso Espejo was the first Engañadan *Doctor* Max had met who was a physician.

"Yes, the poor man was close to death," said Vice-President Suárez in his flat voice, a trace of a grin on his face. The others laughed. Even Espejo smiled as he defended himself: "It wasn't I who killed him, but that speech."

"I'd like to hear about the speech," insisted Max. "Just in case the one I'm supposed to give later might make the same mistake, whatever it was."

There were chuckles, and comments that it was unlikely. Ramírez began. "Well, Morales asked Lively as acting Director and Vice-President—the Vice-President is always supposed to be an American, even though we usually can't find any. Thank God for Mrs. Bowman! But, the speech: it was supposed to be a summary of the past year, of the Center's cultural program, plans for building, significant visitors, that sort of thing. The Treasurer gave the financial report. Anyway, Morales had prepared such a speech and supposed Lively would just read it, or write a similar one of his own. But no. Lively made quite another kind of speech."

"He certainly did!" confirmed Gonzales.

"I'll never forget the opening," Ramírez went on, "although I can't remember the first line exactly. No one was really paying much attention; you know how these things are. You have to know that Lively was a strange-looking man, tall and–"

"And rather like a buzzard, with a voice to match." Suárez commented with a smile.

"Well, yes," Ramírez allowed. "So he said–and in that voice, it came out like a croak, or a shriek, or something—words to this effect:

'Gentlemen, let us begin with the premise that there are in the world today two imperialisms: the North American and the Soviet. Tonight I congratulate you, the people of Engañada in particular, as I would congratulate Latin Americans in general, on having the good fortune to find yourselves within the North American Empire.' Well, that got our attention."

Max was afraid to say anything.

"But he never finished the speech. For a while they let him

talk. They were too stunned to react—but then the catcalls began and soon everyone was shouting and talking, or scribbling out letters of resignation from the Center. But the points Lively made before he was forced from the stage were more or less these: that yes, the U.S. intervened in Latin America, most recently Guatemala, and had done so for years. Cuba, Nicaragua, even Mexico were included. He went back that far. But, Lively insisted, all these interventions, except perhaps that in Mexico in 1848, had been ultimately for the good of the invaded peoples since they established a benign empire much different from the malign empires of Britain, France, and the present alternative, the Soviet empire. The Soviet invasion of Hungary was even more recent back then." Ramirez polished his glasses and continued.

"In the American Empire, according to Lively, subject peoples were allowed to handle most of their own affairs, enjoyed freedom of religion and travel, and generally a higher standard of living. The subject nations of Poland, Hungary, the Ukraine, and East Germany had no freedom at all. No liberty of the press, for instance, whereas Washington allowed newspapers throughout Latin America to criticize any American policy. He was lamenting the nature of those Latin criticisms, describing most of them as 'childish ingratitude,' when he was finally chased from the hall."

"A speech," remarked Gonzales, "that changed the course of history."

"That's not much of an exaggeration," allowed Pristino. "Espejo was never as anti-American as he sounded and at that time hoped to improve relations. But after that speech it was impossible. Of course no one remembered that it was the speech of a private individual, that it had no official standing whatever. It was made by the American Vice-President of the American Center; that was enough."

"But even if it had been made by someone with no position at all," said Ramírez, "it would have had the same effect. Lively's ideas were just too humiliating, and too close to what a lot of people thought anyway. The economy was a mess then—not so bad as now, but bad enough—and many would have liked more business with the Americans. Anyway, Espejo himself told me later that Livesly's problem was mainly his choice of words: why not 'community' instead of 'empire'?"

All were silent for a moment. Then Caballero said, "Poor Morales! His wife tried to hide the paper from him, but he finally got a copy."

"And that," diagnosed Dr. Espejo, "was the beginning of the end."

Damn near for the Center too, I'd think. Must have been fun for the next Director.

"So Espejo turned virulently anti-American for a while," added Suárez, "and completed the nationalization of the fruit companies. What was the line he used? 'Engañada will not be crucified on a banana'?"

"He didn't say that," chided Max in a *you're-putting-me-on* tone.

"He did," confirmed Gonzales, "but only in San Andrés. He could get away with it there. But that particular phrase really dated from long before, from the '35 campaign. Anyway, Jorge here benefited: as a national he could pick up the remains of the American companies and grow fat."

Max looked around the now-crowded room and decided he'd better start acting like a host before the ceremonies began. He was excusing himself to the *Sociedad* members when he suddenly remembered something: Ramírez' account had Livesly here in the fifties, but Livesly's 1938 book had references to Alcalá. The Society members were drifting away and Max grabbed the nearest one, the pale Architect José San Martín, and quickly asked about the dates.

"Oh," answered the architect softly, "I think he was here many times, perhaps for a very long time. But Livesly only became a public figure around 1956."

"I see. Did you know him yourself?"

"Oh, yes. I helped him escape. The night of that speech."

"You did? How? Or where did he go?"

"I'm not sure. He asked me to get him a boat and meet him downriver. He thought he would probably row out to a departing ship and just climb aboard somehow."

"And you did it?"

"Of course!" San Martín responded as if Max had questioned his integrity. "He was a friend! He was very sad and kept saying, 'Too soon! Too soon! They weren't ready.' He called himself an *honest fool.*"

Max heard restlessness in the crowd and knew he should be getting things going or at least greeting people. He asked urgently, squeezing San Martín's arm: "Too soon for what? What weren't they ready for?"

The old man closed his eyes and shook his head. "I'm not sure. I never did understand it very well, but Lively had a name for this...philosophy of his, or maybe it wasn't a philosophy but a moral code or something, or even a political program. He called it 'The Higher Hypocrisy.'" San Martín smiled apologetically, removed Lacey's hand from his arm, and moved off after Caballero.

So Lively snuck onto a freighter in the middle of the night— just like some Director Gonzales mentioned on the ship, something about an affair of the skirts. Wonder how I'll leave.

Max moved across the room smiling and shaking hands with a few people he knew, Jorge Pinzón and the artists Pablo and Pedro, and a great many he did not know. He sensed a sort of low-boil animosity between different groups who formed closed circles of four or six people glaring from time to time at other groups. *Just make nice,* he urged them silently. *No nasty words, no fights.* He stood on tiptoe looking for Gloria or Washington, only to hear Gloria's chatter suddenly behind him. He turned to see her enter with Harvey, now dressed incredibly in a neatly pressed white suit. *Where the hell did he get that?* Several of Harvey's admirers arrived in his wake.

Max had to grab Gloria's arm to get her attention. "We'd better get started. Where's Blanco?"

"Poets always arrive late! But he should be here any minute now it's only 7:30 nothing starts before a half-hour after but oh! Is your speech ready?"

"Yes, but I thought maybe Harvey would be willing to do the honors."

"Oh that's a wonderful idea! Harvey's the Cultural Attaché and he makes the most wonderful speeches and he knows everybody and it would be perfect! Do you think he will?"

"I think he might," Max predicted.

"¡No problema!" Harvey assured them when asked. "But introduce Blanco first. I might want to play off something he says."

Max nodded. "Where'd you get the suit?"

"You'd be amazed what you can stuff into the saddlebags of a hog!"

Within ten minutes Blanco arrived with a distinguished-looking man Max didn't recognize. Gloria soon helped.

"Oh, que maravilla! It's Dr. Ibarra!"

Max spun the name through his memory bank. "The rector?"

"Yes! Dr. Carlos Ibarra Gonzales! Now you can meet him at last!"

The short man somehow combined the dignity and dapperness of a Ramírez with the studied casualness of an academic, as if he were wearing a tuxedo with elbow patches. Max wondered what political calculation had brought him here as he shook hands. "Dr. Ibarra, thank you so much for coming. It means a lot to us."

The Rector appeared wholly at ease. "Delighted to meet you at last, and to join you for this occasion. And thank you kindly for the beautiful art book that Dr. Gonzales passed on to me." Max would have liked to talk to him more, but he now had a poet to greet and a show to get started.

Max exchanged a few words with Blanco and then stepped up on the speaker's platform. It took him a few minutes to get the crowd's attention in the overheated room, but only twenty seconds to say what he had to say: Welcome; we have an art show and two speakers. Here is the first speaker, the renowned poet Simón Bolívar Blanco. Thank you. As he stepped down to light applause, Max thought his introduction at least had the merit of brevity.

Blanco's reading did not. First he recited several of his very free translations of Lively, without naming the source or even saying they were translations. Presumably Max was not the only one to recognize them, but no one objected. Then Blanco read several of his own poems, and in forty-five minutes inquired the whereabouts of everything from artichokes to zebras ("those that wore for all to see/ The prison garb that bound my heart?").

Max thought it was all good. Even if it was too hot and Blanco went on too long, people seemed to enjoy it.

Blanco finally exited the platform to enthusiastic applause. Next came Harvey, who had them applauding every sentence.

He began by greeting half the people by name, then announcing, "I am not simply *pleased*: the word is wholly inadequate to describe the way I feel about being here tonight." He grimaced and shook his head. "How? How can I tell you what this means to me? And what," he shook his head again and smiled self-mockingly, "am I to say after you've heard one of the finest poets of our age so beautifully, so powerfully, probe the questions that haunt us all? And what am I going to tell *you* about the art of Luis Delgado?

"What can I say? That Luis is one of the finest—I mean the very finest artists that I personally have had the privilege and the honor to... No. No, there's no way." He let out a heavy sigh, like an exasperated salesman making an absurdly generous offer to a stubborn client. "Look, what is an artist supposed to do? Create beauty? Well, look at those paintings!" He pointed at them and shrugged, spread his arms out palms up with a smile that asked, 'What more do you want?'

"You want the artist to give you insight?" he went on. "Look at that canvas there, the second from the door. You want more insight than that? Ha?" He laughed at the absurdity of his suggestion. "You people don't need me to tell you about the art of Luis Delgado," he insisted. But he did so anyway for another twenty minutes, certainly to the delight of Delgado, and to the interest of most.

But not all, all the time. Max slipped to the back of the room for a whispered conversation with Carlos Ramírez.

"Anything new about the lawsuit?" he asked, hoping to hear that Ramírez had an old classmate on the bench who would throw the whole thing out.

"Only that someone is pushing hard to get it listed in the Record of the First Instance, which means to get it officially recorded. It usually takes at least two months, but in this case may happen within two weeks. Very strange." He pushed his glasses back on his nose and looked significantly at Max.

"But what does that mean? When might we have to pay the five million?"

"Not for years. Getting it recorded is only the first step. The problem is this: once recorded, it is a possible judgment against the Center that reduces our patrimony by five million honores. And if that happens, then our current debt of some ten million is no longer covered by the value of the building, which would be reduced from twelve million to seven. You see?"

"I follow the figures." A few people glanced at Max in disapproval, and he lowered his voice. "But would this affect us with the bank?"

Ramírez nodded. "Without a full guarantee for the loan, they could foreclose."

"But that's stupid! As long as we make the payments, why would they want to foreclose?"

"I hope they wouldn't, but they could. It's the law."

The law, thought Max. *They really should have killed all the lawyers first thing, like someone in Shakespeare said.* "Look," he asked, "don't we know anybody at the bank, on the Board of Directors of the bank, say?"

"Yes." He raised his eyebrows. "Henry Gandig."

Max looked at the fluorescent light flickering at the end of the room. It would burn out altogether pretty soon. Replacing that fluorescent tube would constitute perfect happiness. "Gandig's resignation from the Board, could it be connected?" he asked.

"I can't speculate on motives, of course." Ramírez began. "But the law prohibits a bank's foreclosing on a loan if an officer of the bank has a connection with the institution granted the loan, except with the approval of the Superintendent of Banks. It takes a long time to get that permission. Gandig has no connection with us now and, an important point in law, has not had since before the filing of the Braden lawsuit. Which is to say, from the moment his bank would have had reason for wanting to foreclose."

Max digested this for a moment. "What can we do about it?"

"Well, we could borrow the total amount of the debt if we could find another bank to loan us the money. That would be hard if our patrimony is reduced to seven million: we'd lack three million of the guarantee. Four, since fees would add another million. Maybe we could avoid some fees, but—?"

"Yes, but will they loan it without more patrimony?"

"Probably not. We'd have to increase the patrimony. Now, although patrimony is usually understood as real property, it can include the value of the business. If a firm has yearly profits of ten million, say, then a bank might loan five million on that basis, the idea being that they'd get their money back if they foreclosed. They could sell the firm for so much."

"So," Max calculated, "we'd need a yearly profit of six to eight million?"

"Yes, that's it." Ramírez smiled at his pupil's aptness.

"But if we had that kind of profit, we'd have no problem to begin with!"

"True. Banks everywhere prefer to loan to people who don't need the money. But if we could show that we're making such profits now, or that our profits are on an upward curve and rapidly approaching those levels, we'd find a loan."

Max did some rapid mental calculations, but found them discouraging. The Harvey applause began to die down, replaced by renewed conversation up front. Manuel and Juan and two other janitors appeared in white coats, carrying trays of drinks and the canapés upon which Gloria had insisted, and which Max now grabbed by the handful to make up for the dinner he'd missed.

When Harvey started with his balalaika, it struck Max but apparently no one else as out of place. Yet it provided the guests a choice of muses, as Blanco would say, and some of them gathered around Harvey while others looked at the paintings; most fled to corners for conversation and serious drinking. Almost all took off their coats; it had grown very warm. Max looked for Washington.

"What you gonna do?" shrugged Maldonado, and Max muttered an obscenity. The ever-present heat kept the air conditioning system working constantly, when it worked, so any number of things could go wrong. He loosened his tie and returned to the guests, moving from group to group like a good host, smiling and exchanging banalities, or standing by with an interested look as two or three Engañadans argued, for the most part, in friendly fashion. These debates usually dealt with Espejo, or the price of property, or investment opportunities, but they might also concern the best fertilizer for tomatoes. Whatever the topic, Max the host made what cheerful comment he could and moved on. He stopped by Cheryl Fletcher, Pablo and Pedro, and a few students as the two painters argued about Art and the Revolution. Cheryl followed it all wide-eyed and silent but kept glancing toward the platform, apparently torn between listening to this profound political discussion and sitting in with Harvey. Her Spanish had improved a lot, so Max supposed she understood most of the political argument. This was perhaps not such a good thing: she nodded in agreement with Pablo's view that Delgado's art was so counter-revolutionary that the painter must have studied with the CIA. "They have schools for all kinds of spies," he assured her.

Max moved on yet again, pleased that everyone, even those who apologetically took their leave, seemed in good spirits. After he'd spoken to everyone at least once he stopped longer with the artists, entering enthusiastically into their discussion of the relation between art and revolution. He couldn't take the subject as seriously as they did, but it was fun to argue either side of the proposition that a change of heart required new forms of architecture.

Around midnight Harvey stopped playing, looked around the room grandly empty save for dozens of dirty glasses, and laughed, "*Bueno,* now that the children are in bed, what shall we do?"

"Let's go to the *Café Tropical!*" suggested Gloria. Besides her, Delgado, Washington, Pablo and Pedro, Cheryl and her student Miguel remained. All applauded the idea. *Ah,* Max finally made a connection, *that's the Miguel whose art I liked at the exposition. And why not go? I can sleep in tomorrow.*

Harvey disappeared briefly to reappear dressed again in his

faded jeans and pale blue *guayabera*, and led the way outside. Max asked for a minute, ran into his office to exchange his own suit for light pants and a *guayabera,* and emerged feeling as if he fit in. Wherever it was that they were going required no coat and tie.

Chapter Fourteen: Late Night Culture

They traveled upriver in Gloria's car, a taxi, and on Harvey's motorcycle. Max somehow ended up on the cycle behind Harvey, the balalaika slung across his back. He recognized streets or buildings for a while, then it all seemed new and unknown as they left the tall buildings far behind.

In time they reached the well-named *Café Tropical,* the ground floor of a wood frame building with bamboo matting. A slowly revolving overhead fan brushed faint shadows over the battered furniture. The owners and waiters greeted Harvey as an old friend and immediately provided his rum and Coke.

Harvey sat on the bar and played while most of the customers clapped and sang. There were women who might have been respectable, short fat men in seedy suits, lounge lizards of several varieties. Only the corners remained indifferent to Harvey's music: one group played cards in near darkness, their game marked by angry shouts, profanities, cards thrown on the table, and recurrent hints of impending violence. Another shadowed corner near the men's room held a table with three figures seated at it, impossible to see clearly but disengaged from the bar atmosphere. Max felt there was something odd about them but brushed the thought aside as he sat near the bar with Miguel, Washington, and Cheryl, who had apparently left her guitar at the Center. He was equally suspicious of the glass of cloudy liquid before him on the uneven table. Something was floating in it. "What's that, Washington?"

Maldonado eyed it critically. "A pisco sour, I guess."

Max sipped cautiously, finding the sweet-tart musky flavor different from that of past pisco sours, but pleasant. *The glass is covered in slime. But surely the alcohol will kill anything really nasty. Anyway, this isn't the kind of place where you complain about dirty glasses.*

No, this dark and damp-smelling café on the edge of the jungle was for other things, other ways of being. He turned to Miguel to compliment him on his powerful art, and received a smile and shrug in return.

Harvey asked one of the men in seedy suits whatever happened to Pancho who used to have the tailor's shop next door, and was told that Pancho had fled the city months before when his brothers-in-law promised to kill him for having said something about the honor of his wife, their sister, "the fat one who carries grown hogs home from the market!" Max joined in the laughter, drank some more and laughed again at the local version of the story about the guy whose wife, mad at him for something, denounced him to the police as a chicken thief, only to seek his release days later because "we've run out of chickens!" He even sang along with the others, assuming a blanket permission to make a fool of himself.

When a large ugly insect skittered across their table, he gazed at it and muttered that for all its faults, it was authentic. Only Cheryl understood him.

Well, he decided, looking around the café at the dark shapes in corners that could be revolutionaries or drug runners or anything, *this is something. Sitting in a tropical café in the wee hours with a collection of characters. The guys at GSA never did anything like this. Maybe I should learn to play the banjo or something.*

"Washington," he said suddenly, "we've got to save the Center."

"What?"

"The Center. We've got to save it."

"Hey, we're trying. I've got two more weddings lined up and a lecture on Transcendental Meditation—they pay almost as well as the evangelicals."

"Not enough," Max shook his head. "The situation's changed."

"What now?" Washington's tone was that of a man used to bad news.

"I'll tell you." Max leaned close to Washington in the same

conspiratorial attitude as the shadowy figures in the corner. "I...forget."

"Come on. You joking or what?"

"No, no. It's just that I forget the details. Something about we're not worth as much as the building's worth because...hell, it doesn't matter. The point is we've got to make a lot more money. A lot more. Millions."

Washington looked at him closely. "Rent to anybody?" he asked in an eager voice.

"Anybody with money."

"Sure? Barbers? Hairdressers? Fishmongers?"

"Sure. We're desperate."

"Okay. Boy, we're gonna have fun," Washington grinned.

Harvey wound up his Caribbean routine with 'Kingston Town' and announced it was time to move on. First Max had to make a pit stop. As he crossed the floor, someone pushed open the swinging bathroom door and illuminated the corner where he had been gazing. *Verde? And Gandig?* He almost waved, though there was something out of place. *Thought Verde and Gandig hated each other. And is that Braden? What the hell?* He stared at them dumbly on his way to the restroom, stumbling into a table and excusing his clumsiness to the card players. Max looked again at the corner on his way out, lit up intermittently as the bathroom door swung back and forth. The demonic figures grinned at him in contempt. Max told himself to cut back on the drinking lest he start imagining pink elephants.

The air was not cold or even fresh, but at 2 AM it was as cool as it would ever be. The motorcycle ride even farther upriver revived him. The road got worse and worse and at some point the river on their right was replaced by an estuary on their left, but Harvey slalomed expertly around the potholes. Finally they rounded a bend and came to a sudden halt, almost running into tables and chairs strewn haphazardly in the way, and just missing a pig asleep in the middle of the road. The pig grunted as Harvey killed the motor. Max noticed there was no longer a taxi with them, but only Gloria's Fiat. As the car emptied he realized that Cheryl and Miguel had disappeared.

"*¡Hola!* Enrique! Where the hell are you, you damned Conservative?" Harvey shouted up at the second-story window of a building similar to Café Tropical, but smaller, seedier and leaning heavily to the left. Max unconsciously leaned with it as he read the sign: *Club Huntington*, and the slogan below it, *¡Viva Espejo!* Harvey threw an empty bottle through the glassless window for emphasis. Shouts and laughter came from the tables as Harvey's greetings awakened whoever was inside, if only for a moment. *Definitely seedier. At the last place they were gamblers, small businessmen, and accountants. No suits here, not even seedy ones.*

A fat woman of indeterminate age waddled over from one of the tables, a wig flopping on her head. She embraced Harvey, who returned the embrace and asked, "Conchita, how are you? How's business?"

She whispered something in his ear and they giggled obscenely. Then she asked aloud when he would take her away from all this as he had promised: "I want to be a great lady and live in the White House!" Everyone laughed along.

Harvey demanded to see the old confidence man, Enrique, and Conchita said she'd wake him again: "he so drunk now, you got to drag him out." She went inside; first there came curses and pounding, and then she appeared at the window with a short fat bald man who gazed drunkenly until he recognized Harvey. "You misbegotten son of a syphilitic goat!" he shouted cheerfully, and ordered drinks served while he dressed.

The unshaven waiter refused to believe Max wanted only a soft drink until Max called him close and whispered that he had this "little problem." The waiter grinned and said he understood. Everyone but Max partied on; dawn began to dawn, corresponding to Max's increasing clear-headedness. *We've heard all Harvey's songs at least three times. Whatever world he goes into when he plays, eyes shut, big smile on his face, must be wonderful.* He was surer than ever that he was happy to be here, to see the world at a different hour and in a different place and with different eyes— eyes ready to see other worlds and hours. With light dawning, Max now saw that they were virtually in the jungle, right between the forest and the estuary. Dark canoe shapes lay along the shore. The fishy smell that permeated everything proclaimed the livelihood of people here, probably including that of the sleeping men at the next table. *I'm glad Harvey came, but I'd like to come back here, or someplace like it, on my own and not as one of Harvey's followers. Maybe I'll bring Rosa. Well, maybe not here. Not her kind of place with all these drunks and such. But a bit farther off we could share the jungle, and the dawn, and the rich varied smell from the sea. She'd feel at home. Could teach me about the fish.*

"Max! How you holding out?" Harvey clapped a heavy hand on his back. The Cultural Attaché was visibly drunk now, as drunk as the smiling Enrique beside him. Max found it reassuring. He had begun to wonder if Harvey was human at all, or some sort of bionic man, knocking back twelve hours of rum-and-cokes without effect. Now he was as blitzed as any mortal.

"I'm all right, Harv," Max answered. "Just fine."

"Yeah, but what's this? Soda pop? You're drinking soda pop?"

"With gin in it. Gin." Max hoped he had slipped one by the master bullshitter himself. "Say, Harv, ever know anything about a guy named Woodrow Lively?"

"Lively?" echoed Tyrone, successfully distracted. "You ask me if I know anything about a guy named Woodrow Lively?"

"Right," confirmed Max. "Woodrow Lively. Was on the Board of Directors of the Center years ago. Made a speech and then got out of town."

"Woodrow Lively!" Harvey shook his head and smiled. "Never met the man."

"Seriously?"

"Seriously," Harvey explained, "I wanted to. Looked for him. But whenever I was in Engañada seems he had just left, or I'd leave and then hear later he came back." He shook his head again. "Wish to hell I had met him. A real nut, but what a character he must have been. Jeez! You hear about that speech he made?"

"Yes, I did. Must have left you some fences to mend, that speech."

"That's ri - - right," Harvey burped. "I can tell you where he's buried."

"So where's he buried? Here?"

"Yerp," Harvey burped again. "When I was here in '69, I said this time I'm gonna meet the guy. Chased all over the places they said where he was or he'd been, and finally got a line that he was off there—" he waved downriver and to the north— "off in the estaber—the estuary—up past San Andrés in Bahia...something. Funny, can't remember. Anyway, I arrange to go there with these fishermen—no roads there, nothing—telling them I want to find the guy, the poet. And the fishermen say 'What? You want to see the crazy *gringo?*' And they said I'm too late, that they buried him the year before."

"Damn shame," Max said.

"Yeah." Harvey looked at the ground and shook his head. "I thought I'd at least visit his grave but then this tennis tournament came up, and I guess I've never been much for visiting graves anyway. But he's out there, somewhere."

Enrique had sat down while Harvey related all this, and Max thought he'd fallen asleep, but now he stood up and growled in a hoarse, happy voice, "Harvey! Look who's coming!"

Max saw him point up the road at a small red Japanese pickup truck, and Harvey walked off muttering "No, no. This I - do - not - believe." Max turned away and looked at the river.

Half asleep and half observant, Max watched the deteriorating party: Gloria and Conchita seemed to have words about something the latter had said to Washington. Washington and Gloria, in turn, were evidently not on terms as grumpy as Max had thought. At least, they showed signs of a reconciliation before slipping into her Fiat and driving off. Some fishermen at the next table wandered drunkenly to their canoes and pushed off. *How can they fish half-drunk?* He watched the canoes disappear against the dark opposite shoreline.

A breeze off the estuary brought a new mixture of heavy but pleasant odors, and Max, falling further towards sleep, dreamed of miles and miles of banana trees beyond within the forest, and lithe girls climbing down from bamboo huts to carry the sweet ripe fruit to the bank. Yes, that was a pleasant dream, that in the deep cool jungle he'd find something—bananas, gold, poetry, it didn't matter–to carry to the bank, to solve everything, to save the Center. He saw himself going back and forth, back and forth, in a canoe, bananas piled high, carrying them to Gandig who scowled, not really wanting them, wanting instead to foreclose on the Center. But Ramírez stood on the dock, weighed the bananas honestly when they arrived and wrote down the numbers, forcing Gandig to sign. A dark-robed judge–somehow Max knew it was Woodrow Lively–sat on a banana cart behind them, overseeing the operation.

Max paddled his dream canoe faster and faster, Rosa helping him now, and others raced beside him in their own canoes–Harvey Tyrone, Lively again, Espejo, both Espejos, President and *Vocal*. Washington and Manuel and everyone helped, loading the bananas onto the boats in the deep jungle as soon as they arrived from the plantations on high wooden carts drawn by oxen. Braden tried to restrain them, but Washington pushed him away. *Way to go, Washington!* A wedding was taking place in the jungle, and Max walked through the guests excusing himself, carrying a huge stalk of bananas. Rosa, wearing a long white dress, helped him put it in the canoe and they raced quickly through the estuary to Alcalá, to the dock. "This is it, Rosa!" Max cried. "The last one! The last! With this everything is paid off! We're saved!" In her happiness she embraced him and they lay on the floor of the canoe kissing joyously as they drifted slowly through the calm waters of the Cholo River, pushed gently, gently downriver by the current.

The canoe struck something, and Max fell heavily against the side. He looked around to see the dock, and from the top of the dock—which Max couldn't see because the sun was in his eyes—a scornful voice fell towards him:

"U.S. Guv'ment didn't send you down here to pick no bananas, boy, no way. Uh-huh. You here to do *program*, you understand? But first thing you gonna do is fix *this!*"

Something fell into the boat. Max picked up three papers held together by a paperclip: his Provincial Press Activity Proposal I, and the words slopped over the margin lines everywhere, carelessly and brutally. "How?" Max asked beseechingly. "How? I swear to God they were inside..."

"Max! Damn it, Max!" Harvey revved up the motor again and Lacey came fully awake. "Come on, throw in your forty *honores* so we can get going!"

Max looked around in the full daylight, blinking stupidly. Behind Harvey stood two Indians, one holding a guitar and the other a flute; they both grinned at Max.

"You slept through the best part," Harvey said. "Here, meet Chiquito and Poquito, two of the absolutely finest musicians it has been my pleasure, personally, ever to play with!"

They were certainly short, but Little One and Little Bit?

"Stage names," Harvey explained. "Why don't you come up to Alpaca with us? We're gonna have a great time, right?"

"*¡Sí, Señor* Harvey!" Both grinned and nodded.

"Can you believe this? There I was, just plucking and sipping, when right out of the blessed gray morning with the wind just picking up off the brown water there, in walk these two guys! And you know what today is? It's Chiquito's Saint's Day!"

"Is that right? *Viva el santo!*" He shook Chiquito's hand before walking over to the nearest table where some bills lay, threw on a couple twenty-*honore* notes, and caught up with Harvey by the motorcycle.

"So do you know what they had the incredible goodness to do?"

"To invite you to Alpaca for the celebration." *No*, Max decided, *Harvey isn't human. They just programmed him to act drunk, that's all.*

"Right! And we've got to get this old torture machine on the road if we're going to get there. You coming?"

"You know I'd love to, Harv, but the Center—you know how it is."

"Do I know how it is? Oh boy!" He shook his head. "Well, okay. Look, can you get back to town by yourself? Alpaca's the other way." He tilted his head vaguely southwest. "Bus might come along, or you can hitch a ride."

"Sure, go on. I'll get back. Thanks for coming, Harv."

"Max, thank *you!* This has been one of the outstanding nights in Alcalá for me. This is the way to run a cultural program! Keep it up, and when you get to San Genesio we'll do it again. Man, do I envy you! What I'd give to be out of the Embassy and down here in your Center!"

"We can't all be lucky at once, Harv."

Tyrone agreed, waved, and turned his cycle northeast. Chiquito and Poquito climbed into their pickup and followed, weaving to avoid the potholes, or maybe because they were drunk. Max watched them disappear; he knew they had gone around a bend, but it seemed as though the thick patient forest had swallowed them up. He studied the jungle as one might a new acquaintance: now a bright green on top where the sun shone, passing through various and deepening shades of green as the eye descended, broken here and there by a violent splash of orange or yellow or blue, until it became an impenetrable greenish-black at ground level. Max stretched and yawned. Perhaps a truck or bus would come down that road soon, perhaps not. He was in no hurry. It wasn't yet hot on this equatorial June morning, no more than it would be on a January or September morning.

He looked across the water, now a bright gray. No, Max supposed, this estuary would never be blue; too muddy. So it was brown or gray or black, depending on the time of day. Last night Max had seen nothing there but deep shadow to rival that of the impenetrable stands of trees, which now stretched as far as he could see, and he wondered just how far they had come from the city anyway. Max himself would now come down out of the jungle to the city, just as Harvey had appeared, and Lively, years ago. That jungle suddenly seemed more real to him than the city, more fruitful certainly and more stable. The Alcalá of high buildings and air conditioning was fragile, but this foliage was indestructible. Max imagined it marching scornfully through the city one day, burying the bank beneath gigantic fronds. And in the mountains, where the jungle thrived up to very high altitudes, it would advance on San Genesio. Persistent tendrils would slide up the steps of the Embassy, through the offices and into the files, curling around and crushing the *Country Plan* as Jackson looked on in horror. Meanwhile in Alcalá, the jungle had surrounded the Center, not to crush it but to wrap it in powerful limbs and roots, a bulwark and a protection.

Chapter Fifteen: Creative Reporting

The changes came fast in the coming month. Washington gleefully executed his commission to raise income by any debatably legal means. Max watched, cool and bemused in his white *guayabera*, as pinball machines lit up the cafeteria and the Student Lounge, a superfluous classroom now made useful again. Other classrooms became a beauty parlor, a record shop, and a bookstore, while the Lecture Hall was leased to the *Sociedad Historica Patriotica*. This last agreement had surprised Max because he couldn't imagine why the *Sociedad* needed that much space, nor did he see how they could afford it. But Guillermo Pristino had paid a month's rent in advance as well as a damage deposit and, since the Hall had more square meters than any of the classrooms, this was the most profitable rental of all.

Within a couple weeks, the small accounting firm recommended by the Archbishop's agency could confirm that income was rising steadily. They would surely survive if they avoided an early foreclosure by the bank, which had just requested a balance sheet. Now intimate with the finances, Max knew just why and how a foreclosure at this point would mean the loss of the building, the end of the Center and his career, and unemployment for Rosa, Washington, Gloria, and dozens of others. Beyond these considerations, Max was more determined than ever to save the Center itself, though he could hardly define the Center apart from its people, or say why it was so important. He had an absurd feeling that the Center represented the coast, the sea and the jungle, Rosa and the warm fertile climate. Gandig and everything that threatened the Center was associated in his mind with Jethro Jackson and San Genesio; not with the mountains, but with the arrogant dead hand of bureaucracy, Engañadan as much as American, that reached out from the capital.

Max increasingly suspected Gandig and Verde of dirty dealings.

The curly-headed young accountant with the constant shy smile, Ricardo Sánchez Gómez, shook his head when he first saw the books. There were accounts in which no money had ever been credited. Or debited; Max could never keep the terms straight. The remodeling expense records were more than a million *honores* out of line with the General Balance.

"Here," explained Ricardo. "Over the past three years, more than five and one-half million *honores* have been spent on remodeling, apart from the ten million for the new wing. But in the General Balance for last year, it shows the value of the building as increasing only four million: what happened to the other million and a half?"

Other problems included personnel contracts badly written, materials purchased at grossly inflated prices, and services never performed. Max's favorite was a fifty thousand-*honore* 'honorarium' paid to Hernan Magaña Verde for "independent revision of Center accounting practices." Finally Max cut the young fellow off, asking him to put all this in the form of a written summary.

And what do I do with it then? Until I know, it's painful as hell to contemplate proof that I was right: that Verde was incompetent where not dishonest, and that he must have been in league with Treasurer Gandig. I wonder why Gandig wanted to close the Center, or for that matter why Verde would want to leave, when both were making so much money from it.

Whatever the case, Max would do his best to thwart the bastards. He got himself invited to various high schools to speak on "U.S.—Engañadan Cultural Exchange," or any other nonsense, in order to urge students to study English at the Center. The girls' schools had a lot of giggling, while the boys' schools tended to obscene catcalls that set the assembled student body laughing. *Don't care. If just one in ten would register. Even one in twenty!*

At the Center he counted the rental money with Washington and toasted Pilar San Martín when registration for the second trimester produced six percent more students. The increase was mainly due to a lower dropout rate, which Max credited to Pilar's direction. But the number of new enrollees had also risen, which Pilar attributed to the advertising on Radio Alcalá. Rosa's doing, as Max made sure to acknowledge.

It was a strange happiness: the Center was fighting for its life, but holding its own. An exhibit on American Founding Fathers had arrived with some water damage to a few posters, but Gloria cleverly cut away or disguised the damage. He learned to enjoy sending perverse monthly reports to the enemy, as he now thought of Jackson. He allowed the Monthly Cultural Report to grow of itself, like a jungle vine, with distinctions merely blurred:

Center Demonstrates U.S. Art Influence: One of the outstanding cultural events of the month in Alcalá was the Luis Delgado Art Show in the Engañadan-American Cultural Center, which proved an excellent showcase for current U.S. leadership in the plastic arts.

Delgado, one of Alcalá's most celebrated young artists, acknowledges both in word and work his debt to such U.S. artists as Homer, Grandma Moses, and Jackson Pollock, and his exhibit prompted many observers, including noted local critic "Pablo," to comment that Delgado's technique and themes seem to reflect specific U.S. training. Most were quite surprised to learn Delgado had never studied in the U.S. (he is in line for an Embassy Travel Grant), and that the U.S. influence came primarily through his studies in the BNC Library and through books presented by Center Director Lacey and his predecessors. The event also proved a good opportunity for Director Lacey to discuss U.S. foreign policy, especially Latin American policy, with such local political figures as Luis Gonzales Carvallo and Dr. Carlos Ramírez, leading local attorney.

The presence of Cultural Attaché Harvey Tyrone, who was invited to deliver the inaugural address, was especially well received by the audience which deeply appreciated the interest of the Embassy in the Alcalá art world, and also the knowledgeable and constructive commentary of Tyrone who, as always, embodied the best of the U.S. cultural tradition.

Jackson, of course, showed no enthusiasm for such reports, but neither could he deny their apparent reality. More importantly, whether Jackson liked them or not had little bearing on the Center's survival. In the most important sense, Jackson and indeed the entire Embassy were simply irrelevant where not annoying. Except for Harvey, of course, but Max couldn't think of Harvey as part of the Embassy. So when Rosa announced a call from Jethro one afternoon, he took it as just another chore, and not a real challenge.

"That you, Max?" Jackson's friendly tone ought to have sounded alarm bells. Instead it inspired the irrelevant thought that, had he been sent to San Genesio rather than to Alcalá, he probably would have gotten along just fine with Jackson. "How's everything goin' down there?" brayed Jethro.

"Just fine, Jethro. You see the last report?"

"Uh-huh. Looks all right. And Harvey Tyrone, he finally showed up here again. He say you doing real good down there."

"Well, I'm glad to have his good opinion." Max almost added, *'he's your Cultural Attaché, Jethro: how you gonna discount his report?'* Instead he stayed nice: "And that poster exhibit on Founding Fathers arrived. Looks real good for the 4th of July reception."

"Hmmm," grumbled Jackson. "Well, I got some important news for you boy. You ready? All right: the Ambassador gonna visit you!"

"Oh, Christ," Max muttered, and kicked the wastepaper basket.

"What that? Max? What you say? You hear what I said?"

"Yes, Jethro. Guess I was just overcome with the honor. Harvey was telling me what an honor it is, having the Ambassador visit your Center."

"You don't sound too damn happy about it."

"Well, Jethro, to tell you the truth it's something we could do without just now. Really busy here. But, we'll handle it, I guess."

"Oh." Jethro sort of popped the interjection out.

Max grimaced at himself. *Damn. Dumb thing to say.*

"Oh," Jackson said again, settling into it. "Mr. Lacey says it's 'something we could do without.' Y'all hear that now? Mr. Max Lacey, the most junior member of this here Embassy staff and so damn junior he ain't even in the Embassy, he say he could 'do without' a visit from the Am-goddamn-bassador of the United States!"

"All right, Jethro, all right. Sorry." Max didn't want to hear the rest, though he had to admit that Jackson's Southern cynic routine entertained almost as well as Harvey's World Adventurer song-and-dance.

"Well if it ain't too much *trouble*, we sure appreciate it! Don't think he going there just to see your Center. No sir. He got business down there, important business. Gonna give a talk first at the Chamber of Commerce. And he got the idea to go see your Center after that. I probably never should have taken you up to see him— that's what gave him the idea."

"Well, okay, Jethro. If he comes, that's fine. We'll have the place looking good for him. And if he's too busy to make it, well, we won't complain."

"Oh he'll make it all right!" Jethro assured him. "And you better have it lookin' real good, hear me?" He went on to harangue Max about the Ambassador's concern with the U.S. image and that he, Jackson, would know about the Ambassador's displeasure if the image weren't right, since he too was coming, though very much against his will.

"Right, Jethro." Max wondered if he should get a milkshake machine. "When would this trip be, anyway?"

"This trip 'would be' three weeks from now!" came the biting reply.

Max tuned out the rest of Jethro's exhortations, thinking: *so what can I do, and what can't I do? Guess we'll just have to risk His Excellency's displeasure at finding stores in classrooms and the Lecture Hall leased out. And coming soon, karate classes in the former language lab. Can't run the clients out now, so Mr. Ambassador and Jethro will just have to understand. They can't be that stupid.* Max got through the parting banalities without thinking, heard the click and hung up.

The more Max thought about it, the worse it looked. Yes, they really could be that stupid. Grandly uninterested in the Center's problems, they cared only about its images. *Tough. I'm not going to lose the Center just to make those clowns feel better about our image.*

Of course, when Jethro wrote Max's Efficiency Report in a few months, that would begin the end. There was a place on the report for a response, where one could briefly and within the black margins rebut negative statements. If done well, this might delay one's dismissal for a year or so, long enough to hope for a different job with a different supervisor and a new chance at survival. "Big frigging deal," he muttered to his own surprise.

Maybe I can satisfy both demands. If the Center looks good enough, and I attribute the improvement to the rental income, we might be all right. Of course the place looks lousy right now, especially the unfinished patio. Maybe there was another way. He turned thoughtful as he looked out at the patio, which despite daily sweepings looked the same as when he had arrived: dirt and even pieces of concrete magically reappeared overnight. And of course the plywood windows remained a disgrace. But now Max thought of an opportunity to polish not only the Center's image, but his own. The Center had always held a reception to celebrate U.S. Independence Day. He would make this 4th of July more special, with a morning event to kick things off.

He spoke to his staff. Events were set in motion. The great day was soon upon them.

Chapter Sixteen: Home Improvement

A flattened cardboard box above the Center entrance announced, in Gloria's artistic letters:

FIRST ANNUAL CULTURAL CENTER JULY 4TH
SWEEPSTAKES AND PATIO PARTY

By the time he arrived at eight, Max was delighted to see half a dozen students already standing around the patio. Washington had predicted that not even the prospect of free beer could get them out on a Saturday morning, and especially not to clean up a patio. The middle-class students, he had insisted, considered manual exertion beneath them while those from poor families would dismiss it as a con game. Max thus worried about both snobbishness and cynicism, but by presenting it as a typical U.S. cultural activity, it seemed he had awakened their curiosity.

They looked even more curious beholding the Director in jeans and a work shirt. When Max picked up a hacksaw from Rosa, who issued brooms and tools and paintbrushes by the door, their mouths fell open. He invited them to watch as he sawed off one of the dozens of rusting steel rods that projected from the unfinished new wing. When he finished, a neat cut flush with the wall, he passed the hacksaw to an eager student. The rest caught on quickly and were soon at work patching holes, or sanding off the stairway railings that had rusted for lack of paint.

One student, ladder in hand, paused on his way to where the new building joined the old and asked Max whether the beer would be cold. Max assured him it would. More students arrived, caught the developing spirit, and laughingly set to washing the remaining windows and walls.

Max greeted Luis Delgado and Pablo and Pedro, the first of the artists Gloria had promised. The latter two seemed embarrassed to be there, but curiosity had won, especially after

Max himself had seconded Gloria's invitation.

Gloria had explained their task: each was to paint something on one of the plywood sheets that covered broken windows, emphasizing the opportunity to paint true People's Art with basic materials in a public place. She had herself already made a good start on her panel, covering the whole thing with a thick coat of orange. "For background, you see?"

"I can paint anything I want?" asked Pedro suspiciously. "Revolutionary scenes?"

"Well," Max answered cautiously, "yes...but I think the American Revolution would be the most appropriate, don't you?"

"You have your Weathermen," Pedro allowed thoughtfully.

"I was thinking of Jefferson, Franklin, people like that."

Pedro's face fell. "Bourgeois," he said glumly.

"Oh, all right. You can paint Tom Paine."

Pedro considered. "A theoretician...perhaps, but I prefer your Patrick Henry: 'Give me Liberty or give me death!' I could paint that, yes."

"Please, be my guest. Your window is here, on the corner."

Manuel's grizzled old *compadre*, Lenin Jaramillo Gómez, arrived in a small Japanese pickup truck loaded with cement and sand. Upon proposing the project to his staff, Max had been delighted to learn that Manuel's friend was a self-taught mason "who can, I assure the Señor Director, do whatever thing is needful with cement or brick; my *compadre* is, if I may say so, more of an artist than a workman." He also had two children who wanted to learn English, so an arrangement was reached despite Gloria's objections. She had warned that if the Center allowed someone else to finish the fountain, it would constitute intellectual theft from the artist who began it, and that he would surely complain when he returned from France.

"If he does," advised Washington, "we threaten to sue him for abandoning the project. I know he was paid. His father is Verde's cousin."

"Good," Max agreed. "If he complains, we'll offer him intellectual compensation. He can design our next fountain for free." *Besides, as Harvey would point out, how do I know that either the artist or I will be alive in six months?* After his formal introduction to the Señor Director, *Don* Lenin set to work on the fountain. Max watched with satisfaction as the mason nailed up the loose forms and prepared to mix the cement.

Meanwhile, as more hands arrived, Juan dragged out a hose and sprayed the cement walls while students scrubbed them with rags tied to long bamboo poles. There were some curses when water splashed on the artists' works, but the mood grew increasingly cheerful and the patio rang with laughter bouncing off the three enclosing walls. The students laughed partly at themselves, at their doing such a thing; but they seemed to sense, as Harvey Tyrone surely knew and Max was learning, that absurdity is demeaning only if one refuses to incorporate it. Some students showed initiative with the gaping holes and empty spaces where the buildings joined; several disappeared and returned shortly from somewhere–*and I do not want to know*–with plywood panels of various sizes, two-by-fours, and an electric drill with a long cement bit. Soon the ugliest parts of the building were covered with panels which the students, scrambling about the haphazard scaffolding like monkeys, then painted in the national colors of Engañada and the United States. Max liked the clash of the Engañadan orange-yellow-green with the red, white and blue.

At one o'clock the cafeteria crew brought out Max's beer and a table laden with hotdogs and salad. The pace of the work slowed after lunch, but the patio was already transformed. As a final touch, a photographer from *La Voz del Pueblo* arrived and snapped a roll of film before joining the beer drinkers. Who could say where those pictures might appear?

By 4:30 they'd done about as much as could be done: the place was spotless, the windows either clean or covered with bright paintings. Solid loud colors dominated Gloria's panel, and revolutionary ones that of Pedro: Patrick Henry addressed a peasant crowd with his fist raised high, long curling locks falling from beneath his beret, beard visibly agitated by the force of his passion. You might not have known it was Patrick Henry rather than, say, Che Guevara, except for the American flag held by one of the peasants.

It was a little off, especially the fifty-star flag, but Max didn't object. Indeed, he thought it the best of the lot, making Patrick Henry into an 18th century Guevara, as Pedro intended. With the other paintings it was hard even to know what the artist wanted to do, let alone whether he had succeeded. But that didn't matter either: the great thing was that the patio was bright and cheerful.

Maybe Webster will even agree.

He slapped Manuel on the back as he and his *compadre* proudly demonstrated how the fountain worked, actually getting water briefly to shoot up thirty feet in the air. "It is a problem with the pressure," Manuel explained, "a problem which I will resolve at the earliest opportunity. But first we must allow the cement, so adequately poured by my *compadre*, to dry properly, or the effects of the water would present the inconvenience of undoing that excellent labor."

Max thanked the students as they left, while helping collect and turn over to Rosa the last of the tools and rags. When a newsboy came by with the afternoon tabloid, two headlines had pushed the usual murder and sex stories from the front page:

ESPEJO WON'T RUN!
EXILES TO RETURN!

The first, from Panamá, quoted the old President on the prospects of mounting another campaign at his age and with his party divided: "Who would think of such a thing?" Espejo had asked.

The other story was brief but important: the government had published the Implementing Decree of the Resolution of Return, which had been expected for some time. Exiles could return as of September 1st. Max moved over to where Manuel and Lenin sat by the last half-case of beer, looking as if they intended to sit there drinking until the fountain dried. They smiled, made room for Max, and opened a beer for him.

"What do you think of that?" Max asked, showing the paper.

Manuel and Lenin looked at one another and grinned. "*No sé,*" shrugged Manuel. "I don't know. What does the Señor

Director think?"

"I think that Espejo himself didn't exactly say he won't run."

"Ahh," breathed the two Engañadans, nodding in agreement.

"And I wonder if the second headline has anything to do with the first."

"The Director is very perceptive," judged Lenin. "Indeed, maybe the government wanted Espejo to promise not to run before they let him back. If that's what they thought, Espejo fooled them again!" He laughed, showing several gaps in his teeth.

"By the way," asked Max, "how many exiles are there, anyway?"

They laughed. Lenin held up one finger. "*¡Uno!* Always–almost always–when they say 'exiles,' there is only Espejo!"

Rosa joined the laughing men, sitting next to Lenin. He called her *mi hijita,* pronouncing it *mi'ita,* "my little girl" in the truncated coastal dialect.

"Well," Max asked, "when he returns, do you hope he runs?"

"Of course," answered Lenin, "so long as he comes to San Andrés—eh, Rosita? I'd go home for that, for the pig!"

"That's right," agreed Rosa. "In San Andrés, we always looked forward to his visits. They were like a carnival with everyone happy and big parties and lots of pigs roasted. Some people save their best pigs just for his visit!"

"In my present neighborhood this also occurs—" began Manuel, but Lenin cut him off to extol the uniqueness of the San Andrés Espejo pig roasts. "They are something! And they are the reason that my father stopped being a communist, along with others. The communists turned against Espejo and said no one could go to the pig roast for him, so he said 'to hell with you, then, I won't be a communist anymore!' He even tried to have my name changed, but it was too late. Besides, the official who came to register names was of the party and wouldn't allow it anyway."

"Communists in San Andrés!" Max marveled.

"Not now," Lenin clarified. "After my father left, they didn't have enough to play hearts or any other card game, so the party sort of fell apart. But let me tell you about the pig roasts!"

He launched into stories of the great cookouts in San Andrés, working up to what he considered the best of them all: when Espejo stood as Rosa's godfather. "You don't remember that, *mi'ita,*" he informed her, patting her on the head. "Ten pigs! Ten!" He held up both hands with fingers outspread. "We said it was one pig for every administration and the *Presidente,* he said 'yes, because every time I am President I kill a fat pig to feed the people, even fat foreign pigs!'"

"And aside from the pigs," Max asked, "will the people of San Andrés be happy that Espejo is back?"

"Of course," answered Lenin, "we're always glad when he comes back. It's the best time, when he's running for president. So many beautiful words! What speeches! He makes us think we'll all be fat like the pigs and that he'll teach the oligarchs a lesson. So we're all happy, except poor Don Jorge. He owns the market and is a big conservative. He gets nervous and the children taunt his fat wife when she goes to church, because she thinks she's better than we are because they have a house with a tin roof which is a fancy stupidity because they die from the heat! And Don Jorge says if Espejo wins he'll sell everything and go to another place, and then where will we sell our fish and pigs and bananas? And we laugh at him and tell him Espejo will give us our own market. 'Nonsense!' he says. Then Espejo wins and everyone's happy except Don Jorge and his fat wife, who don't go anywhere like we knew they wouldn't, and there are lots of pigs roasted. Then in a little while, everything is the same and we wait for the Army to throw Espejo out. Don Jorge, he laughs at us and says 'don't worry, the communists will get what they deserve!' and his fat wife turns up her nose even higher on the way to church. Then the Army sends *El Presidente* into exile and we roast pigs in farewell and wait for him to return, when it will be our turn to laugh at Don Jorge again."

"Yes," Max said, "but are things better with Espejo or with the Army?"

"Eh!" Lenin shrugged. "Things they're always the same, or they get better or worse no matter who's on top in San Genesio. Sometimes I wake up in the middle of the night and I can't remember who's President."

"Well then, I'm glad nobody gets killed in all these coups."

"Of course, but why do you say that?"

"Because it would be terrible for anybody to get killed for nothing."

"What do you mean, for nothing?" Lenin asked, finishing off another beer. "That I laugh at Don Jorge, or he laugh at me, is that nothing?"

Max pondered for a second. "No, it's not nothing."

And that night he was pleased to find that Center Board members, and other dignitaries who came to toast U.S. independence, thought that the work on the patio was not nothing. They congratulated him as they sipped Scotch amidst an exhibit of American Founding Fathers.

Chapter Seventeen: "I'm Not That Dumb"

Max now turned his attention to the inside of the Center, walking through the building with a critical eye for whatever should be fixed or dusted or scrubbed. He got the karate people to suspend classes voluntarily on the day of the projected visit, and made sure that the Casino Night scheduled for the auditorium would not begin until well after the Ambassador had left, with the roulette wheels and crap tables to be kept covered in the Library until late in the day. They looked like reading tables, sort of. So far, so good. Ideally the *Sociedad Historica Patriotica* would have promised to disappear as well, or at least take down some of their posters and book exhibits. They seemed most patriotic about the Espejo presidencies, and his portrait covered their walls.

"But Engañadan history *is* the Espejo presidencies," joked Jorge Caballero.

"I grant the point, but it would be helpful if you could temporarily remove a few paintings, lest the Ambassador mistake the *Sociedad* for some sort of political organization."

"Of course, of course," Caballero agreed.

Hoping the man would follow through, Max turned to his next problem: Cheryl Fletcher. *If she latches onto the Ambassador, he'll conclude that the Center has become a hippie hangout. But if I say anything to her, I'll guarantee that she shows up at the worst possible moment. And yet if Caballero does what he promised, and we find a way to keep Cheryl out of sight, we might get through it.*

With the visit four days away, every reasonable preparation had been made. "Can you think of anything else, Rosa? Washington? Gloria?" he asked at the end of a meeting.

"We should have a photographer," said Rosa.

"Are you kidding?" Washington exclaimed. "The newspaper people will be crawling all over the place. Take all the pictures you want."

"I mean our own photographer, for souvenirs for the employees. Did you know," she asked Max, "that Manuel has pictures in his house of himself standing next to every ambassador or other important man who ever visited us? They mean a lot to him—and the others would want one too."

"You want a picture of yourself with the Ambassador?" sneered Washington, softening his grin as Max glared at him.

"Of course," said Rosa, as if that were obvious.

"So do I," added Gloria. "I mean after all it's really an honor."

"That's right," Max allowed. "The Ambassador represents the President of the United States. So even if he is a...never mind. Whoever he is, it's an honor. But what will it cost?" They ended by agreeing to contact a photographer who had asked for darkroom space and was now thinking about their offer. Maybe they could take the photos off the rent.

While The Visit took on a life of its own for the Center, it caused little stir elsewhere, though announced prominently in the press. Local interest centered on politics, the papers full of charges and countercharges between different groups that had won seats in the last Congress and were already maneuvering for control of the next. An editorial in *La Voz del Pueblo* alerted the public to choose candidates in the upcoming elections with an eye to the primordial task facing the nation, the repaving of the Alcalá—San Ramón highway. The next day the *Telégrafo* editorially observed that the owner of *La Voz* had a large farm near San Ramón and that, "however important the welfare of that gentleman," it ought "not to distract the public's attention from such pressing needs as the enlarging and modernizing of the port."

"The *Telégrafo* people are also in the import business," explained Washington.

But it was not only the papers. The streets too were full of politics, full of posters backing Espejo mostly, but some asking General President Morales to stay on as elected President. The Madera posters caused quite a bit of laughter: Washington pointed out to Max, "Look! The official seal! These came right from the

Government Printing Office and they forgot to drop the seal!"
These posters tended to get torn down. Others promoted yet other
names—Gómez, Rivera, Valenzuela, Morales—which meant little
to Max and, apparently, to anyone outside each man's small
coterie. Washington tried to explain, but Max could not keep track
of the interwoven family alliances and feuds, business and military
connections, and both old and new political groupings. Most
parties had no more members than could fit into the living rooms
in which said parties were born.

"Anyway, it seems to get everyone excited," Max observed,
recalling a heated argument he'd overheard between Manuel and
Juan, with the former insisting Espejo was a great gentleman who
helped the poor while Juan insisted as strongly that it made no
difference except that different people got rich.

"Like soccer games," shrugged Washington. "It's something
to talk about. But you know the biggest party? The
quemeimportista!"

"Ah yes. *What's It Matter to Me?* A worldwide movement."

"I belong to it," said Washington proudly. "And you?"

Max caught himself before proclaiming his unrestricted
loyalty. "I try to," he said at last. *Yes, I might be dead in six
months and certainly in fifty years, but is that a reason not to care,
or a good reason to try doing something right while you can?*

In the café that had become his morning coffee stop, Max
overheard three business types exchanging projections. One
assured the other two that Espejo would get nowhere, would find
the city completely closed to him. Another allowed it was
probable, despite Espejo's popularity even among many
businessmen, for he had a friend in the Provincial government, and
this friend had seen certain instructions from San Genesio...

Max found it all rather unreal, for no election had been
scheduled or even promised. Everyone simply assumed there must
be one, since it was tradition for the military to return the
government to civilians that way. Then the civilians would write a
new constitution, usually a revision of some previous one, which
would uphold as the first traditional point the non-political nature
of the Armed Forces. The military traditionally swore allegiance to

the new constitution on Inauguration Day, while the new President (Espejo, traditionally) tried to suppress a smile.

Max looked forward to observing it all, but disliked seeing political interest bringing crowds to visit the *Sociedad Historica Patriotica*. It was one thing to turn his Lecture Hall into a museum or private club, but something else to make it look like a campaign headquarters full of excited young volunteers and cagey veterans. Then he saw Luis Gonzales there one day with his student, Raúl Rojas.

"I've been a member of the *Sociedad Historica* for years," smiled Gonzales, "and Raúl needs some materials for his project."

"That's right," Raúl agreed, but his smile was not as practiced as was that of his mentor, to whom Max now turned suspiciously.

"Dr. Gonzales, I think—"

"Please, I told you before, call me Lucho."

"Right. Anyway, Lucho, a wise man advised me once to be very careful in Alcalá. Maybe I wasn't careful enough: I'm beginning to wonder about the historical motivations of the *Sociedad*."

"My dear friend," Gonzales smiled wanly, as if Max were incredibly naive. "You acted as necessity compelled you to act, and that surely is the essence of caution. But I understand your concern: all this activity, which resembles political activity, does look a bit unusual for an historical society. But please understand that in Engañada every organization gets excited about politics at times like this."

"It's one thing to get excited, and another to do all this!" Max waved at a pile of brochures entitled *El Señor Presidente,* which detailed the progress made under Espejo, "especially when it's visited by the head of the Loyal Espejo Party."

"But Max, we all have various interests. History, music, politics, food...no?"

"I'd think that these days politics was your only interest. I read this morning's paper."

"Good! You mean about Espejo's return? Well, I should not try to deceive you. The fact is we looked for other places to set up a little office, and no one would rent us anything." He raised his eyebrows and then said in a low voice, "That's not an accident."

"Come on, Lucho. I'm not that dumb, to believe you can't find a place to put a desk. And this should be the last place you'd want. Isn't it politically unwise even to be seen in the American Center, and Woodrow Livesly's American Center at that? So why set up a campaign headquarters here?"

"It's an Engañadan Center too, and doesn't belong to the Government," interrupted Raúl Rojas, unsmiling. Gonzales hushed him and turned again to Max, a sad look on his face.

"Max," he said reasonably, "let's not call it a headquarters. And anyway, what's the problem? We pay a good rent and you needn't worry. We have, after all, the approval of one of your Board members. Dr. Ramírez was so kind."

"He did? But he can't! He couldn't!"

"But you work for the Board, do you not?" This, as if teaching a slow pupil.

"For the Board, yes, but no one told me this, and anyway no single member of the Board can decide such things by himself! There has to be a quorum!"

Gonzales shrugged. "That's a matter for the Board."

"Damn it all," insisted Max, losing patience. "We've got the Ambassador visiting us on Friday. What's he going to say about this?"

"We've thought about that," said Gonzales calmly. "We'll be discreet."

As he fumed, Max remembered something. "Lucho, I have a scroll in my office proclaiming me Honorary President of the *Sociedad Historica.* As President, I order that all this stuff be removed!"

Gonzales nodded. "Well thought of, Max. But of course you know that 'honorary' means in name only, without power or even a vote. I doubt that Jorge Caballero would support your order in his capacity as official President."

Yes, Max did know. He sat down beneath Miguel's picture of Espejo speaking from a balcony, one hand reaching out toward his audience.

"But–" Max began before falling silent.

I have no idea how I'll ever sort out this mess. They get Webster mad enough and he'll pull me out. By the time they send a replacement—if they bother—the bank will own the whole place.

"Poor Max," said Gonzales sympathetically.

"It will serve the People," comforted Raúl.

"You think this is trouble for the Center," Gonzales went on, "and you can't understand why Espejo, who has always been more or less anti-American, would now accept an association with the American Center. And I'll tell you the truth: I don't altogether understand it either." He sat down next to Max, looking as if he had confessed a great weakness and, in doing so, made it downright rude to question his sincerity or his proposal.

"You don't?" Max asked, playing dumb.

"No. You're quite right, you know: the problem of space could have been solved in some other way. We could have used my house, if nothing else. But this was the alternative chosen."

"Who chose it?"

Gonzales smiled. "Events here are followed closely in many parts. Anyway, I expect the Center will be convenient in countering the line that we expect from the generals, that Espejo is the tool of the Communists. Especially should the U.S. Ambassador visit. That would answer the generals but alienate the left—except that many on the left would think it merely another cagey move by the old fox. But that's only speculation."

"Which Communists? Maoists or *Rusos* or what?"

"In this context, it doesn't matter. No, Max, don't think of me as a Maoist now. With regard to the businessmen allied with Madera, I am what you would call a moderate progressive Republican."

Max stood up. "Lucho, you're pretty good. As good, I think, as Harvey Tyrone. But I'm not buying it, and I think you'd better start packing all this up. I'm not going to let the Center be sacrificed in a political maneuver. We've worked hard to save the place and you can take your headquarters elsewhere. Whatever the Center ever was or is, it's never been mixed up in politics."

Gonzales nodded. "Are you sure it hasn't?"

"Lively doesn't count. He was a nut. An unauthorized nut."

Gonzales didn't smile, but his eyes laughed. "I admire your spirit, but did you look into the motives of all those students who worked on the patio? And as for saving the Center, well, have you checked your mail today?"

What damn thing now? "I'll do that, Lucho," he said, unable to hide his worry. Max went downstairs, dreading what might await.

"There's a letter from the bank," Rosa said nervously, as though she already knew what it said. Max tore open the envelope and read the ornate legalistic prose. "Call Ramírez," he said. "Time to look for another bank."

To Max's annoyance, the lawyer was neither surprised nor particularly upset by the notice of foreclosure. "Our banks are very touchy about guarantees."

"You don't suppose they got even touchier when they heard Espejo was setting up his headquarters here, do you?" Max asked sarcastically.

"Ah, yes. I meant to discuss that with you, but the details were not quite clear. And in any event, there was no clause in the rental agreement specifically prohibiting such activity. So in law, we really have no grounds for complaint, nor even any problem: the Center is not engaging in any improper activity, for we in no way sponsor the *Sociedad*. It is strictly a business arrangement. They rent space, like a hair salon or any other tenant."

"And can we get a bank to see it that way? Or the Ambassador?"

"That may be a little difficult, though I have hopes. About the bank: send me a statement of current income. I understand it's increased? With that, we can begin. In any case we have thirty days before the foreclosure takes effect. A lot can happen in thirty days."

"The first thing that should happen is we throw out Gonzales and the *Sociedad* before they manage to outrage the Ambassador. If they do, it'll ruin the Center. I know we can't afford to pay a Director, if I'm sent home and they don't provide a replacement."

"I am sure the Ambassador would not dream of such a thing. As for evicting the *Sociedad*, however, that truly could bring problems. You know that Espejo is very popular here in Alcalá, as is the *Sociedad Historica* itself."

"But not so popular that anyone will rent him space."

"That's just politics. Anyway, if we were to throw them out now, when they haven't even done anything yet, and just before Espejo returns, it could do great harm. It would look as though the Center were acting politically. Probably no bank would dare loan us money."

The strange beauty of this utter absurdity enchanted Max for a moment. To evict a political organization, in order not to involve the Center in politics, would involve the Center in politics. It was as if words themselves, like the wood that went into docks and houses, decayed in the humidity and retained but a trace of their original grain. But he had no time to think of that now, nor to waste further with the lawyer.

I could just ask Ramírez whose side he's on, anyway, but I think I know. Meanwhile, the man is both my lawyer and President of the Board. But I still have one bureaucratic card to play. "If the Board agrees with you, fine. But I want it in the minutes, in a meeting with a quorum."

"Very wise," Ramírez agreed. "I'll set it up myself and let you know."

I lose. He's way ahead of me.

Max pushed papers around on his desk, looking for his Office Diary so as to make careful notes. He could imagine the questions that would be coming. Below the Diary was the *BNC Guide,* which he thumbed through to see if this situation was covered. Alas, he found only the generalized warning that "BNCs must at all costs avoid even the appearance of involvement in local politics."

Max started to think about those costs. But not for long.

"Max?" Rosa said, sticking her head into his office. "Esperanza Romero is..."

Through the main door burst the Regional Secretary of the Ministry of the Child. Today she wore solid blue, giving her the aspect of a beach ball.

"I here!" she announced. "Lectures almost ready I haf. Where the materials?"

Max smiled. *This is a test. Remember, not a word in edgewise for her. Deep breath first.* He jumped up and ran to her to guide her to a chair.

"Dra. Romero, what a pleasure! But at the same time, do you know that it pains me to see you?"

"What?" She started to get up, but Max smiled more broadly, filling his lungs as discreetly as possible.

"Because I have the most painful duty to tell you that the materials are stuck in Washington somewhere! I don't know how many times I've called the Embassy, or how many telegrams Mr. Tyrone has sent, but nothing moves! But! But we have some good fortune too! You know I've been talking to everyone about this project and guess who has taken an interest in it? None other than the *Sociedad Historica Patriotica de Alcalá!*" He pitched his voice toward the door. "Washington! Immediately, please!" Back to her: "And Dr. Luis Gonzales is up there right now and I know he'd love to talk to you about it—you know they have their own contacts in the U.S. and Washington! D.C., I mean. I know Dr. Gonzales would be glad to see you—"

"You call?" Washington had his head into the office. Max motioned him in. "Right. Dra. Romero, my associate here, Mr. Maldonado, would be privileged to take you right up to Dr. Gonzales where you can see the various points in common, and I'm sure there are many such points. Dr. Gonzales is fond of pointing out that every great historical figure was once a baby and then a child, and we all know the importance of childhood, so thank you very much, and I'll be consulting with Dr. Gonzales as well as Mr. Tyrone and I'm sure we'll soon have something definite. Thank you, yes, goodbye, thank you, Washington, fine, fine." He'd maneuvered them through the door, which he now shut. He sat down and smiled, and Rosa came over to smile with him.

"That was very good," she said.

"Thank you. Now if I can just think of some way to keep the Ambassador out of here, just in case." He also wondered if Esperanza would storm back after being brushed off by Gonzales, and was happily surprised when she did not.

"Why would you want to keep the Ambassador away?"

Max looked up at Rosa. "It's a long story. Very long. If you want to hear it, I think it would go best with *linguado*."

She accepted. The *linguado* was very good. They forgot to talk about the Ambassador.

Chapter Eighteen: Discouraging Guests

Never had Max seen business transacted so quickly in Engañada. Two days after Ramírez said he would set up a Board meeting, the Board met. Only Dr. Ramírez and Mrs. Bowman appeared. Ramírez suggested they invoke Article XII of the Center Statutes that allowed the Board, however constituted, to declare vacant the positions of any members who had neither attended nor sent written excuses for three consecutive meetings. In this case, that meant everyone except the two of them and Gandig, who had resigned. Mrs. Bowman seconded Ramírez' nominations for replacements, as allowed by Article XIII. Thus Luis Gonzales joined the Board, as did Jorge Caballero and other *Sociedad Historica* officers. These new members arrived within half an hour, and there was one more: Mariana Guzmán, the longtime secretary.

She had returned sooner than expected from her travels and greeted Max effusively. The first thing she'd said to him in her rapid English was, "if we have somebody like you before maybe this doesn't happen." Max felt he already knew her through stories he'd heard from Rosa and others and from seeing Mariana in various photos. But she seemed warmer than he had expected, not at all the harsh taskmaster of some accounts. He was glad she was there, despite everything.

In a final demonstration of unprecedented speed, the new Board held its first meeting just one hour after the last meeting of the old Board.

"Amazing coincidence," Max remarked to Ramírez, "that

they should all be available."

"Hmm." The lawyer polished his glasses.

The new and quorate Board ratified Ramírez' arrangements with the *Sociedad,* confirmed him in the Presidency, and then congratulated Max on his efforts to save the Center. Ramírez graciously acknowledged that he really hadn't understand the situation before Max arrived. "We're in your debt that you not only found out, but have done so much to solve the problems."

Too suspicious to feel grateful, Max nonetheless enjoyed the compliment. He asked what they could do about Gandig and Verde, describing the indications he'd found that the two had conspired to cheat the Center and finally to ruin it.

"Hmm. Difficult, difficult," muttered Ramírez.

"At present," said Jorge Caballero, "very difficult. But later, yes, I think we should look into this."

There they had left it, and Max had to content himself. Proving Gandig a crook wouldn't help with the Braden case. That was in the hands of Ramírez anyway, just as the *Sociedad* business was now in the hands of a Board that had become the *Sociedad* in a different room. The old bureaucrat in Max might have rejoiced to be so neatly absolved of responsibility, but the same old bureaucrat knew Jackson wouldn't buy it. Max could imagine his comment on the creation and decisions of the new Board: *If you'd been doin' yo' job like I tole you I didn't want you screwin' it up, them people would have come to those meetings like they supposed to and there wouldn't be no new board!*

If the Board were part of the U.S. bureaucracy, Max could absolve himself of all blame by citing its orders. But it wasn't, and the U.S. bureaucracy recognizes no power outside itself.

Of course, Max could just relax and yield responsibility to them, accepting that they pulled off a deft power grab. But no, he couldn't. The Board wouldn't do his job for him, and he doubted they could save the Center. On the contrary, their politics would finish it off, at least as a joint American-Engañadan operation. And once Espejo had no further use for the place, this Board would lose all interest again. Except Mariana: she seemed to care for the Center, unless she was just another flatterer for obscure purposes. He refused to believe that. After the meeting she'd promised to have a long talk "when things they more quiet." He had told her that he'd been really disappointed to find her gone when he arrived, that her advice could have saved him many problems. She seemed both pleased and a bit ashamed.

Things won't be quiet for a while, Max thought grimly as soon as the Board had left. He asked Rosa to find Washington for him, then sat down to think.

He had to prevent the Ambassador's visit on Friday. If Webster saw that the *Sociedad* now hardly even tried to hide its true identity as the *Partido Espejo Leal,* the Center's political involvement could not be denied. If the Ambassador visited the Center now, he would seem to endorse Espejo. That would create a firestorm when the government charged him with interfering in internal politics.

What if Webster understood the situation? He wouldn't come! *Yet if I warn him, the Embassy will have to cut all connection with the Center. And it would probably mean my own ruin. I'll just have to save the Ambassador without the Ambassador knowing.*

Besides, aside from the politics, Max wasn't even sure now about the record store and the rest: maybe they couldn't be justified. If Webster believed the necessity argument, he might just identify Max as a man who couldn't find dignified solutions to problems. Grimaldi and Jackson would look bad too; fat lot of good that would do Max.

To hell with them all. Max imagined himself standing on the steps greeting the Ambassador with "Hey, Webster! You want to know what you can do with this job?" Tempting, but he knew he wouldn't doom the Center and his own career like that. Neither was he going to sit passively as disaster approached. *No. I will save them both or lose them both with my best shot. If I lose, then I'll tell Jethro and Webster where to go.*

But how to keep them away? No point in citing scheduling conflicts at the Center: Max had to adapt to the Ambassador's itinerary, not vice-versa. He had to make Webster unwilling or unable to come. Back in Mexico, George had suggested he tell the ambassador the building was being fumigated. That wouldn't fly; George had been joking, and in any case, a Center Director could reschedule pest control work. What then? A crisis in Washington would keep him in his embassy, but that was too much to hope for. A revolution in San Genesio? Yes, but equally unlikely. Tell him about an outbreak of yellow fever in Alcalá? Too easy to disprove, and Webster probably kept up his shots anyway. He was the type.

Max saw Washington crossing the patio on his way back from lunch and knocked on the window to get his attention, then waved him in. "Sorry I'm late," Washington began, but Max cut him short:

"Never mind that. How can we keep the Ambassador away on Friday?"

Washington considered the question as if he'd been expecting it. "We could tell him a pipe broke and that the place is flooded."

"He might want to inspect the damage."

"We could break a pipe," Washington suggested reasonably.

"Would cost too much to clean up, and he'd still be here and ask why all those Espejo posters were floating past."

"How about a death threat?" asked the Activities Director, fishing in the pocket of his *guayabera* for a toothpick, with which he began to clean his teeth.

"Don't be silly."

"What's silly? Just a few phone calls and why would he take a chance just to visit us?"

"The security people at the Embassy would want him to cancel," Max allowed.

"You want to call, or should I?"

"Come on, Washington!" Max tried to laugh scornfully. "Couldn't they trace it?"

"I doubt it, but you're right; there is a problem. To call long distance you have to give your phone number, or else go to the phone company and call from there. Yeah, calling San Genesio is a problem."

"I thought so."

"But hey!" Washington brightened. "We don't have to call them. You could just tell the Embassy you got this call, see? And say the guy said such and such. And we could call the police here, but they wouldn't do anything until next month...but the newspapers. Yeah, we call the papers, threaten to kill Webster, and then the papers will send reporters to San Genesio to ask Webster how he feels about being killed in Alcalá!"

"But—" Max frowned, unable to think of any objection to this plan. "But just lie, say I got a call when I didn't?"

"No need to lie. I call you, right? Then you call Jackson and say you got a call and a voice threatened to...no, that's putting your interpretation on it, an interpretation you know is false."

"Learn that in law school?"

"Yeah. So you say, 'the phone rang and a voice said: such and such.' Right. And I'll call some newspapers."

So the Ambassador will postpone visiting the Center. I can hope to work out the problems before he schedules another visit. The Center and I will survive. It will serve the U.S. national interest. "All right, Washington. But what if something goes wrong?"

Maldonado shrugged. "We'll think of something. But if the worst happens, well, Caballero can get us work picking bananas."

"With my experience in management, couldn't I get a job running one of those banana stations?"

Washington thought he probably could.

Max went back to his apartment that night thinking to get his mind off all his problems by losing himself again in Hemingway's complete works. But after he'd washed down his ill-cooked dinner with several beers, he read only a few more pages of *For Whom the Bell Tolls* when he felt drowsy and lay down on the bed. He told himself he should be grateful: like Robert Jordan, he was having adventures in Spanish, but unlike Jordan, he didn't have to worry about getting shot. A few more pages put him to sleep. The book was still on his chest in the morning.

Chapter Nineteen: Fair Warning

He'd not been in the office fifteen minutes when Rosa said he had a call. A familiar voice mumbled, "Your Ambassador might find his visit dangerous tomorrow." Good old Washington: he'd thought Max foolish to insist on the actual call, but now his own careful statement suggested he'd entered into the appropriate bureaucratic spirit. He at once tried to call the Embassy, but the phone wasn't working. No matter; Washington's other calls had worked. Jethro called him early in the afternoon, so unsettled he hardly bothered to sneer.

"Max? Oh, real glad you on the job there, boy. Real glad. Now suppose you just tell me what sort of security arrangements you got set up for the visit of the goddamn Ambassador?"

Max had begun to smile at Jackson's panic, but soon stopped. Why should he ask about security arrangements for a trip that would be cancelled? "Security arrangements?" he asked stupidly.

"You deaf, boy? That's what I said! Security arrangements! Like against the damn communist terrorists that been calling I don't know who all saying they gonna kill the damn Ambassador down there!"

"Right, Jethro. In fact, I got a call this morning myself that said the Ambassador might find his visit dangerous."

"You too? Why in hell didn't you tell us right away?"

"The phones—"

"Oh, hell. What you plan to do?"

"The fact is, Jethro, well, you know these centers aren't bomb shelters. I mean, we're open to the public and I really don't know how we can guarantee anything. Matter of fact, the first thing I thought of was that maybe the Ambassador would just want to postpone the visit."

"That's what I said! I told Ambassador right off we ought to just forget the whole damn thing! But he stubborn, said he ain't gonna let no crank or no terrorist neither scare him off. Well that's fine, I said, but if it's all the same to you I'll just stay right here but he said no way, I have to go too. So now I want to know what sort of security you got set up there! You call the police? The Army? I want all of 'em there, you hear?"

"Is that what the Ambassador wants, Jethro? I mean, wouldn't look so good."

"Hell no! He said he don't want to look like Lyndon Baines Johnson visiting the troops in Vietnam!"

"Well, Jethro, you and I know it would take an army to protect one of these places. Maybe you can convince the Ambassador of that. Of course, he's right that it doesn't look good to—"

"I don't care how it looks! I just know don't want to get blown up in Alcalá, Engañada, visiting no damn bi-national center! And your job as Director down there is to get the Army and bomb squads and anything else it takes and do it so he don't know you did it and especially so he don't know I had anything to do with it!"

Max smiled coldly. *Welcome to Alcalá.* Then he said easily, "That's kind of hard to bring off, Jethro. Even without considering the, well, moral aspect. I mean, deceiving the Ambas—"

"What are you talking about, boy? Ain't a question of deceiving nobody. I'm trying to save the man's life! *And* protect the U.S. interest: how you think we look if the communists can kill a U.S. ambassador right in our own Center?"

"You're right, Jethro. I guess in this case we'll just have to take some creative measures."

"That's just what I say, damn right. Creative measures."

"I'll do what I can. Of course, you know how things go in this country. The Army might not show up until after it's all over, to help dig out the bodies. Hope they have those heavy rubber bags, with all this heat."

Max heard Jackson suppress a whimper. *We play rough down here, Jethro. Don't mess with my Center.*

"You do what you can, huh, Max?" Jackson asked in a weak voice.

"Sure thing, Jethro."

"All right." There was a resigned pause, then his voice started to gain strength again. "There was something else I wanted to ask you about, about that Center of yours. Yeah, just what the hell going on down there?"

What's he unhappy about now? "I don't understand what you mean. You don't sound too happy about something."

"Darned right I ain't too happy about something, and I can tell you right now the Ambassador ain't none too happy about it neither, and that's seeing pictures in the newspaper of a U.S. diplomat dressed up like a bum with a broom in his hand and a great big old communist picture in the background!"

Max rested the phone on his chest and silently mouthed *damn* in the general direction of the river. He'd been pleasantly surprised by the *Voz's* account and photos, and he'd received only compliments from local Engañadans for the resulting publicity. Free publicity was always good. Why couldn't they see that in San Genesio?

"Well, Jethro," he answered evenly, sliding the phone up to his shoulder again, "since you don't want to hear about the money problems this place has had for a long time now, even while reports said it didn't have any, which it did, I'll just say we try to save money where we can and I work cheap on Saturdays. Sure do. Anyhow, every tin can and every scrap of angle iron we've picked up will be that much less shrapnel flying around here tomorrow."

"Oh," Jackson said, the spirit gone out of him again; he muttered a goodbye and hung up.

Max then mouthed a vile Spanish expression, one involving mothers' milk, that he'd picked up in *For Whom the Bell Tolls,* though he'd never heard it elsewhere. Its vulgarity conveyed his present anger and disgust rather well.

He next summoned Washington. "He's coming anyway. We have to find another way to stop him."

Washington pondered for a moment and said, "A

demonstration. We'll arrange a demonstration."

"Hmm." Max rubbed his chin. "A demonstration in front of the Center. Right. Crowds like that are as dangerous as bombs. And then the Army or at least the police will come to break it up, but if they come too soon then he'll still get in here."

"Are you kidding? The police and the Army don't go near demonstrations, not unless they threaten the government buildings, or a factory or something that some general owns a piece of. They'll show up when it's all over."

"Maybe we could dress up a couple of the janitors as soldiers and put them where Jackson can see them?"

"No way. They'd get killed by the demonstrators. But if we do it right, there'll be so much confusion that Jackson won't know if the Army was there or not."

Max frowned skeptically, but let it go. "Where do we get the demonstrators'?"

"At the university, of course. But..." Now Washington frowned, "It will be touchy. Some of the groups are too violent."

"This has to be peaceful, Washington!"

"I know, I know."

"But not too peaceful. I mean, they should look threatening."

"Right. That's why we have to get the right group. The Espejo people might cause problems...well, leave that to me."

"That's right. You're a student too. Sometimes. Gonzales' student, in fact. When will you finish so we can have our own shyster right here in the Center?"

Washington shrugged. "I finished my courses six years ago, and now I'm working on my thesis. If you finish too fast they won't approve it. Anyway, you leave this to me. We'll have to work with Raúl Rojas' enemies." Before leaving he added, "There will be some expenses for placards, renting a bullhorn, some old tires to burn. Okay?"

"All right, but don't let them rip us off." *I'll just check my* BNC Guide *for handy tips on economical ways to sponsor anti-American demonstrations.*

In the afternoon Mariana Guzmán stopped by to visit, surprising Max, as things weren't quiet yet. She said it was *importante que* she see him but began by apologizing for leaving just before he arrived. "I so sorry to go, but *no veía* any alternative," she explained in a fluent mixture of two languages. "Besides, I was here so long, it was time I leave and let young people work. Rosa, she *buena muchacha,* but I don't come to talk about me."

Mariana reached into her purse and pulled out a handkerchief, with which she dabbed her eyes and then blew her nose. She bore a superficial resemblance to Esperanza Romero, but this plump, graying woman was on the angels' side. She even looked a bit like one in her white ankle-length dress. She had come today, she said, to warn Max and encourage him, and to excuse herself. "A little while ago I don't care what happens to the Center," she said, because the "shameless ones" (her translation of the harsh Spanish *sinvergüenza)* who should have helped were instead using it for their own ends, "especially that Gandig!" She spat out the name. "Why you think he quit the Board?" she challenged, and immediately answered her own question: "Because he don't want to be tied down by the Braden *denuncio o como se llama, demanda,* the lawsuit that he start himself!"

"How's that? Started it himself?"

"You see that lawyer Braden has? The *compañero* of Gandig's lawyer? You think Braden have the brains to sue, that nothing of a man? Ha! But he must be happy now! Don't worry, Gandig will take care of Braden with a job or something at least for a while, until he doesn't need him anymore! And how did Gandig know about the contract and the visa? Because he worked with that thief Lucho Verde! Oh, Mr. Lacey, the things I see in this place they make me sick! Worse than that poor Woodrow Lively...you know about this maybe?"

"Yes, I do."

"Oh. Well, poor Mr. Lively, he almost get our Center closed but he not a crook, he just say what he mean, poor crazy *gringo.* But we work so many years to make the Center a nice place, like it was for so long, and then these garbage get in it! But, it not my place to say anything. I was just a secretary even if they call me Executive Assistant after twenty years. Now I wish I said something. Dr. Ramírez, he tried but he always too busy to see, and then it was too late." She dabbed at more tears of sadness and rage.

"But why does Gandig want to wreck the Center?" Max asked. "I agree that he and Verde are in this together and that Gandig wants his bank to foreclose, but why? I could understand a political motive, but Gandig has no interest in that. I don't see what's in it for him."

"He only interested in money," Mariana asserted. "Tell me, don't you see the empty old buildings near to the Center here? You know who owns them now? Gandig! You know that he and his friend Roberto Molinos—by the way, Verde working for the Molinos Brothers now–Molinos, the one that do the remodeling here so bad, that they have this big plan to build a giant building in Alcalá? You know Gandig is on the Board of the bank that it wants to foreclose now? Who you think will buy this building, and cheap too?"

Max found it clear enough, but almost too banal to believe.

"I try to make Mr. Grimaldi see this. I give him hints. Maybe I should have told him *claramente*, but he just smile and write his reports to San Genesio."

'A-number-one good shape.' A cold-blooded careerist, this Grimaldi. A few months ago, I'd have envied him that. Now he looks like another sinvergüenza.

Mariana went on to complain that San Genesio was just as bad, especially Jackson with his insistence that the Center do Embassy work at almost no cost to the Embassy. With the gradual reduction in recent years of the American colony that had helped found and sustain the Center, Mariana had grown increasingly disillusioned. Disheartened by the treachery and indifference that promised a shameful end to the Center's very existence, she had quit and promised never to return. "But now I'm on the Board," she smiled proudly. She had followed events despite herself, even from abroad. She had, she said, at first thought Max just another non-entity, but had rejoiced at the firing of Braden and the efforts to increase income.

"Who told you all this?" Max asked.

She smiled and went on. "I don't like the beauty shop in our Center but I know there no other way. But it too late now, maybe *fue ya tarde* when you come here. The bank, they don't wait: now they asking the court to let them foreclose right away, without waiting thirty days. Even with thirty days we don't get a loan, though. Dr. Ramírez, he try, but I know people in all the banks." She shook her head sadly. "It's business, Mr. Lacey. Lots of people make money if Gandig build his building. I don't know why he's that way. We had so many nice American businessmen here, like Mr. Bowman of *Molinos* and Mr. Michael Gandig the uncle of *este* Henry that inherited it all. What a shame that his uncle *no tenía* children but he didn't, and this Henry shows up not speaking Spanish or caring about anything, so different from his uncle. And Mr. Harold Riley that had the textile mill, they do business a good way, to give jobs to people and they didn't just care about profits. *Pero* now..."

"Then, *Señora*, I have a question. If all is lost, why did you agreed to serve on the Board?"

"*Señora!* Please, call me Mariana! Well, that's why I come to see you. Maybe we have a chance—with Espejo. Maybe he save us. That's our only chance, I think."

The idea was in the best Engañadan tradition: to ally oneself with a powerful politician and so benefit from special decrees, exemptions, and rulings. And what politician more powerful than Espejo, when he wasn't exiled? "You think he would push through some sort of law to help?"

"*Por supuesto!* We call them laws with Christian names and surnames," Mariana laughed. "So that's why I come really, to tell you not to throw out Luis Gonzales and the *Sociedad*."

"You needn't have worried." Max laughed with her. "Luis Gonzales and the *Sociedad* control the Board. I can hardly throw them out if they don't want to go. If anything, they could throw me out."

"You find a way if you want to," she decreed. "But don't fight them. Luis is a good man. I've known him a long time and he's godfather to my second son and help me so much when my husband died."

"I'm sorry."

"Oh that was a long time ago. But if Espejo is elected he can do a lot, and even if he's not elected he is very powerful with lots of friends. You understand now?"

Max did, and didn't. For one thing, time was short. They had thirty days; less, if Mariana was right, and no time to wait for elections which might or might not occur. *But this is not the time to argue with her. I'm still figuring out on how many fronts I'm supposed to fight.*

He thanked her for her advice and "your help and loyalty for all these years." After she had embraced all of the employees and left, Max reflected.

Everything she says might be true. Even before I came, I was told I could trust her, at least...well, by Gonzales. But if she truly is honest, what then? She could still be mistaken on some level. Is Espejo really going to expend any political capital in saving the Center? And even if Mariana's best-case scenario plays out, will it be worth it? Do I want to lend both the Center and the Ambassador to Espejo's purposes, even if Espejo's success saves the Center? It was one thing for Max to frustrate the bothersome plans of the Ambassador to visit, in order to save a Center that did good things for the United States. It was another thing to let foreign politicians manipulate the personal representative of the President. *And yet*, Max frowned. *Always an 'and yet.'* The Ambassador could probably afford to lose a little dignity, and the United States would survive in all its majesty. And the Center might be saved. He walked over to the window and looked for the green hill he knew was out there and which he suddenly wanted to see, but he couldn't find it. The only window in line with the hill had been replaced by plywood. The afternoon wind was rattling all the panels now, and Max remembered a question he'd long meant to ask.

He called Rosa: "How did all these windows break, anyway?"

"The windows? They broke one by one after this new wing was finished. Something about the foundation, that the building sank and then broke them somehow. Don't you notice how the floor slopes there by the corner?"

Yes, there was a definite slope. He pushed gently against the remaining windows: those closest to the corner seemed to have more tension. He looked cautiously at the edges, expecting them to shatter any second. *Damn. Friends of Gandig, of course. He probably told them not to worry, that the building would soon be knocked down anyway. How many people have made money out of this place? Now it's to be used yet again, and with it the Ambassador—who has his own uses for it.*

Something of patriotism, but more of pride settled the matter: they weren't going to manipulate his Center, or him, or the President's representative, and they wouldn't reduce him to Gonzales-style scheming, either. He'd handle this like a man and an American. "Rosa," he said, "would you get the Ambassador's office for me?"

She looked at him curiously but went to make the call, which, amazingly, went through almost at once. Max recognized the voice of the cool secretary he had met in San Genesio, asked how she was, then requested to speak to the Ambassador.

"His door is closed," she said, as if that were final.

"Could you tell him it's urgent?" Surely he would agree it was urgent, and in appreciation for Max's forthrightness, would probably get the Center a grant.

"Wait a moment." Max heard himself switched to *Hold*. He drummed his fingers on the desk, rehearsing what he would say to the Ambassador and contemplating this irony: he had been told to rely on Mariana, and had lamented that she was not here to guide him. Yet now, when she advised him not to oppose Gonzales in this, he was doing just the opposite. A snap on the line ended his contemplation. "Mr. Lacey? The Ambassador says he's busy, and that in any case you should communicate with him through Mr. Jackson. And he told me to remind you that he would visit your Center tomorrow. You can talk to him then." Her tone invited zero argument. Max said goodbye.

All right. I tried. If he wants to talk to me tomorrow, he'll have to get through one hell of a demonstration first.

Chapter Twenty: Play It, Sam

"Where are they, Washington?"

"I don't know. They should have been here by now. I'll call Pablo." He picked up Max's phone and began dialing.

"Tell him to hurry." *Not a good time for jokes about* mañana, *also known as 'Engañadan Daylight Time.'* Max didn't like relying on Pablo, even though he liked him well enough personally after discovering that his politics were both serious and better thought out than his pious rhetoric would suggest. That made him unreliable. If Pablo decided his politics were incompatible with Max's purpose, he might undermine the plan. But as in so many things, Max had no choice. Washington related that Raúl Rojas, probably at Gonzales' bidding, had tried to prevent the demonstration and that Pablo was the only student leader willing to oppose Rojas, with whom he had some sort of rivalry. Anyway, Pablo had promised a couple of hundred students who didn't care what they demonstrated for or against. But now it was after ten: the Ambassador was due at noon and they needed the demonstrators now. Max had directed Washington to tell the projectionist, Sam, to record gunshots and a bugle call from an old John Wayne western that had, somehow, been left stranded in the Center for twenty years. If need be, they'd play the tape through two large speakers hidden near a second floor window, making it sound both like the Ambassador was under attack and that Max had got the army here as requested. But it wouldn't work without some kind of disorder.

Washington turned from the phone. "There's a problem with the placards: they don't know what to paint on them."

"Can't they handle that?"

"He says they need some ideological direction, a theme. Are they protesting U.S. intervention here or in Vietnam or where?"

"Does it have to be anti-American?"

•   Washington looked impatient.

"Well, Vietnam then. Don't remind him the Americans have left already."

"Okay. Pablo? *Dice que sea de Vietnam, sí. Que más? Momento.*" He covered the mouthpiece and turned again to Max. "They want to know how much they're getting paid."

Max tried to laugh it off, but Pablo turned out to be serious. After quick negotiations, they settled on 150 *honores* per demonstrator, students to be counted jointly by Pablo and Washington. But Max held firm against free beer.

"He says they had it for the sweepstakes," Washington relayed.

"If they come back tomorrow to clean up their mess, okay. But only if this is a peaceful demonstration: no rocks, no beating anybody up, and stay away from the windows." Max quickly calculated about thirty thousand *honores* for two hundred demonstrators, and with the placards and old tires and beer, the total could get close to some sixty thousand. He decided he'd pay for the beer himself. *More of my money for free beer! Goddamn Webster to hell. Maybe I should ask Jethro for a cultural grant to cover it. I know what he'd say:* "Hell no! This ain't the Lyndon goddamn Baines Johnson administration, ya know!"

"He wants to know if burning tires is still all right," Washington reported loudly, recalling Max from his reverie.

"Of course, but in the middle of the street. And tell him to hurry."

Max spent the next hour glancing at his watch: *still no demonstrators. Ideally we wouldn't need them. Ideally the papers will stop Webster where the phone calls didn't.* The *Voz del Pueblo* on his desk had a front-page story on the official visit with a subhead advising, "Terrorist Group Promises Revenge for '62." Max learned from Washington that some political group had been banished in the coup of 1962, for which the United States was still widely blamed.

Unhappily, the reporter to whom Washington had telephoned anonymously about threats to the Center was one of three journalists who now came through the door to await an interview with the Ambassador. In the meantime, he sought one with Max. Upon hearing Washington speak, the fellow eyed him with suspicion as Max rambled on for a bit about the honor of the Ambassadorial visit. Begging off an immediate interview, Max invited them to wait in the cafeteria, where he instructed the manager to keep them supplied with free drinks. He had learned in Mexico that, *the drunker the reporter, the better for us.*

At 11:15 there were still no demonstrators, but Luis Gonzales arrived to welcome the distinguished visitor on behalf of the Board. Max was glad to have the advantage of his old shipmate: "Only if he can get through the demonstration," he smirked.

"I think he will," Gonzales smiled back.

"Did you mess up my demonstration?" Max asked angrily.

"Not at all. Improved it, perhaps."

Which might mean that Rojas managed to get it shut down. Is that why they haven't shown up yet? "Any demonstrators yet?" he asked Rosa, nervously.

"No, but there's an elephant."

"Huh?" He and Gonzales both rushed to the window. Sure enough, an elephant was lumbering across the patio toward them. A second elephant appeared from around the corner with a small dark man in a turban astride its neck. A truck with a lion painted on the side was parking by the curb.

"Washington!"

The Activities Director came in carrying a placard, "Stop Exploitation of Local Labor," and began to explain his own plans for the demonstration when he caught sight of the elephant. He slapped himself on the forehead. "Damn. I forgot it was today!"

"Washington, just what in the hell is going on here?" demanded Max, vaguely aware that he sounded Jethronian. "Are you working for Gandig too? Or for Lucho here?"

"Max. For shame," said Gonzales disapprovingly.

"No, Max, really! I'm sorry," blurted out Washington. "I was going to surprise you! They're paying ten thousand for just one day, to advertise—"

"Ten thousand?" Max exclaimed, thinking how welcome this would have been at any other time. Some kids might have come to see the elephants, and stayed to study English.

"Right. They set up on the edge of town always, but they come through the center and stop someplace to attract people, you know? And I know you said once 'no circuses,' but then when you said everything was all right, I thought it would really be...you see? Anyway, it's only for today."

Max sat on the couch and rested his head in both hands.

"And they said they'd clean up everything."

"Why don't you get some donkeys," suggested Gonzales, "and call it an exhibit of the U.S. political process?"

"Very funny." Max stood up and faced Washington. "Your initiative is appreciated. Any day but today, this would have been wonderful. But today," he pointed to the patio, "elephants out! Right now!"

"Right," Washington agreed. "I'll just go look for the guy I talked to—"

The sound of distant chanting reached them all at once. The chants were unclear but rhythmic, growing louder and louder until they could distinguish: "¡Viva Espejo! ¡Viva los Estados Unidos! ¡Viva la amistad!" Washington looked puzzled.

"Your demonstrators, Max." Gonzales slapped him on the shoulder in the way of a graceful winner.

Max looked at him in shock. "You've sent pro-American demonstrators! How could you?"

"We want the Ambassador to feel welcome, of course."

But now new sounds disrupted the friendly chants. Gonzales might have gotten his own people here, but he had been unable to prevent Pablo's group from showing up. The new arrivals chanted anti-American slogans, and mixed with the first group to form a crowd with a split personality. Placards proclaiming friendship with the U.S. waved next to those demanding *U.S. OUT OF LATIN AMERICA AND VIETNAM!* Espejo posters waved next to those denouncing the CIA or the Espejo Party that had disowned Espejo. The first placard to enter the patio called for closing 'the Center of Cultural Imperialism.' A few kids held up anti-Espejo posters, like "Espejo is the Past," but these soon disappeared.

Max wanted to believe it would be enough to discourage

Webster, but the demonstrators were too cheerful. A few argued but that wasn't chaotic enough. A lot of them were laughing.

"Washington, aren't they going to burn a tire or something?"

"Doesn't look like it."

"Well, see if you can get one of your buddies there to burn one. Maybe it will stir them up. Right now they look like a welcoming committee."

"What if it scares the elephants?"

"So much the better."

Max watched Washington greet friends as he worked his way through the crowd toward a pickup truck down the street. From his gestures and conversation with Pablo and others, it seemed they had brought a few old tires; they just didn't want to burn them. A pair of giraffes walked past as they argued, Pablo pointing at the animals. Finally they pulled a tire and a small gas can from the pickup and walked past the Center toward downtown, from where the Ambassador's party would come. At the corner they threw down the tire. "Good man, Washington." But why didn't they set it afire?

"You can't depend on anyone anymore," sighed Gonzales.

"Señor Lacey, can you tell me if you think these demonstrations hurt U.S.-Engañadan relations?"

Max turned to see two of the journalists at his office door. Fortunately, both looked half-crocked, unsteady on their feet. He put an arm around each and guided them back to the cafeteria, while delivering a set speech on U.S. respect for and even encouragement of the expression of all viewpoints, even those critical of the United States which, while not perfect, shared a vibrant tradition of unfettered debate with freedom-loving peoples everywhere. So it was hardly surprising that in Engañada, so noted for the independence and forthrightness of its citizens, differences between friends should be frankly discussed. He left them with their third colleague, who had lost all interest in politics for this morning, and promised to advise them as soon as the Ambassador arrived. "Do have another drink while you wait."

Back in his office Max found Washington, who said Pablo and company refused to burn the tires unless they were given an

American flag to burn as well.

"I'm glad they respect tradition," said Gonzales. "Surely you can afford a flag, Max?"

"In his capacity as a member of the Board, will the Señor Director Gonzales approve the expense?" asked Max, elaborately sarcastic.

"Come on, Max," insisted Washington. "It's almost noon, and they won't burn it without the flag."

"No. There are some things I won't do even for my country. Look, why don't they draw a picture of Uncle Sam and burn that?"

"Is there time?"

Then came a distinct change in the crowd noise. The laughter and happy chanting were replaced by shouts of alarm and anger. Someone shouted, "The bastards have sent the tanks!" From the office window they couldn't see much now, with demonstrators pressed against it and the elephants moving back and forth. Max ran to the second floor and looked down the street, happy to see the students getting hostile and that someone had set tires on fire, but wondering who could have ordered tanks. Jackson didn't have that much clout.

A pair of bulldozers advanced on the Center, their motors purring heavily, *Construcciónes Molinos* stenciled on their sides. Cameras flashed. Max ran back down to his office wondering if there was time to call Ramírez, almost colliding with Rosa who ran in to tell him the lawyer was on the phone.

"Bad luck, Max. They found an *Espejista* judge, one recently assigned from San Genesio, and got the waiting period waived. I'll appeal it this afternoon. There are Espejo judges on the Appellate Court, but of course they're at lunch now."

Even as he insisted it would be too late, that the bulldozers were almost at the door, Max wondered what amazing grace enabled him to understand what Ramírez was talking about.

"Yes, I know they're there," Ramírez said. "The Court granted foreclosure at nine this morning, and by ten the bank had sold the building to Alcalá American. I found out that's a company formed last week by—"

"By Gandig and Molinos," Max concluded.

"And others. Lucho Verde has some shares. But they can't knock down the building while there are people inside. That's illegal."

"We'll just stay, then."

"No, don't do that! Once the bulldozer driver or someone shows you the eviction notice, to stay would be contempt of court. Just avoid them until four o'clock or so. Can you do that?"

"I'll guarantee the next hour or two. Then we'll have to see."

"Do your best. I'm working on the papers now."

Gonzales was no longer smiling. "The fools have made them mad. Look at that!"

The patio had cleared somewhat as students sought cover, and Max could see tires burning right in front of the bulldozers, whose drivers stood warily on the other side of the street. The elephants watched everything closely but remained calm, munching on the hay thrown before them. Someone threw a rock at a bulldozer, but the students were more a crowd of nervous and irritable people than a real demonstration. Nonetheless, the scene was chaotic. Max hoped it would be enough.

Rosa came downstairs to tell them, "There's a big car trying to come here." Max ran back up the stairs.

He looked out a second story window and saw a black Chevy Impala sedan at one end of the street, stopped behind yet another truck, this one carrying a heavy cage from which an ape stared at the Embassy party. Webster and his dignity stood out amid the strange scene as if in a spotlight. A husky Engañadan-looking fellow stayed close to the Ambassador, looking warily about. They in turn stared uncertainly at the scene before them: jugglers, a Fat Lady, and some clowns, but not for long. The Ambassador started walking forcefully toward the Center with Jethro Jackson following reluctantly, staying close to the Webster's equally nervous-looking Engañadan bodyguard.

"Hey! That's that Bradford Webster guy. I remember him. My dad helped him get his job. Looks kinda straight, doesn't he?"

Nooooo! Not you! Max had no time for Cheryl now. "Right," he agreed, and started downstairs with her jogging beside him.

"Where'd you get the elephants? They're cute. I really like

animals, you know? But why do they put chains on their feet? I think that's cruel. I think you should just let everything be natural and fly around instead of caged up, don't you?"

"Yes, absolutely." He grabbed Manuel at the foot of the stairs. "Play the tape!" he ordered.

"Perdón?"

"The tape! Play the tape!"

"Perdón, but I have not the honor to be aware of the matter to which the Señor Director refers."

"Didn't Washington tell you to get the tape ready?"

"I have not had the pleasure..."

Right! It was the projectionist! Max ran back up two flights of stairs, losing Cheryl as he darted into the auditorium. He saw the projectionist through one of the windows in the projection booth.

"Sam! Where's that damned tape?"

"Right here, ready to go."

"Then play it, Sam, play it!"

Running back down to the second floor, Max located the Ambassador. He stood no more than twenty feet from the patio, staring haughtily at everyone. Jethro and the bodyguard flanked him. The demonstrators glared back. Webster turned to scowl at the Center again: his eyes met Max's. Sam finally threw a switch.

"SERGEANT, SOUND THE CHARGE! BANG! BANG! *CHIEE-WHIIING!"* the loudspeakers blazed. A bugle charge then mixed with the gunshots.

"Damn it all," Max muttered, "I told them just the shots, no dialogue, just the damned shots and bugle. Why can't anyone get anything right? And why didn't I check it myself?"

Webster's bodyguard was better trained. At the first sound of shooting, he embraced the Ambassador and pushed him toward the car, which had gone over the sidewalk to get around the bulldozer. The vehicle now rushed forward, almost running over Jackson, who scrambled in as it passed. "Thank God," sighed Max, but his relief was short-lived: he saw Cheryl Fletcher running across the patio, Manuel at her side, her long hair bouncing back and forth. They reached the Ambassador as the car did. Cheryl said something, smiling brightly. The Ambassador turned to look at Manuel, who for his part turned to smile at the photographers. Then the bodyguard pushed the Ambassador into the car, Cheryl piled in after him, and the sedan spun around in a cloud of blue smoke and squealed loudly down the street.

"I think Manuel got his photo," Rosa said.

Chapter Twenty-One: Conjuring Dark Powers

The following Monday, after watching a repairman reattach the phone, Max awaited the inevitable call from San Genesio. He did so in an office darker than before, thanks to a new plywood window replacement. While dodging an elephant, a demonstrator had jostled a juggler, causing him to send a heavy wooden ball through the middle pane behind Max's desk. But someone – perhaps a high circus wagon or an elephant – had done happier damage, taking down the phone line that ran from a pole on the corner. Max was glad to have no phone service in his office over the weekend, and of course his apartment phone wasn't yet installed. Surely Gonzales had contacted some friend or relative to get the Center's line fixed so quickly; the *Sociedad* needed communications.

At least the disorder had kept the bulldozers at bay until Ramírez secured the Appellate Court order canceling the immediate foreclosure. After the bulldozers left, the atmosphere had eased, with the day ending in a friendly circus promotion complete with children and cotton candy. Max even got to ride on an elephant. And the next day, sure enough, many of the demonstrators returned to help clean up and drink beer. At the same time, Pablo contributed some new artwork to the Center. On the plywood sheet covering the newly-broken window, he rendered what Rosa called *El Día de la Auto-Manifestación* ("Day of the Self-Demonstration"). It was a circus scene complete with demonstrators, and Max thought it among the best of all the patio's now-extensive exhibit.

At first, Max had worried what in God's name Cheryl Fletcher might have told Webster in the car. But she'd returned from the outskirts of Alcalá, where she had bid farewell to the Embassy party, to ask Max to pay off the taxi she'd had to take because "I'm like broke again and in this heat I mean who can walk?" Then she reported, to the extent he could understand her, that she had told the Ambassador the Center was a wonderful place and she couldn't understand why the U.S. government didn't support it better. She'd ask her father about that, she said.

The media coverage cheered him less, for both papers carried pictures of Manuel smiling beside an angry, crouching Ambassador and a bouncy Cheryl Fletcher. The photos had been taken from slightly different angles and a split second apart, and the two newspaper accounts of the "incidents at the American Center" reflected the differing political alignments of the respective publishers. Both accounts agreed that the reporter filing the story had been forced to barricade himself inside the Center with the American Director. But whereas the *Telégrafo* reporter claimed to have sought protection from a mob of communist and other elements intent upon disrupting the honor of an Ambassadorial visit to the local center of "friendship and amity between the sister republics of Engañada and the United States," the *Voz del Pueblo* journalists were threatened by elements "controlled from San Genesio as well, of course, as by foreign interests" who were determined to prevent the Ambassador's courtesy call on the *Sociedad Historica Patriotica*. Webster's purpose, according to *La Voz*, had been to manifest his respect for the Society and for the democratic traditions embodied in the persons of Don Luis Gonzales and Don Jorge Caballero, trusted advisers to Don Juan Francisco Espejo Suárez, who had looked forward to conferring with the Ambassador on matters of mutual interest.

Max consoled himself. If the Center had been all too clearly identified with local politics, he had nonetheless chased Webster away without manipulating him, no matter what drunk journalists wrote.

"Max! It's Jackson," advised Rosa from her office door.

He waited for the switch to be thrown. "Hello, Jethro. How's it going up there?" *I'll just bet he's in full cry.*

"You ask me that. You got the nerve to ask me how things goin' up here. A bullet damn near takes my head off and you ask me how it's going up here. Well let me ask you something. Just what in the *hell* are you doin' down there? And what's the matter with your phones? I been trying all morning to get you!"

Poor Jethro. The Ambassador must have got on his back. "Phone got knocked out in the violence, Jethro. Only got fixed this fast because strings were pulled – and I'm working on my home phone. Sorry you couldn't get inside the Center, but you know these demonstrations are the best evidence of our effectiveness. Show we're having an impact that the bad guys don't like."

"Yeah. Well, the Ambassador is not impressed with your effectiveness and neither am I. An effective BNC director doesn't let his center get mixed up in politics. An effective BNC director doesn't have no elephants in his center. And an effective BNC director don't embarrass the press section by messing up no damn visit by the Ambassador of the United States!"

"Sorry the Ambassador got on you, Jethro, but you can tell him that I can't help it if people decide to demonstrate, and I can't keep circuses out of town, either. What I could do, I did: you wanted protection and you got it. Who do you think was covering your escape, anyway?"

"Yeah, that's another thing. Where were the army and police like I told you to have them there? Maybe I heard something, but I sure didn't see 'em."

"Jethro, you said yourself Webster didn't want to see no Army, so I worked it out for you. You know about plain clothes, undercover stuff?"

"Harumm," growled the public affairs voice of the Embassy. Then he shifted tone: "Hey, anybody get killed? Sounded like a damn war."

"Nothing serious. Some damage to the building; big plate glass window."

"Uh. Well look here, Mr. Lacey," continued Jackson, shifting back to his sarcastic tone, "I called to tell you that you in real big trouble. You understand? Real big trouble. You know what the Ambassador said to me when we left? He said, 'I am not pleased.' That's just what he said, those his own words, 'I am not pleased,' and he told me to tell you just that, that he ain't pleased, and that you walkin' on thin ice. So maybe you think you can fool old Jethro Jackson, which you can't no way, but you'll never fool that man. No sir. So I'm telling you right now, boy, you better not screw up no more, like we don't want to see no more articles in no papers about how U.S. Ambassador getting ready to get in bed with an anti-American demagogue which this mission is not at all interested in seeing get elected again. How you let them go print something like that anyhow?"

"Jethro, you really want me to answer for the imagination of the press?"

"Seem like that Center of yours just inspire them to imagine things. Anyhow, I think there's only one thing saving your ass right now. That girl climbed in the car, that Cheryl Fletcher?"

"One of our most popular teachers."

"Damn hippy you ask me. Can't understand a word she says. Anyhow, when it turn out her daddy's a senator, which I never heard of no Senator Fletcher but her daddy got divorced or her mamma did, or something, damn politicians as hard to keep track as movie stars anymore, this girl anyhow, she going on about how great the Center is, *you know?* And how everybody loves everybody down there. Thought she was talking about a bunch of perverts. Anyhow, she says she'll tell her daddy all about it, so Ambassador, he tell me to just hold off until he see which way this Senator jumps."

Max sighed. *Maybe hiring Cheryl was the best mistake we ever made. But no matter when or which way the Senator jumps, things don't look good. Not with an ambassador out for my scalp.* It wasn't fair. "Jethro, I can't see what Webster's ticked off about. Does he blame me because some Engañadans have a demonstration?"

"'Course not. But what he does blame you for is for not preventin' the demonstration at a U.S. cultural center on the day he visits the damn place!"

"I don't see the difference."

"Well, that's just why you won't cut it in the Foreign Service, boy. He said, 'Lacey's lost control.' See, you ain't got control of things down there. Why don't you have contacts with people so you don't get no demonstrations–and no circuses neither—*and*," Jackson raised his voice as he remembered something, "and they don't go publishing no pictures that make the U.S. Ambassador look like a damned idiot right on the front page?"

Max couldn't help himself. "He should have smiled, Jethro. Manuel came out real well."

"Boy, don't you—"

"I'm not your boy," Max cut in. "Now look, Jethro, you remember our phone conversation of last week, when you practically begged me to save your ass from getting blown up down here?"

"And a great job you done, with a bullet missing my head by an inch!"

"Jethro, trust me, you were never really in danger."

"Like hell I wasn't! Didn't you hear 'em? Anyhow, you talking about a memo or something? Something in writing?"

"No, about a phone call where you—"

"Where I told you be sure you don't mess up the Ambassador's visit! That the phone call you mean?"

"All right, Jethro," said Max resignedly. "Have a good day, hear?"

As he hung up, disjointed words from *King Lear* ran through his mind: "I will do such things... What they are I know not, but they shall be... terrible." Yet he soon forgot about impossible revenge, and set his mind more happily and fruitfully to other problems, and other loyalties.

The next day after lunch Max wondered why he hadn't thought of it before: all they had to do was to get Braden to drop his lawsuit. The figures on Max's notepads were beautiful: income was up, and most expenses were holding steady or even down a bit since they had started buying paper supplies and other things from new vendors rather than those with whom Verde had some connection. They became pitifully inadequate only in the shadow of Braden's demand. Or Gandig's. Take that away and everything was manageable. They could pay off the loan, get the foreclosure cancelled for good, and move on. Moreover, it would undercut the Board's argument from necessity for allowing the loyal *Espejistas* to use the Center—something Max still opposed, even should the Ambassador never schedule another visit.

Gonzales had now gone so far as to discuss housekeeping arrangements in preparation for Espejo's return "which, I have reason to believe, may be imminent." He thought only the Director's office would serve. "Of course we'll do something about the windows."

"Are you kidding?" Max had asked in disbelief. Gonzales had replied, "We can hardly put the President in a broom closet." Max resisted; Gonzales cited necessity: "Espejo is the only hope of the Center, as indeed of the country."

Ramírez had then played his part by reporting sadly that no bank would give then a loan even though current income was "impressive, yes, quite impressive." Max doubted the lawyer would lie outright, but Max could imagine the manner of his approach to his various banking contacts: "You wouldn't lend ten million to a struggling cultural center with a lawsuit hanging over it, would you?"

But could Max get a loan without the intervention of Ramírez? No. He'd tried it that very morning, right after talking to Gonzales. He visited the manager of the *Banco de la Costa*. This gentleman, after sharing a cup of coffee and chatting about life in general, had asked after his *compadre* Carlito Ramírez. When Max raised the subject of a loan, the response was that these were difficult times but, if Carlito and the Board cared to present a formal request, it would be considered in light of the generally accepted banking criteria. Max got the message.

All right, no loan. But if there were no lawsuit, there'd be no need for a loan, no need for Presidential protection, and no justification for installing Espejo in my office. Of course, the Board could then simply order me to stand aside, but that would be too blunt an admission for Engañadan taste: it would confirm that they worked for Espejo, not the Center. I doubt they would do that. What I need is another queen in my ongoing chess match with the Board.

Wasn't there something else? He pondered a few seconds before remembering the other face of Armageddon: *The possible fine for having an illegal foreign employee!* Ramirez had said that could cost even more than the lawsuit. *So just give up?* No. Max decided he could worry about only one problem at a time. First up, Braden. Dodge that bullet, then worry about the next one. His mother always said, "Some saint will provide;" that would have to be his plan for now.

So Max grabbed Washington and together they set off in search of Braden. Max hoped to appeal to his better nature, or offer him money now to drop a lawsuit that would take years to settle. Braden's landlady had not seen him for more than a week, nor had anyone in his usual hangouts. He had to be around somewhere, because Max was almost sure he had seen Braden in the Café Tropical with Gandig and Verde. In the last café they checked, they ran into Braden's former student Javier, who thought Braden had taken a trip.

"To where?"

"I don't know," Javier shrugged, "but the last time I saw him he said he was going to work for the revolution. Something about Cuba. Some day."

Good luck with that, Bertram. They'll lock you up as a CIA agent, maybe shoot you.

Javier finished his coffee and lit a cigarette. "Braden was into politics, or at least into 'fighting the system,' as he put it. In the poetry class, he said the only justification for poets is if they help the revolution." He looked at the ground and smiled. "Strange fellow, Braden. I sort of miss him, though Cheryl is a nice replacement."

"He should have read more Lively," Max sighed. "Or understood better what he did read."

"He said Lively was an unwitting reactionary."

Washington asked where then, in Engañada, Braden would

221

have gone to work for the revolution? None of the three had a clue. There had once been an insignificant guerrilla group up in the mountains somewhere, but they hadn't made any noise for years. And, as Washington himself pointed out, "If Braden went looking for them up there, we'll never see him again. He'll freeze to death. Or starve."

"Hell," sighed Max, "we sure don't see him here."

As they returned to the Center discouraged, Max got another idea: What if they asked for some sort of court hearing and Braden didn't show up? Maybe the suit would be thrown out?

"For God's sake don't do that!" exclaimed Ramírez when Max called to suggest it. "You'll have us all in jail!" He explained that the law had indeed contained such provisions at one time, but they were changed long ago after several suspicious incidents in which people who had lost cases for failure to appear at court had gone missing, or had washed up downriver. So the fifth Espejo Administration had transformed the unexplained disappearance of a plaintiff into presumptive evidence of murder by the defendants. "A good law in its way," Ramírez added, "except that some plaintiffs have abused it by disappearing in order to put the defendants in jail."

Max told Ramírez that he'd forget the idea, and hope that either Braden would show up or that no one noticed his absence. *I will also insist that law student Washington Maldonado show me the relevant statute in his law books.* Meanwhile, Ramírez soothed him about the possible legal consequences of Braden's disappearance: "I wouldn't worry about getting jailed. That usually happens only in family cases, and the law is rather skeptical now in the absence of any proof of wrongdoing. Of course, the judge in a particular case may have particular views, so it always helps to have friends who can put in a word for you."

"I see."

"And, just as a point of interest," continued Ramírez with a touch of superiority in his voice, "even if Braden lost the case, or dropped his demand, it wouldn't solve our problems. Have you forgotten the possible fine for employing an illegal alien?"

"No, I haven't forgot it." Max saw no point in confessing that it had indeed slipped his mind for a while. "But one thing at a time."

Ramirez couldn't argue with that, and Max pushed the question to the back of his mind along with a mental note to light a candle to St. Jude, patron saint of hopeless cases.

He went next to Washington's office, where Maldonado rummaged through a few law books and produced the statute in question. There it was, all right. Max saw his queen carried off the board in triumph by the opposing king, bishops, and knights who had attacked her simultaneously.

"So I guess you're going to let Espejo move in, or whatever they want?" asked Washington.

"You mean, you guess I'm not going to try to sabotage the Board's decision."

"Right. Are you?"

"You want to organize another demonstration?" Max asked cheerfully. Then Rosa interrupted to announce a call from Jackson.

"Two days in a row," Max muttered. He went to his desk and picked up the heavy old-fashioned phone as Rosa threw the toggle switch in her office. There was the usual heavy click and then Jackson's voice inquiring, as always, if he really had Max Lacey on the line, as if the phone might have betrayed him.

"Yes, Jethro. What is it?"

"Oh. I'm real glad you there, and not out in no demonstration or nothing."

"What do you want, Jethro?"

"You ask me what I want. Well, now..." Jethro began a longwinded display of sarcasm and outrage that Max heard with decreasing interest and fear. Jethro ranted that Max was in more trouble with the Embassy, enumerating once again his various shortcomings in procedure and result alike, punctuated with the customary rhetorical questions. *Nothing I can do about all that crap. Nearing bottom, though, one sees the silver lining. Mixed metaphor? Big deal. If I'm out of the Foreign Service career, at least I won't have to deal with thirty more years of Jethro Jacksons.* He listened to the tirade as if it concerned somebody else until Jethro finally came to the point.

"Ambassador talked to this Senator yesterday. This Senator's the father of that Fletcher girl?"

"And?"

"And nothing. Didn't mention a word. So look like he ain't got no interest at all in this business, so Ambassador told me to tell you to just pack it up 'cause you'll be getting on a plane real soon now," Jethro gloated.

"And who's going to replace me?" Max asked.

"That ain't your problem, but my guess is ain't nobody going to replace you. Ambassador and me, we about up to here with that damn bi-national center that ain't nothin' but one problem after another. So my guess is that he'll just tell Washington it's not worth it and he don't want no replacement 'cause he don't want no more connection with the place."

"I see." Max imagined the maneuvering that would begin among the Board members, with each one trying to get his nephew into the job—if they found a way to pay the salary. He also wondered what Jackson, or the Ambassador, or Washington D.C. would have in mind for Max Lacey, but he wouldn't give Jackson the satisfaction, and didn't ask. *I think it'll be more fun to ruin his day.*

"I'm confused, Jethro. I mean, what about those guys that were down here?"

"What guys?"

"The guys from Washington. You know. I'm not supposed to talk about it, I know, but I thought they had you all tied in."

"What you talking about?"

"Of course, they never actually said you were, and that I was to say nothing until they passed the word. I guess I just assumed the Ambassador had to be in on it. Of course, they did come straight from Washington."

"When was this? What guys from Washington?"

"Geez, Jethro, I really can't say."

"Where you say they were from?"

"From Washington. You know. Sort of. Across the river."

"Oh. Them."

Max imagined his mind and Jethro's simultaneously flying north on the George Washington Parkway that led to CIA headquarters.

"What the hell they want down there anyway?"

"They wouldn't say much, and I wasn't encouraged to get nosey. Just gave me my instructions and said they'd be in touch." *Let 'Hetro' worry about what the spooks might want in Alcalá.* He recognized it was a pointless and petty revenge, but pointless and petty seemed about right for Jackson.

"What instructions?"

"Sorry, Jethro. But on the timing here of this move, I can't leave until they say it's okay. They said this was important. Really important. Maybe that's why they didn't tell you."

"I'm gonna have to see about this," Jethro snorted, a little uncertainly.

"You do that. He—they—said something about a 'Delta Channel.' Maybe you could check that out. I don't want to say more on this insecure line."

"Yeah. But hey, don't you go thinking this changes nothing. You can still start packing and better tell that Board of yours to start looking for somebody to take over."

"We'll see."

After hanging up, Max savored Jackson's confusion for a moment, but soon returned to worrying about the Center, and himself. He stretched back in his chair and looked around the office. "This is it!" he laughed. "This is my life!" What now? Might the Board select private citizen Max to replace Foreign Service Officer Max? They well might, so it would be foolish to fight them on the Espejo thing. But the Center Max wanted to direct wasn't a tool for political scheming. It was dedicated to understanding, culture, all that good stuff.

I should win some prize for naiveté.

Max tried to think realistically about both his prospects and himself, what he could live with. *To join them willingly and for a purpose would be one thing. To be used by them, or to join just to have a job, would be something else. But what other options do I have? I'm not good at starving. I am good at forms. Even Jethro admits that. So I should be able to get on with the government somewhere, maybe even stay in the Foreign Service.*

Two voices in his mind argued over the prospect of another bureaucratic job: one sneered "Big deal," while the other answered "Sour grapes!" Max soon tired of their squabbling.

He told himself to stop thinking about it, and returned to thinking about it. A third voice broke in, asking if he shouldn't have become a priest after all, as Sister Monica had predicted when he was in the second grade.

He doubted it. With his luck, he'd have drawn a poor parish under an indifferent bishop. The roof would leak and collections fall off. He'd have ended up renting the basement to a Masonic lodge while a group of evangelicals set up shop in the empty parochial school building. And anyway, Sister Monica had long since married a sociologist and moved to a commune in Oregon. But then, come to think of it, she had predicted he would become not just a priest but a missionary.

In a way, she'd been right. He tried not to remember how many missionaries had also been martyrs.

Chapter Twenty-Two: Booing the Messenger

Max was surprised that he heard no more from Jackson in the following weeks. He couldn't imagine that his silly CIA suggestion had caused Jackson or the Ambassador to back off, and thought it more likely that they were sick and tired of dealing with the Center. Absent another outrage, they were probably content to ignore it for a while. Maybe they were too occupied with Engañadan political developments.

In mid-August came an evening event that would interest all Engañada: the official announcement of a new constitution. Max moved the Embassy-loaned television set, normally used to show videotapes of American ballet or Presidential press conferences, into his office and invited the staff to watch with him.

Washington thought the constitution had been rushed to completion. It usually took longer, and he suspected something sinister. Gonzales had told Max that morning that it was better back when he was a boy, before radio and television, when they heard it from criers who went from town to town. He also disliked the relatively recent innovation of the outgoing military junta writing the constitution, rather than having the new government call a constitutional convention. Sometimes, of course, both happened.

Max sat next to Rosa on the couch, her hand in his, while Washington and half a dozen others completed a semicircle around the television set. Precisely at eight o'clock, the National Anthem blared out while the screen showed the flag of *La Republica de Engañada* evidently blown by an electric fan off-screen. Then a small balding man with large glasses appeared behind a huge desk as a voice announced, "Dr. Jorge Chilela Gómez, Honorable President of the Constitutional Committee of the Supreme Directorate of Government."

Chilela jiggled his papers, cleared his throat, and began. "My fellow citizens: I have the supreme honor tonight to put into the cognizance of the Engañadan citizenry the fundamental charter of the Republic, approved on the fourth of the present month by the Supreme Directorate of Government, and which will henceforth guide the destiny of our beloved fatherland."

Looking often from his notes to the camera and back, Chilela proceeded to review the errors of the previous constitution and the long and careful process by which the new one had been drafted "with the collaboration of the most patriotic and distinguished jurists."

"Tailoring it for themselves," sneered Washington.

Chilela described the many benefits to be obtained under the new document and the noble principles that had inspired it. The Preamble, which he next read, amply confirmed these principles.

Then followed an incredible number of clauses and provisions that made Max think he was hearing not a constitution, but a legal code.

For example, under the general heading of Natural Resources came an article guaranteeing that "the export of seafood must forever remain under the control of those legally constituted organisms empowered to regulate it in such a way as to protect the maritime heritage of the entire nation."

"That's for the Suárez family," explained Rosa. "You know, of the packing plant by the Customs House?" But Chilela's long exposition bored them until he got to "The Presidency." That brought them all to the edges of their seats.

The description of Presidential duties and powers passed without comment, but the short Article XLIII brought cries of treachery and betrayal: "Article the Forty-Third, of the Age of the President: No person shall assume the Office of President, or present himself as a candidate for the Office of President, if he will not have attained his forty-fifth year prior to the date of inauguration of the term of office, or the term of office for which he would be a candidate, or if he has or will have completed his eightieth year prior to such aforesaid dates."

Chilela rushed nervously to the next point, as if facing a mob rather than a production crew in his own office. Based on the reaction around him, Max doubted many people were now listening anyway. Rosa declared it a plot, a cowardly trick to keep Espejo from winning, and that the people would not accept it. Washington, whom Max had never thought of as a conservative, railed against the violation of tradition. Manuel told Gloria it was a San Genesio trick, and Gloria assured Rosa that they would not get away with it. Juan smiled agreeably. Max looked indignant for Rosa's sake.

All ignored the television until Chilela finished, except to curse his somber face now and again. At the end, Chilela arranged his papers and set them aside. Instead of saying good night, he reached for another document. His silence got their attention.

"Citizens," he resumed, "we are all aware of certain events that have taken place in the Republic in recent days, and more particularly in the city of Nueva Alcalá. In addition to seditious and unauthorized public meetings, there have been riots, disorder, and chaos. I refer most particularly to a cowardly attack on the cultural center, symbol of peace and friendship, which bears the joint name of our beloved Republic and that of a great sister republic of the Americas, an attack which resulted in the death of twenty-six innocent people and the hospitalization of hundreds more."

Washington softly hissed a vulgarity impugning the chastity of Chilela's mother.

"What's more," Chilela continued, "only the rapid and professional action of the Army and the National Police prevented the assassination, by terrorist elements, of the esteemed ambassador of a great sister republic of the North, a crime which, had it not been prevented by the forceful action of the government, would have besmirched the national honor forever."

Max slid down until his head rested on the back of the couch and laughed softly.

"These and other incidents, my fellow citizens, have given rise to rumors of all kinds, rumors which have as their obvious purpose to disturb the public tranquility and confidence in the government and in our scheduled return to the elective process.

"My fellow citizens: the highest authorities of the Supreme

Directorate of Government have authorized me to assure you tonight that this will not be allowed to happen, that we will not be held hostage to hoodlums, criminals, and subversive elements. The government will act decisively to curb this totalitarian attempt. The Supreme Directorate of Government, in its untiring endeavor to assure the security of the nation, has recently completed arrangements to receive much-needed security assistance from a sister republic and so—"

"Max!" broke in Washington, "Why are you selling the bastards more tanks?"

"The better to protect the Center," Max responded innocently. "But listen!"

"I am authorized to inform you," droned Chilela, "of the following resolutions which will take effect immediately:

"A) The elections for President of the Republic and for other offices as called for in the new Constitution will take place immediately upon the reestablishment of a democratic climate in all regions of the Republic;

"B) There will be a reorganization of the military structure, with all commands now to have their headquarters in San Genesio under the direct supervision of the Minister of Defense;

"C) Henceforth and until further notice, public meetings are banned and a curfew is in effect from eleven P.M. to five A.M.

"My friends, you may rest confident that these wise measures will quickly restore the viability of the peaceful and democratic processes traditional in our country, and in the firm benevolent stewardship of the Armed Forces. Thank you, and good night."

The fan-blown flag reappeared. The curses of the gathering were aimed at Chilela and other interests. Max got up and turned off the television. "Think Espejo will back off?" he asked the company in general.

"You'll see," answered Rosa grimly.

Chapter Twenty-Three: The Exile Returns

Max stood on the Center steps and reflected that the tropics probably never knew the tension of colder places. The electricity generated by the fall of a government might crackle through a cool Parisian morning, and certainly Berlin must have been palpably nervous on the day Hitler met with old Hindenburg. But the Alcalá humidity absorbed everything, even emotion, so on this September Saturday the city was merely a bit less lethargic. Max imagined a man lying in a hammock slung between palm trees, evidently at ease, yet glancing at his watch every few minutes.

People were preparing for a parade on the Center's street, hanging flags and banners. Most were ordinary enough (*¡Viva Espejo!*) but others were quite elaborate. Max especially liked the one Raúl Rojas had draped across the Center itself: "The People United With Espejo Will Overcome Elitism, Imperialism, Centralism, and Inflation." Loudspeakers hung from the walls. *Can't even see the Center. Jethro will love it.* Then he decided he might as well go in and have another cup of coffee, and actually read the newspaper story he'd been avoiding, the one headlined:

ESPEJO RETURNS TODAY!
WILL DEFY EDICT ON AGE!
Official Reception at American Center!

The headline pretty much told it all; the rest of the article consisted mostly of details or historical padding. Even a few days earlier, the idea of an illegal Engañadan candidate defying the government in his center would have sent Max into shock. Now it just seemed inevitable, almost old news. Still, these headlines disturbed him, announcing the end of his career on the front pages. It didn't matter that the article didn't mention his name, and he even felt a bit insulted. *I am the Director, after all.* But these were Great Events, unfolding the nation's history, and minor bureaucrats didn't much factor.

The article might have addressed this question: Why are Alcalán authorities not preventing Espejo's return, or at least his 'official reception?' Max had asked Lucho Gonzales this question, receiving the vague yet sufficient response, "The arrogance of San Genesio produces nothing but resistance in the provinces. They never learn."

By eleven o'clock the streets had filled with happy, shouting people. Police efforts to keep them behind barriers failed. After the street was closed to traffic, every distant horn was taken as a sign of Espejo's arrival, and every disappointment increased the crowd's enthusiasm. Max kept an interested eye on the throng, chatted with those few of the staff who were not making welcoming signs or polishing something, and spent some time arranging his new second-floor office. He joined Rosa at a window just before the first car arrived. "Quite a reception," he said.

"Isn't it wonderful? Look at the people! I feel so happy, don't you?" She wrapped her arm around his and smiled.

Her happiness made Max happy, even as it intrigued him. *Why should another Espejo return make her so giddy? It can't just be the prospect of a pig roast in San Andrés.* He answered his own question as he remembered his Dad getting misty-eyed at Kennedy's speeches. Like JFK, Espejo evoked hope in people in, Max supposed, some wonderful way. He would soon see, and hear. Max squeezed Rosa's hand and felt suddenly part of all this now, whether he wanted to be or not. The Board's decision to receive Espejo would be the final *coup de grace* to any link between the Center and the U.S. Embassy, as well as Max's diplomatic career. The Board would have to hire their own Director now, and surely that would be Max, wouldn't it? He'd always have a place in Alcalá. *If only my VW had arrived.*

A place in Alcalá! The voice of George jeered in his head. Max ignored it.

"Look!" cried Rosa. "There—a car!"

Mine? he wondered briefly before focusing.

A Ford sedan appeared. A huge board mounted on the front bumper proclaimed ESPEJO in bright letters. Loudspeakers blared discordant music from its rear windows. A convertible full of pretty, waving young women followed, then a police car and a military jeep.

"They were stupid to insult the local commanders and still expect them to enforce their dumb rules," commented Rosa.

And then the man himself appeared, standing very tall in the back of a 1966 Cadillac convertible, waving with his right hand while his left rested on the steady shoulder of Luis Gonzales. Otherwise, Espejo stood majestically alone. Max had expected to see an old man. He saw more. He wasn't sure what. The father of a country?

"His wife died, didn't she?" he asked.

"Yes, poor woman. She was always so sad-looking. They said it was because they didn't have children. And when she died, Espejo gave up politics for a while."

Max had trouble imagining that, or that the Patriarch could be childless. More than Age, Espejo could have been Time itself with his flowing white hair and lined face and deep eyes, and authority in his confident smile and the paternal wave of his hand. Or he might have been Hope, an image of another and better Engañada. It was something beyond prosperity or even politics, as if the old man would somehow inspire a better Max, a better Rosa, and a Manuel as Manuel imagined he might have been. *Very strange,* Max reflected, but very powerful; to be within sight of this tall gaunt old man was to want to be always within the magic circle where one was more than himself. Max fought to retain respectable cynicism. *How does he do it?*

The caravan stopped in front of the Center. Max sighed, thinking what an honor this visit would be under different circumstances.

"Aren't you coming down?" Rosa asked.

"I don't think so."

"Oh. I understand. But Max, he especially asked that you sit with the dignitaries."

"I know." *And no, you don't understand. I'm not afraid of Jackson or Webster anymore. I'm afraid of Espejo.*

"Please come."

"All right." Max wondered how to prepare himself to resist the magic of a wizard; he couldn't even resist the plea from Rosa.

They reached their seats as Espejo made his jerky way to the high platform erected in front of the fountain. Thanks to Manuel, it now worked: water spouted from the top, rose a few feet and then fell back down over the various flanges and projections into the pool. Together with the circus poster and the revolutionary portrait of Patrick Henry (both relocated to walls after the window replacements the *Sociedad* had contracted), it made a nice background as Gonzales waved for quiet to make his introduction. It was brief by local standards, barely five minutes. Then the grand old man moved to the microphone and the cheering began again.

Espejo waited a moment and then slowly stopped the cheering with gentle gestures and a tranquil smile.

"Bueno, my friends: it's good to see you again." He began quietly, his tone that of a simple man returned from a journey and now greeting his neighbors. His voice, rich and strong, set the crowd cheering once more. When they grew quieter, he went on. "But it is good to be home. Old men should stay home, and you know I am very old."

"NO! NO!! ESPEJO!"

"Please, my friends, no flattery! It is so. Even my faithful friend Dr. Ramiro Gómez Gomez, President of the 'Espejista Party,' says I am old, that my work is finished—"

"NO! DOWN WITH GÓMEZ! VIVA ESPEJO!"

Max also heard several obscenities from the crowd, comments on the prior experiences of the ladies Gómez, mother and wife. He wondered briefly at the unjust custom of insulting women because you disliked their men.

"Please! Dr. Gómez says my work is finished, and I am glad

to hear it is so. For my work—our work—was very important. Our work was to feed the children, care for them and educate them, and provide decent work and decent housing for the poor of all Engañada. I am glad these things have been accomplished in my absence."

"NO! THEY LIE! VIVA ESPEJO!"

"What? Are you telling me I've been misinformed? Can it be that the babies of Alcalá do not have enough to eat? Tell me, have they or have they not?"

"NO!"

Espejo managed to look surprised. "Well then, do they have clothes?"

"NO!"

He managed now to look shocked, and then led them in a litany of denial that the children had schools, medical care, or playgrounds. As one, prompted, the people denied that the children's fathers had work or that their mothers had running water. Espejo finally shook his head in sadness, then opened his eyes wide in sudden comprehension. "My friends, I think I have the answer. My good friend Dr. Gómez was merely mistaken. He didn't understand my work. He thought, perhaps, that my work was to help the oligarchs. Tell me then, do the oligarchs eat well?"

"YES! DOWN WITH THE OLIGARCHS!"

"I see. And do owners of the factories—the shoe factory in barrio Villacruz, for example–do they have sufficient cars, enough Cadillacs and Mercedes? They do? Then surely they must bend under a tax burden so high that they cannot go each year to Miami and London and Paris? No? Then perhaps they have no servants, since the salaries are so high they cannot afford to keep a maid and a cook and a gardener?"

These propositions were loudly denied.

"There, my friends, is the answer. Dr. Gómez was mistaken, that's all. He thought my work was to make life better for the oligarchy, and of course that work is finished. But I am sorry to see that my dear friend and colleague Dr. Gómez, a man dedicated completely to the welfare of the people...yes, you have but to ask him! I am sorry, I say, that he is so mistaken. For this is not my work."

He stood silently studying the crowd for several moments, as if assessing the reception. *Isn't he afraid he'll lose them? That was masterful; he has them on a string. Isn't he afraid to break it? Yet...maybe, here, a long pause is exactly right, just as the whole rest of the speech is verbose by American standards. The lazy casual introduction, the invocation of the straw man Gómez, both were drawn out and savored as if neither Espejo nor his audience could possibly have anything better to do on this September Saturday than this, or that they'd want to be anywhere but here, participating in the perfect denunciation, the perfect return.* Finally Espejo broke the silence, dropping all sarcasm and proclaiming in a rising voice,

"This is *not* my work! This *never* was my work! This will *never be* my work!"

Thunderous ovations lasted for several minutes. Espejo was truly back.

"No, my friends, I have other work. And that work is not done. My work is to feed the babies of Alcalá and San Genesio and Algernón and Santa Ana!"

"ES-PE-JO!"

And so he continued telling them his true work for some time, playing them like a violin as he produced the responses he wanted, a YES or a NO, loud or soft, or an interlude of chanting or laughter, until he had described his mission fully: the elimination of all misery and all indignity. Then he turned to a new theme, again beginning with references to his esteemed friend of the '*Espejista*' Party:

"I am afraid that someone has deceived our companion Dr. Gómez. Not only did they deceive him about my work, but about my friends. My presence in Engañada, he says, would serve only the oligarchs, and the United States, and the Marxists. Tell me, my friends, we know that one cannot serve God and the Devil. How then can one serve three devils at once, all of whom hate each other? Well, let us see. Do I serve the oligarchs?"

"NO! VIVA ESPEJO!"

"I think we can agree, my friends, that I do not. The oligarchs would not have thrown me out of the country twelve times if I had been serving them! Do I serve the Yankees, then? Did I serve them when I reclaimed our beloved land from the U.S. fruit companies?"

This got an especially loud cheer, even from the Center employees.

"No, my friends, I don't believe the Yankees think I have served them well, not after I'd fought them for half a century! Not after I taught them that Engañada is a sovereign country that must be treated with respect, and not a colony to be exploited. They didn't like that lesson much. They resisted. But we the People did not surrender: not to U.S. Banana Corporation, not to North American Shrimp, and not to Tropical Gulf Mining Corporation! We fought each of those battles and won, and the Yankees learned at last."

The invocation of old struggles drew loud cheers from the older people, but more perfunctory applause from the youngsters.

"Then do I serve the Marxists? What does that mean? That I am a Marxist—I, who have always defended the freedom of the press, of education, of religion, of work and movement—and outraged the Communists by doing so? Or that I serve the Russians then, or the Cubans? Does Dr. Gómez forget the time I expelled the Soviet ambassador because he was meddling in our affairs?"

That brought cheers too, though less enthusiastic than those directed against the Americans. Max supposed it was inevitable, at least until Engañadans had reason to envy Russians. And he was pleasantly surprised to see students applauding at all, even Raúl Rojas clapping and *viva*-ing in the second row with the best of them.

"No, my friends," said Espejo, returning to a quiet reasonable voice. "I defend the right of any Engañadan to be as Marxist as he wishes or as anti-Marxist as he wishes. And I defend Engañada against the interference of any country, north or east!" He smiled. "Look about you; is this the place for a meeting of Marxists? Hardly. But Dr. Gómez is not simply mistaken, my friends. No. I am afraid he is out of date. He has not kept up. He is fighting old battles that are over and done with. The world changes, my friends! Engañada changes, even as we never give up those principles received from our fathers. Is Dr. Gómez worried about the Tropical Gulf Mining Corporation? I don't remember that he joined us when we fought them, and now that they are defeated, he says that I serve them!" He shook his head sadly. "That battle is over! One might as well call now for our independence from Spain! And because I don't bother to fight a battle already won, Dr. Gómez says I serve the Yankees. Even the Yankees change, my friends. Even they learn! And never, never have I or the Engañadan People had anything but the highest admiration and affection for the great *people* of the United States!"

The cheering was sincere enough, if subdued: this wasn't what the crowd wanted. Now he turned to what did matter to them: the neglect of Alcalá by the central government.

"But you know," he began, "I am reluctant to disagree with Dr. Gómez, for he and the other patriots who opposed my return are San Genesiaños all, and as you know—

He stopped to let them jeer the nation's capital.

"As you know, they are best able to judge these things, as are the military who govern us, San Genesiaños all." He kept up the irony for several minutes before promising to finish another task he had set himself long ago: "to restore to Alcalá the dignity, the freedom, and the prosperity which our fathers left us as our birthright, and which has been stolen from us by the San Genesio oligarchy!" The crowd roared. It was a popular theme since any Alcaláño could give a long list of abuses: that the taxes paid in Alcalá never returned but instead paved the streets of the rich in the capital; that local schools were under-funded, the port neglected, and coastal authorities denied the autonomy that might permit them to address these problems. *Makes me wonder what sort of speeches the old man has given in San Genesio over the decades.*

Espejo now changed his tone in some subtle way, as if shifting down for a difficult task. "Yes, my friends, there is a little work still to do. I am an old man. These hands are feeble now. These legs cannot carry me as they did in '25 when I helped you dam the river, or when we fought the fire on the docks in '37. Yet I am come to spend my last strength in this work, this little bit of work that remains to be done." His voice dropped to a confessional whisper and he paused for five, ten, fifteen seconds. When he resumed, it was in a rising angry indignant voice:

"Tell me my friends, may I do this? May I do this work? Have I your permission?"

"SI, SI, ESPEJO! ES-PE-JO! ES-PE-JO!"

"Have I your permission?" he shouted, his amplified voice colliding with the crowd's roar. "Do I? Despite my years?"

"SI, SI! ABAJO CON EL ARTICULO CUARENTA Y TRES!"

Max wondered what sort of communication allowed thousands of individual tongues to chant the varied responses in unison. How, in response to a speech they were hearing for the first time, could so many agree so perfectly in form and rhythm in condemning Article Forty-Three, on the age of the President?

"Am I not too old?"

The crowd chanted that he was not.

"But the generals have said I am too old! They know, my friends, they know. They know I am old, that I have grown old in the struggle, that my many years have been spent in many battles against them and their masters in the banks!"

The crowd went wild as Espejo stopped to catch his breath. Max feared he would have a stroke right there on the platform, so red was his face. The veins in his temples throbbed visibly and his grip on the podium displayed white knuckles. *This is more than speaking*, Max thought, feeling the sweet anger of those around him, delighting in the denunciation of the shameful traitorous self-servers who would deny the great man his chance, his destiny, to serve the people. Then, mercifully for all of them, Espejo changed his tone again.

"Thank you," he said quietly. "Thank you. I know–how could I not know?–that I am old, but am I too old?" He shrugged. "That is for you, the people, to decide. No one else.

"Yes, I am old. I am old enough to remember when age was honored in our country. So," he smiled wanly, "you must know that I am very old indeed. Permit me an old man's pleasure. Let me sit in the park with friends of an evening, and talk of old times.

"My father used to tell me of very old times, when he was a boy and there were those still alive who remembered the Revolt from Spain. There were rich and poor, he said, and the rich rode in carriages and the dust from their wheels covered the peasants who walked on the edge of the road carrying sixty-pound loads of bananas. And in those old times there was rivalry between San Genesio and Alcalá, and they fought in the Parliament, but they were all Engañadans and fellow citizens and loved their country.

"And my father told me of the times when he was a man and Alcalá grew rapidly with sailing ships from all the world arriving for provisions and for trade: whaling ships from North America and Germany and England, and merchantmen from France and Holland on their way to China. And the workers on the docks moved aside for the gentlemen from the stock market who came to see how much money they had made in a morning, and some of the gentlemen came from San Genesio and took the money of the workers. For the 'country,' they said, but they were all Engañadans, and any fight between them was a family fight.

"And in the old times when I was a boy, and the workers brought wood or coal for the steamships, it was the same. But by then, they had only to send telegrams from San Genesio to tell us how much of our money to pay in taxes. And when I was a young man, the railroad was built—what a wonder it was! And the merchants of Alcalá could go to the capital in a single day to invest their money where it was safe, and while there was a governor of Alcalá sent from San Genesio, he could go to visit his parents every week. And we thought that Engañada then was truly united, for this railroad laughed at the mountains.

"And we were sure it was so when a citizen of Alcalá was elected President for the first time: I remember well when Don Miguel Roberto Urrutia Blanco got on the train–at the old station in the center of town across from the park–and waved goodbye to us. And when we saw him here again, he was on his way to his first exile. But this exile—as unjust as the rest—they demanded for the good of all Engañadans."

240

He continued in the same quiet, sad, even voice through the history of his own administrations, always emphasizing two things: the tradition of elections open to all parties, and the loyalty of Alcalá and the coast to the idea of national unity, a loyalty which had withstood many tests and had cost them dearly. The sadness in his voice changed to restrained anger as he concluded:

"So these are the old times we old men like to talk about in the park, these times old and gone. And now? Now the elections will be more orderly and there will be no surprises, for the unacceptable candidates will be eliminated before they begin. And the nation, our Engañada? That will be old times, too, for Engañada will be smaller. How strange, that as a country becomes an empire it grows smaller! For San Genesio will be Rome and Alcalá will be Palestine, a mere colony, and they will call us not fellow citizens, not brothers, but rather their colonials, or their slaves. Yes, it is better we talk of old times in the park.

"For if we were to talk of these new times, would we remain tranquil? As old as we are, would we sit quietly and await the orders of an imperial governor? Would we, Alcaláños and Engañadans, dare to place flowers on the graves of our fathers while we their children dishonored their bones by our cowardice?"

The crowd muttered angrily as Espejo boomed out the last few lines. Sharing their anger, caught up in the drama, Max was glad he had boomed them out: they needed to be shouted, broadcast everywhere, hurled against the mountains and the smug walls of the palaces and embassies of San Genesio. But Espejo was motioning for quiet again, and neither Max nor anyone else in the huge crowd could deny Espejo anything. Not now, not while the words came.

"No, my friends, I don't think such a life is possible. I don't think there can be such an empire, such an Engañada. There can be the Engañada of our fathers that we love and want to preserve. Let us pray it is so! Or there can be...something new. There cannot be a country half slave and half free: there can be no empire."

The cheering, guided by his detached tone, was restrained. Max again marveled at Espejo's ability to play the crowd like an instrument even while recognizing that he himself had become another string of that instrument, and even as he wondered if Espejo had consciously plagiarized Lincoln.

"The old ones who sit in the park are not all fools, not all senile. No. And in some places age is even honored. It was honored once in Engañada. And if there were someone from San Genesio who asked the old ones in the park for their wisdom, what would they tell him? They would say: do not do this thing. Do not try to destroy Alcalá for the sake of a few oligarchs in San Genesio, for thus you will lose Alcalá and Engañada and all!

"That, my friends," and here Espejo smiled for the first time since early in the speech, "is what the old ones would say. And they would not be angry and violent, for they would be confident in their strength, confident that the charges against them of subversion—of all things!—were nonsense, and confident in their friends who are more numerous and more powerful than some people think, confident that in the moment of trial they would have allies, and such an ally as San Genesio would not care to face. And they would go home to their beds and sleep in the sweet air of Alcalá and dream of the river they hear always, even sleeping, even in exile. They would sleep well, yet eager for the dawn that will confirm their hopes or, if the deaf will remain deaf, call them to a struggle they do not fear. And I too will go to bed in Alcalá tonight, for the first time in many years, and sleep the sleep of an old man, and tired. But never too tired, my friends. Never so tired as to forget that I am an Alcaláño and an Engañadan, and never too weary to remember my duty.

"My friends, it will be good to sleep again in Alcalá, as first it will be good to pass the afternoon with you, to gossip on the veranda after lunch, to watch the afternoon rain make puddles in the street and talk until the sun returns to dry them again and leave the road dustier than before. For I notice," he smiled, "that San Genesio has not yet sent the money to pave our streets!"

When the jeering laughter died down, he continued: "But that is all right. One can endure a great deal when among friends, and respected, and at home. Oh my friends, let us pray that we keep always our homes and our friends in Engañada. To keep our respect, that alone is wholly within our power, and that we will do." He stopped for a moment while he looked grimly, determinedly, from one side of the crowd to the other. "And that," he repeated, "we will do. And that, my friends, is why I have returned. Thank you. Thank you all!"

There were a few seconds of silence before the cheering began, a sudden roar of applause and chants and clapping which seemed to continue forever. Max would remember it always as the setting in which he was swept up to the stage with the crowd as Espejo embraced one ecstatic follower after another. It was the setting in which Max first met Espejo, daring only to take the great man's hand and then being as embarrassed as surprised when Espejo folded him, too, in a great embrace as the cameras continued to flash and the crowd's sustained roar seemed to register at first shock and then approval at Lacey's inclusion in the celebration. And he heard Espejo's soft greeting to him—perfectly audible as though the man's voice had privileged passage through the din—as a blessing: "Ah, Mr. Lacey! I'm so glad you've decided to join us." And Max felt, then, that he had. Indeed, he had never felt so much a part of anything since singing carols in church on Christmas Day. So when Espejo handed him on to Gonzales, he returned his erstwhile antagonist's embrace and then willingly embraced Rosa, Washington, Mariana, the elders of the *Sociedad Historica*, and even as much as he could of the formidable Esperanza Romero Ycaza, who had sat with Gonzales in a place of honor.

The heady feeling was strengthened by the drinking he did through the rest of that day and night–the curfew was a joke–with Washington, Pablo and Pedro, and a changing crowd of artists and students, and it faded only slowly through the long Sunday that followed. It lingered even as the phone rang on Monday morning.

"You wanna tell me what you were doing on a stage hugging a damn subversive?" Jethro got right to the point, but had adopted a *faux*-casual tone, perhaps expanding his repertoire of sarcastic voices.

"I was only following orders, Jethro. You know, from the Delta Channel."

"Oh, I don't know about that so-called 'Delta Channel' even

if it exists," Jethro responded in the same calm tone, "and even if it did I don't buy that they'd want you photographed puttin' yourself right in the middle of local politics. But don't you worry. We'll be taking care of all that real soon. Meanwhile" – and now his voice edged briefly toward his wonted outrage – "I know a whole lot more about the mess you been making down there. Got inside information on the whole thing!"

"What do you mean?"

"Had a nice talk with Mr. Braden this morning, guy you fired 'cause he was trying to straighten out the English program? He had all kinds of interesting things to say, about motorcycles in the lobby and teachers all upset and talking about going on strike. Yessir, bunch of interesting stuff!"

"Braden's in San Genesio?"

"Sure is. Running one of those new English academies someone's been setting up around here. Came by to introduce himself today. Real gentleman."

Max could not picture Jethro Jackson having a friendly conversation with the bearded and disheveled former Academic Director. "You sure it was *Bertram* Braden*?*" he asked. "Tall skinny guy with a beard?"

"Didn't have any beard. All dressed up in a nice suit looked like it was brand new. Said he was glad to have the chance to teach English the right way."

Braden can't be acting on his own. "Who owns that academy he's running?"

"How inna hell would I know? Some company. Glad to let them do it. I sure don't want no more bi-national centers and sure don't want one close to me!"

"Well, say hello to him for me when you get the chance," said Max bitterly. Jethro snorted and hung up after reminding Max "of what I already *tole* you," to pack up and get ready to leave. "Real soon. We'll straighten out this 'Delta' business then you're on a plane! Meanwhile we don't want you nowhere around that Center or that Espejo crowd!"

"No place in Alcalá to avoid them, Jethro."

A snort was Jethro's only 'goodbye.'

Max figured he knew who owned that academy. *Mariana nailed it. Gandig's taking care of Braden and must have told him to go meet Jackson for some reason, maybe to give the Embassy more reasons to get me out. He must be paying for a shadow director too. Unless a miracle happened, there's no way Braden has the sense or energy to manage anything.*

He wondered if Braden had received a bonus to shave off his beard, and if he had really learned nothing at all from Woodrow Lively even after checking out his books a dozen times.

This relationship of competence to salary reminded him of something he'd determined to do. Now he did it, typing a memo to the accountant stating that Rosa Fuentes Serena had been promoted to Executive Assistant, with corresponding salary. He sent a copy to the Board, assuming they would not object. He didn't care if they did.

Chapter Twenty-Four: A Rendezvous With Greatness

San Genesio did not react publicly to the Espejo speech for a week, but their unannounced reaction came swiftly enough: new commanders arrived at the Army and police units on the coast. Most of the existing commanders refused to turn over their commands, either citing a lack of proper documents or simply telling the replacements to go back to the capital. The new commanders who did stay could do so only after reaching agreements with the troops. As a further precaution, San Genesio had suspended the shipment of supplies to all military units not under the firm control of the capital. It mattered little since the order became mired in red tape and didn't take effect for nearly two weeks.

When General President Madera went on television at last, it was to denounce the grave crisis facing the country. He blamed foreign interests for trying to subvert the established order, re-impose capitalist colonialism, and turn Engañada into another Cuba. Max wasn't impressed by the General, and found it hard to believe the guy had headed a coup. He seemed barely to understand what he read and looked like he'd rather be someplace else. *Not in Espejo's league.*

Gonzales sighed when he discussed the speech with Max. "The country is going straight downhill. The generals who used to take power were at least able military politicians, but this fool can't even see that his position is untenable, as we had hoped he would. He hasn't even got the whole army behind him, for heaven's sake! And as for his partners on the junta—tell me, can you name one of them?"

Max thought a second. "Rodríguez Blanco?"

"Fernández Blanco. Good for you! One out of five isn't bad. Complete non-entities, even dumber than Madera. I'm surprised they've stayed in power this long. They've lost most of the support they had when they overthrew Espejo."

"Maybe it's against military honor to overthrow a duly-imposed general," suggested Max.

"Not always. Anyway, most of the general-presidents had some political gifts, while this one seems clueless, a political joke. Old General Vásquez—he overthrew Espejo three times—had some talent as a speaker, and a few people even thought he rivaled Espejo. But this one..." Gonzales shook his head.

Max nodded. "Let's hope he's not a competent soldier, either."

"I'm not sure I'd hope for that. Badly managed wars are the bloodiest. We've had talk of civil war before, though not recently. Always the two sides would arrange their troops so that neither had any overwhelming advantage, and then they negotiated. But if Madera can't handle that, or even worse if he actually wants to impose his terms, there could be real fighting. The man seems a fool but he was bright enough to beat other officers to the Presidency, and even if he's not a competent soldier he has some generals who are. "

Gonzales' unaccustomed concern was contagious. Max imagined young soldiers lying dead on the side of a road, a burned-out tank, and a reporter in battle fatigues looking into the camera and speculating on what effect this offensive might have on Congressional attitudes. So when he got a message later that day that Espejo wanted to see him, and needed his help in preserving the peace, Max went at once to his former office.

It had been repainted and refurnished with rich new furniture suitable for a president. The windows had been replaced, albeit with jury-rigged frames. Max surveyed all this from the door before he noticed Espejo sitting at the conference table playing Solitaire. Rosa sat beside him and watched as the President turned over some more cards, put one here and one there, moved a pile, uncovered another card and grunted in satisfaction. "Finally I win!" he announced. "A good sign!" Then he got up and walked slowly with Rosa toward Max, who wondered how yesterday's towering figure had become this bent man who shuffled slowly across the room with a goddaughter's aid. But when he saw Max, Espejo straightened slightly and became as if by magic a President.

"So here is our American," he said thoughtfully, taking Max's hand. "My little godchild here has been telling me about you. You come highly recommended, Mr. Lacey!"

Max smiled uncertainly while Rosa blushed. Then Espejo kissed her on the cheek and said, "It's good to get reacquainted after so long, Rosa. And soon we'll be in San Andrés again, I hope, for a campaign and a party!"

As she went out she stopped for a moment, took both of Max's hands, and said "Thank you." Max still wore a puzzled look as he accepted Espejo's invitation to sit down in one of the new leather chairs. Max was alone with the Great Exile, the historical figure, a being as much myth as man. Much about him resembled Luis Gonzales: the thin snowy white hair, weathered face, noble Spanish nose, even the rhythm of his speech. Yet he was utterly different, as if Gonzales had been magnified, or re-tuned to a more somber and authoritative key.

"Well, Mr. Lacey," Espejo began, "I'm afraid I'm proving an inconvenience to you. I hope it won't last long. And surely you don't mind: it's in order to further the great work of returning Engañada to the glory which is its heritage, and the people to the prosperity which they claim as birthright."

There could have been a grin on Espejo's face, but Max was unsure. He stayed with the safe, courtly response: "Please, Mr. President, it's no inconvenience; an honor, rather."

"Very good," judged Espejo. "You have a future as a diplomat. You look doubtful? You must learn patience. Learn it of me. Do you know how many times I've been exiled?"

"Several times, I think, sir."

"Twelve times! There's something biblical about it, don't you agree? But I don't speak much of numbers anymore, for obvious reasons. Anyway, an exile more or less hardly matters in a good cause. All of my causes were good: the nationalization of the fruit companies, the Comprehensive Labor Law, etc. What I was exiled for in one term often was realized in the next, or another. And I believe you've joined a good cause now."

Cause? The word sobered Max. What cause had he joined? To get Espejo another term? To ruin Jethro's day? *Or the one Gonzales described, that of making Engañadans believe they were innocent enough to be deceived?* He echoed dumbly, "a good cause..."

Espejo smiled. "Peace, first of all. National unity, among other things. We have great hopes, despite the grave situation into which the generals have led the country this time. I foresee the realization of Engañada's leading role as a member of the Pacific Rim Community and even, if I can change some attitudes, of the Western Alliance."

"I see," said Max warily. *Western Alliance? NATO?*

"So," Espejo resumed, "perhaps you see why I need your office, and why you and Rosita must move to the second floor. You may say it's time for a change in style; I'm tired of hearing myself attack the U.S. even if the public isn't, even if every generation of students is as eager to hear it as were their fathers."

He smiled softly for a moment but then changed his expression, and his voice took on a note of urgency. "Mr. Lacey, you have heard the answer of our General. He does not know how to retreat gracefully, and now we're on our way to the devil unless we manage some solution. Do you know why civil wars are the most vicious? Because they're not about what we possess but about who we are. It's one thing to cede some land, but quite another to give up your identity. And whatever my other failings, I've never brought us to war. I don't want to start now."

"Of course not," Max agreed. "But if it's really such a danger, wouldn't waiting be the surest way to avoid it?"

"Accept the prohibition, you mean? Renounce my candidacy? Yes, I've thought of that. But it's not possible. I don't control everything, and many things have been set in motion that cannot easily be stopped. The military commanders, for instance: do you think they can simply change their minds after defying orders from the Commander-in-Chief?"

"No," Max allowed. "I see the problem. But surely there must be some way to avoid a war–"

"A war," Espejo interrupted, "fought to replace an idiot general with an ancient political joke. I know you weren't going to say that, but it's what you think if you're half as smart as Rosa says you are. And you're right, except that it does make a difference. Or so I think. Or so someone thinks." He gestured toward the conference table where the cards lay arranged in neat piles. "You must wonder why I play Solitaire at a time like this. It is because I think best when I am distracted from thinking."

"Excuse me?"

"So many things." Espejo waved his hand as if chasing away flies. "So many possibilities and dangers and hopes and needs fly around in one's head that he loses all hope of sorting them out. But somewhere else in the head, or in the heart, they are put in order. I play Solitaire to get myself out of the way so that the heart or the imagination or the spirit can do its work."

"I see." Max had been there, getting ideas about a term paper on Shakespeare, say, while playing tennis.

Espejo sat forward and held Max in his gaze, his brown eyes at once judging and appealing and mesmerizing. "I think you've learned something of our history from Lucho. You should learn a little more. You have a right to know more, because I'm going to ask something of you."

Max wondered what that could be, how far he could trust Espejo, and if he could trust himself not to be hypnotized. Part of him wanted to embrace the wonderful rhetoric. The old man seemed to read the conflict going on in his head, with the old Max urging skepticism and the new one demanding poetry.

Espejo had shut his eyes, his face taking on beatific tranquility. "You're suspicious, as you should be. And you probably can't see what difference it makes whether Madera or I wear the presidential sash. I tell you," he said, opening his eyes now and holding Max with them, "it does make a difference, quite aside from the consideration that there would be other candidates to wear it, some of them worse than either Madera or myself.

"I know what the peasants and workers say, with their natural cynicism. The students say it as well, with their carefully cultivated cynicism; that it's always the same in the end, only the rich changing places. But do you really think nothing has changed in the last fifty years? Much has changed. Very much. When I was a boy a landowner could kill one of his peasants, and if the police bothered to investigate at all, they would inevitably find that the worker was attacking his *patrón*. That doesn't happen anymore."

Max started to mumble his approval, but Espejo ignored him.

"Take just one simple thing, the fact that workers are now paid overtime: do you think that was easy? Or that it would have happened without political maneuvering? No, I assure you it would not have happened. And what looks like chaos to you, with elections followed by coups followed by elections of the same people, is madness with a method. It *is* our political process. Other countries may propose something to themselves and reject it once, twice, a dozen tines until finally enough people change their minds and accept it. But no Engañadan politician could admit he was wrong and change his vote; he'd be thought an idiot who didn't know his own mind, or accused of selling his vote twice. But if the country passes from one historic epoch to another, with the division clearly marked by revolution, then everything begins anew and he can vote differently. Do you see?"

"I think so." Max tried to recall a parallel in U.S. history. *Maybe new attitudes about civil rights after the Kennedy assassination was this kind of sea change.*

"Of course," Espejo resumed, "there is more to it than that, but the point you should understand is this: these coups and returns constitute an inherent part of our tradition. Of our democracy, if that's not stretching the term too far. They are the means by which we change course. Did you note Madera's sporadic anti-Americanism? I promoted that theme years ago, and was thrown out several times because of it. But those who replaced me had finally to adopt it themselves, and it spread, making possible the solution of the problem of the fruit companies. Before we could confront that sort of problem, we had to regain some measure of self-respect in the face of American arrogance. It's impossible to deal with someone who patronizes you, wouldn't you agree?"

Max remembered what Gonzales had told him about the contempt Americans had for Latin America. Gonzales wasn't altogether wrong.

"It's very sad, the attitude of great countries towards weak ones," continued Espejo, as if reading Max's thoughts, "but it's always been so. One must work around it or despite it. In confronting the foreign companies we didn't win their respect, but we did make them fear the problems we could give them—enough that they took us seriously. What about you, Max? Have you found anything to respect?"

"Yes. Your loyalty to family and place and tradition. I admire that. Everyone seems to have a place. I envy that, even though it has a price, or effects—"

"When one's loyalty is centered on the family or the village, it's hard to build a nation," Espejo said quickly. "Anything else?"

"Yes…Something about life here as it's imagined rather than as it is. I mean, someone like Manuel, for instance. He's a janitor, but carries himself with a certain dignity and speaks with a sort of eloquence."

Espejo nodded. "You're the second American to tell me that: Woodrow Lively was the first, although he said it more fully. But poor Lively, he wasn't prudent. You've heard of his famous speech, when he congratulated us on being within the American Empire?"

"Yes. I guess it took years for the Center to recover."

"Not really, Max, not really. But they should have let him finish, for do you know what he wanted to say? He wanted to congratulate us also for being members of the Empire: citizens of it, and not merely subjects! Yes! Not only that, but he thought we had a vital contribution to make, precisely the imagined life you mention, though he put it in terms of poetry. This, he maintained, was just what the American Empire lacked. I'm not sure why he thought that and wonder if he ever saw any Hollywood movies. But, that's how he saw things and said our inclusion would perfect northern pragmatism by uniting it with Latin poetry. Indeed," Espejo shook his head. "He thought that Engañada was, on balance, the most advanced part of the Empire, and that's why he chose to live here."

"But that speech of his, it wasn't Engañadan at all! At least the part I heard about: it was blunt and straightforward, an American speech."

"That's true, and that was his problem: he was still very much an American. Yet he'd changed, had become Engañadan in some ways. A real American wouldn't have made that speech, not in Alcalá. He'd have seen the practical consequences. Lively conceived it in poetic terms, but the opening was too blunt, and he never got to the poem he'd included. Do you know it?"

"Not unless it's included in his collections."

"It's not. But here, I have it..." Espejo walked to the book shelf and selected one of a dozen law books, opened it in the middle and took out a single sheet of paper, which he handed to Max:

Two Poles, One Field

Betwixt the poles magnetic
Democratic is the field;
No voices sound splenetic,
But Freedom is the yield.
Hear you Northmen! Cease to vaunt,
Though you be rich and strong;
Cease to take and cease to taunt:
Let the Latin teach you song.
Friends of the South! Nevermore
Begrudge the Northman's varied Treasure:
Envy makes the richest poor—
O flee that sin which yields no pleasure!
Betwixt the poles magnetic
Two countervailing forces,
Meeting not in strife frenetic
But to balance their two courses!

Dynamo and Virgin's fond embrace
Breed the happy, healthy race!

Max looked up to find Espejo studying him with questioning, laughing eyes. "Well?"

Max looked at the floor and then shrugged. "Quite a vision." *Some rather forced lines, though.*

The President reached for the poem and put it back in the law book. "A vision, you say? Strange: that's the word he used, too. Well, the poor man was neither Engañadan nor American in the end. Perhaps he'd spent too much time in the jungle, seeing visions. I hope he found the one he wanted, before he died."

They observed a moment of silence in memory of the poet, and then Espejo got back to business. "So, we were talking about anti-Americanism. Always be with us, inevitable. A tool, and I used it." A smile played across his lips for a second. "But you'll agree it's time for a change, that the sentiment has about exhausted its usefulness and has become rather a nuisance, even a danger as well as a bore. I won't get into the great international realities. No, enough that Calvin Coolidge is no longer in the White House, and that we need investment, even by such scoundrels as your former Treasurer, Mr. Gandig. Better yet, more American businessmen like the late Mr. Bowman of *Molinos de Engañada.* A climate must be prepared. Someday, perhaps, there will be such a climate as poor Woodrow foresaw. In any case, do you see why you had to move to the second floor?"

"I understand what you're saying," Max admitted. He also understood that this might be a consummate con game, yet he pushed that thought aside, preferring to imagine himself part of something new and wonderful.

"You understand," repeated Espejo. "Good. One must prepare the ground. And what better way than that my followers have an interview with the U.S. Ambassador before my return? But you frustrated that plan–I congratulate you on the tactical victory. Anyway, do you see why Madera is so dangerous? He is attempting a true revolution, trying to end this process of redefinition and adjustment. That would mean stagnation, the worsening of the current vices and the progressive loss of whatever virtues remain. Or benefits: Madera, God bless him, has in fact attracted some foreign investment. But not enough, and not in the right places, and government corruption involves foreign companies in bribery. We must do more. To stop the process of renovation now is to see the present government become increasingly corrupt. Corruption..." The old man shook his head and then resumed. "Of course it's always with us; clerks in the records office holding out their hands if you want your marriage license issued today rather than next month, or government purchasing officers getting gifts from merchants. These are irritating but understandable. Clerks make very little and have to supplement their salaries, and usually things go on despite the little briberies. But it has gone too far. Businesses that might expand and hire more workers don't do so because this minister or that secretary wants not just a bribe, but a piece of the company. All those unemployed are paying the price."

Espejo stared at the floor, appeared briefly weary and sad. "You have one example of petty corruption right here, in the effort to bankrupt the Center with the connivance of some judges. Corruption can only increase and bring worse evils as corrupt officials take stronger and stronger measures to protect their corruption. I know. I've seen it happen in my own administrations. The next step is to buy and sell offices and laws openly and arrogantly, once all opposition has been intimidated. So press freedom suffers, and we have arbitrary arrests of those who protest, and of their friends and family, perhaps, and then with a muzzled press and a corrupt judicial system there is nothing to stop even torture. You know these things happen in Latin America. Yet in Engañada, in many ways one of the most backward countries on the continent, we have managed to avoid them, with a few exceptions.

"Nor have our changes been violent: look at me, twelve times overthrown but not a single bullet hole! The generals who overthrow me today know that other generals may overthrow them tomorrow, and that everyone has family connections everywhere. The spirit of revenge, once abroad in a land, is a terrible thing. So we don't get shot; we go into exile for a while, or receive a twenty-year jail term which is converted to parole after a month and then forgotten."

Even while trying, almost against his will, to find some flaw in Espejo's case, Max admitted it was a very civilized system. He felt himself being sucked in as if by a whirlpool. One thought struck him with utter clarity: *I am no match for this man. I can either join him completely, or flee. Choose.* How happy might Eve have been, or Faust, if they had not tried to match wits with the devil!

"So, Mr. Lacey," Espejo resumed, reverting to formal address, "you see what is at stake. Repression and maybe even war in the short term, and decay in the long term. A generation or two or three condemned to hopelessness. I want you to help us avoid that."

Max hesitated only for a second. "All right, if there's something I can do, but–"

"You don't see what. And you're right. Mr. Max Lacey, Director of the Engañadan-American Center, can do nothing.

"But Ambassador Max Lacey could do a great deal."

The hell! "I'm not an amb—"

"An ambassador. I know. But many people do not. I'm sure you've heard that shrewd observation of Abraham Lincoln, that you can fool some of the people all of the time, and all of the people some of the time, but you can't fool all of the people all of the time?"

"Yes, of course."

"I'm asking only that you help me fool some of the people some of the time."

"But...that's almost impossible, and what would it accomplish anyway?"

"What could be more dramatic than a declaration of independence by Alcalá and the coast? It would make all Engañadans see what is at stake: the end of the country as they have known it. It will come to an end if Madera succeeds in his plan, though this is not clear to everyone. But a prospective division of the country? That should turn people against Madera, if they believe he is driving Alcalá to take this step.

"Of course, Madera's first reaction probably would be to declare Alcalá in revolt and send the army to quash the rebellion."

"Doesn't that mean war?" Max asked. "Isn't that what you want to avoid above all?"

"Of course. That's what everyone would want to avoid, and public support for any military action would not last long. Not after some boys were killed." The old man sighed and closed his eyes before adding, "It is vital that we delay it. The Engañadan military moves slowly at best. Every day of delay will make peace that much secure. And here is where Ambassador Max Lacey comes in.

"If they thought that Alcalá's independence was supported by the United States, they would think long and hard before doing anything that might endanger military and economic aid or foreign investment. They would be even more reluctant to take any action that might mean fighting against Americans. The presence of a U.S. Ambassador to Alcalá, and rumors about Marine Corps preparations, would give them pause indeed. They would see, I hope, that they have no choice but to respect tradition and settle things peacefully. Which is to say, we would cancel our declaration of independence. Alcalá is far too small to be viable anyway. Elections would follow."

"Sir, I hardly know where to begin, but I know Ambassador Webster would tell them I'm a fake. Washington would disavow me as a rogue. It would never work!"

"It would not work for very long, I agree. But it need work only for a week or so, perhaps as little as a few days; at most until the end of next month. And in that time, we would hope to have the problem solved. You would have a new problem, of course, with American authorities."

Max thought about his new problem and smiled a gallows smile. "'I'm not sure just how serious a felony that would be under United States law."

"They might have a difficult time defining it. They might prefer to ignore it, and hope not so many people noticed." Espejo smiled in sympathy. "But, Mr. Lacey, I believe you might agree that I am something of an authority on exile. Yes?"

Max grinned. "Yes, sir."

"Well, then believe me, please, when I tell you that there are far worse fates in life. And believe me also when I say this: there would always be a place in Alcalá for an honorary Founding Father, even of a short-lived republic. In the meantime it will be amusing, don't you agree, to watch the news from Washington? If some reporter asks the President if he has recognized Alcalá, the President, who has never heard of such a country, will say it is being studied. The State Department will think the President wants it studied and will form a task force to do so. They in turn will find conflicting reports. Lucho has some ideas for that, with some thanks to you."

"What did I do?"

"It seems you sent Doctora Esperanza Romero Ycaza to see him some time ago, perhaps hoping to transfer a problem to him. He recognized an opportunity. As you may know, she is also a sometime journalist. Well, as I was saying, the White House will want everything confirmed ten times before they say anything. Isn't that the case?"

"Perhaps," Max allowed, wondering why he resented an outsider's ridicule of the American bureaucracy in which he had planned a career. Of course it deserved ridicule, but Max wouldn't be part of it for much longer, and it's the more gracious and manly thing to speak well of a love you are about to abandon.

"More importantly," continued Espejo in a different tone, "it will render much less likely the worst of all possible outcomes, and one which I am told General Madera has already suggested to Ambassador Webster: that the U.S. send Marines to fight on his side in case things go badly."

"They don't do that anymore," Max protested.

"Interesting," observed Espejo with the barest trace of a smile. "The last American to tell me that was your Ambassador to Santo Domingo at a meeting of the O.A.S. in 1961, I believe, or '65."

Max said nothing. No need to confirm the man's memory of Marine landings in the Caribbean.

"So," Espejo continued gently, "may I call you 'Mr.

Ambassador' when the time comes?'"

Max still said nothing. This would put the third or fourth definitive end to his career. It would truly and seriously violate some regulation, or even some Federal law, to do such a thing while on the government payroll. *So I won't cash any more Federal paychecks. Wait. They're deposited automatically. Okay, I won't use any of the money. I'll live on...what?*

The President, reading his face, said quietly, "Don't think only of your own problems, Max."

Max felt ashamed. He saw the soldiers again, lying broken beside the highway, and secret police dragging peasants from their thatched huts in the middle of the night. He pushed those images aside and tried to imagine a new era of good relations, with the United States developing real respect for Latin America. *"Oh,"* said a faint voice in his head–be it George's, Jethro's, or even his own–*"now Max Lacey is setting himself up as Secretary of State!"* Was he succumbing to Pride, that primal sin by which fell angels? *No. I hope not. I don't really want it. It's not even real but only pretending for a while. And it's in a good cause.*

"Max," Espejo's soft voice resumed, "you know your heart's with us; you just can't quite get your head to come along. Even when the heart's mistaken, its sins are soon forgiven. The heart repents and, if one is blessed, brings the head along."

"That's a comfort," said Max, a weak smile forming on his lips and a ringing in his ears, as of countervailing forces harmonizing. "I just wish I had the proper ambassadorial credentials to present."

"There's no hurry. We'll write them later."

Chapter Twenty-Five: A Wary Informant

Cheryl Fletcher stared across the coffee table at Max. "You want me to call my father?" She sounded disbelieving.

"Yes," Max answered somberly, "I do. You called him after the demonstration, didn't you? After your talk with Ambassador Webster?"

"No. Why should I? Except I would like to tell somebody that American ambassadors should be more sympathetic to people you know what I mean? That Webster, he just sat there and growled about how he couldn't get into the Center, and Ambassador Jackson just complained about how he almost got shot, and they didn't even care about all the good things the Center does."

Max looked puzzled. "You told me you were going to ask your father why the government didn't support the Center more."

"I did? Oh. Well, I use that a lot, telling people I'm going to call my father the Senator. It's got me out of trouble sometimes. But I never do. I mean, hardly ever."

Max forced himself to nod sympathetically. "This time you really should call him. Someone should tell Washington about all the good things we do, and all the problems. Especially now."

"Why now?" she asked, wide-eyed.

Exercising all the patience and honesty in his power, Max explained that great historical forces were in motion, that the tyranny of San Genesio had now pushed the coastal provinces beyond tolerance, and that the situation was very dangerous. "It's important the U.S. get on the right side for a change, that it support human rights this time, and democracy."

"Oh, I see," she murmured. "What side are we on now?"

"On the side of San Genesio, I'm afraid. You see, Webster reports from there, and he's naturally sympathetic to the people he knows. Maybe he's even..." Max searched the ceiling and then said nobly, "sincere. But you and I know how things really are

260

here, and how harmful it would be, not only to human rights in Engañada, but to the United States itself if Washington were to support the generals in San Genesio now."

Cheryl curled her legs underneath her on the sofa. "Oh, I agree, absolutely. So you want me to tell my father all this? So vote against supporting the generals?"

"I think he'll be grateful to hear from you. He'd also be glad to know that Espejo is the true friend of the United States down here, and not the generals. I'm not sure Webster has made that clear to him."

"Is that why they demonstrated at the Center?" she asked, "because we're supporting the generals?"

Max shrugged. "What would you do if you were them?"

"I'd have been out there like them. All right, I'll call him."

The connection took some time to go through. While they waited, she recalled all the allegations of repression she had heard from the artists and students she knew. She had no doubt they were true, and when she finally got on the phone, she relayed all these claims to the Senator, "just like I told that Webster guy," along with gushing claims about the Center's good work.

The Senator was evidently surprised and angry at first to learn his only child was in Engañada, that she hadn't told him she was going there, and that Ambassador Webster hadn't mentioned it. Nonetheless, he seemed pleased and grateful she had called.

Am I using her? Yes. But it seems to be helping them reconcile. Still, I owe her something.

She got up to leave. "Cheryl," he said, "please be careful. It may yet dangerous here. And we need you." Cheryl looked first puzzled, then pleased.

Max wondered if Gonzales had any such misgivings about using people, or if he had succeeded in using Esperanza Romero as Espejo had implied he would. As it happened, Max got answers to both questions the next day, starting with a story that appeared in *La Voz del Pueblo* and God knew where else:

STATE DEPARTMENT IN CONTACT WITH ALCALA NATIONALISTS

(AP Exclusive) by Esperanza Romero and Juan Tyrone. Alcalá, Sep. 22. Associated Press has learned that the U.S. State Department has been in contact with Nationalist groups in Alcalá who are campaigning to end the long and increasingly brutal domination of their traditional homeland by the central government of Engañada in San Genesio. Our reporter recently obtained an exclusive interview with one of the leaders of the warily clandestine resistance group who, after being assured of anonymity, revealed that a U.S. ambassador recently traveled to Alcalá for an unannounced interview with Luis Gonzales, aide to then-exiled Alcalá leader Juan Francisco Espejo Suárez.

U.S. sympathy for the liberation struggle was suggested perhaps even more strongly by the site selected for the meeting: the American Cultural Center. (However, to avoid all possibility of misunderstanding, the resistance leader pointed out that the Center is not official U.S. property and not completely under the control of the U.S. Embassy.) Although no specific details of the talks can yet be disclosed, the resistance leader recalled that U.S. Ambassador to Engañada Bradford Webster has on several occasions stated his belief that no nation has the right to dominate another in brutal fashion–a position repeated in the State Department briefing on the very day of the meeting. "Draw your own conclusions," suggested the wary resistance leader to this reporter.

Asked if direct U.S. military assistance could be expected before the rainy season, the leader smiled and commented that one does not reveal in advance the number of tanks, rocket launchers, helicopters (the versatile "Huey" of Vietnam fame, updated with the most recent electronics), or the number of troops in the 7th Marine Expeditionary Force. (Our reporter has learned from other sources that the 7th Marine Expeditionary Force sailed from San Diego three days ago, its destination "classified.")

Questioned whether the U.S. was prepared to recognize an independent Alcalá, the source declined to speak for another government, adding that this was in any case not the moment to publicize agreements which both parties had agreed to keep secret "until the opportune development of the diplomatic process prepares the groundwork."

Asked by this reporter for his estimation of the prospects for Alcalán independence, the representative said, "We are confident, very confident. You may add, we are also deeply grateful."

Max thought that should do it. If it confused the hell out of him, it should shake Madera & Company up even more. Harvey was right: nothing else matters if you have a good story.

Something clicked. Juan Tyrone had to be that journalist son of Harvey's, and got the job of putting Esperanza's English into English. In any case, Gonzales also deserved congratulations. Max dropped by his office to deliver them.

The old man held up his hands and laughed. "Max, I merely made some suggestions to Dra. Romero."

"I see. And I wonder if this Juan Tyrone could be related to anyone we know?"

Gonzales smiled.

"Won't this cost her her job as Regional Secretary?" Max asked.

"It should, even for a force of nature like her. But things move slowly. Has your paycheck stopped yet?"

"No." Max didn't explain his decision not to use the money. Gonzales would just laugh.

"Thank the delays of bureaucracy, both ours and yours. But, just as you have taken a chance in order to become an ambassador and an honorary Founding Father, so too is Esperanza risking the miserable salary of a Regional Secretary for the dignity of a Ministry. She wanted to be Minister for Information, but that's too important. We'll create a Ministry of Child Development right here for her. Or even better, if things go well, maybe we'll give her the one in San Genesio once this masquerade is over. Or maybe not. We have to think of the children."

Max shook his head. Gonzales' grin seemed truly satanic, the look of a man utterly without qualms. "How many innocents have you corrupted in your time, Lucho?"

Gonzales looked him straight in the eye: "None, Max. Not a single one."

Chapter Twenty-Six: When In The Course of Human Events

A hundred meters of plaza separated the Provincial Government Building from Heroic Park. Both plaza and park were full of people, and more gathered at the upper windows of buildings surrounding the plaza. From their seats on the platform, Max and Rosa looked out on thousands of faces awaiting Espejo's arrival with a mix of happy excitement, tension, and determination. Above the space flew the new national colors: the bottom third blue and the rest green, save for a wavy blue stripe: "The blue is the ocean," Rosa explained, "and the green is the jungle with the Cholo River running through it. Isn't it beautiful?"

"Did you know?" he asked. "That there'd be all that blue? Is that why you got that beautiful blue dress?"

"You like it?" she smiled, standing up and twirling around. It swirled gracefully behind her, the hem almost to her ankles.

"Of course I do."

Max glanced again at the *Declaración Solemne de la Independencia de Alcalá* in his hand. Everyone had been given a copy as they arrived, though the *real* declaration of independence would be Espejo's speech. Nonetheless a written document was in order and this one had been composed by the Citizens Committee for the Restoration of Alcalán Dignity. It was signed by many people Max knew – Espejo, of course, and most of the *Sociedad Historica* members – as well as several he didn't. It might have been based on Jefferson's Declaration, or maybe not: perhaps all such documents list a series of grievances for which the only relief is independence.

His gaze returned to the new flag, but before he could ask who had designed it, Gloria grabbed his arm and announced that the Archbishop had arrived. Max took a few steps and waited as the thin, cheerful-looking cleric climbed carefully up the unsteady stairs to the platform.

"I'm pleased to meet you again, Mr. Lacey. I've heard a lot about you recently. This really is a small town, you know, though we look populous enough at the moment." The Archbishop indicated the throng.

"A small town indeed. Everyone's related to everyone."

The Archbishop laughed. "Yes. Yesterday Espejo started naming the children I'd baptized with himself as godfather. The man has a memory, I'll tell you! He asked me what funeral oration I'd give for so many in case of war. I suppose he used similar arguments with you?"

"Yes, Excellency, more or less. But the emphasis was on humane political processes."

"Of course. Well, you and I will be much discussed in Washington and Rome tomorrow. I'll be accused of seeking a red hat, because as you know, every sovereign country needs a cardinal, after all. And you'll be accused of–what?"

"I don't know," Max smiled sadly. "They'll have to work on it; I don't know if there's a term for promoting oneself to ambassador."

"It will all work out somehow, please God," said the Archbishop kindly. "I talked this over with the Cardinal in San Genesio, but I don't suppose...?"

"No, your Excellency. I'm afraid not. Mr. Webster doesn't take my calls, and I doubt he would be sympathetic."

A tremendous roar greeted Espejo's arrival, louder even than the cheering at the previous speech. Not only were there more people, but the shouts had a fighting tone. Espejo emerged from the Government Building, smiled and waved his way down the steps and up the ramp to the platform, all eyes on him. Every voice cheered as he made his slow way, stopping briefly to shake hands with the dignitaries in attendance.

He greeted the Archbishop with a hearty smile. "An innovation indeed! A cleric present at the Creation!"

"Perhaps it's not the Creation," suggested the Archbishop, "but the Fall?"

"In that case, the presence of a cleric is no innovation!"

The cheering rose to yet a higher level when Espejo stepped to the microphone. He let it continue so for several minutes before waving for quiet, then began very formally:

266

"Most Reverend Archbishop of Alcalá; Señor Ambassador of the United States, Señor Ambassador of Italy..."

Puzzled, Max looked around until the Archbishop whispered, "Mazzini the restaurateur. I don't know what Espejo said to him."

"*Señores* governors of the six provinces of Alcalá. People of Alcalá:

"Today is a blessed and an historic day. Let your children note it so that they may tell their children and grandchildren that they were here, in the Plaza of Alcalá, on the Day of Independence!"

Furious roars went up, cheers for Espejo and liberty and Alcalá.

"My People! Today is a day of deep joy, yet not a day for celebration. Is it not strange? For today we proclaim that liberty shall never die in Alcalá, that tyranny has no hold here, that Alcalá shall be for the people of Alcalá!"

They started cheering, but he gestured them to quiet. "And yet we would not have had it so. Did we not ask peace of our brothers in San Genesio? Do we not love them? Have we not proudly formed part of Engañada these many years, and poured forth the blood of our youth in its defense? We have loved Engañada, and it is for us a deep sadness that we must leave it."

He stopped and looked sadly at the huge crowd; they waited silently.

"No, we would not have left Engañada. And we did not leave Engañada. Engañada was taken from us!"

"ES-PE-JO!"

"In Engañada we were respected! In Engañada the public good was the only concern of the public authorities! The cry of the widow and the orphan reached the halls of power! Engañada was a nation inspired by the noble ideals of Bolívar, of San Martín, of O'Higgins: that was the Engañada we loved! And that Engañada, my friends, is no more."

He stopped for a moment of silence in memory of that Engañada, and then continued with some lines of poetry by his friend Bolívar Blanco:

"Oh where has Engañada gone, that Liberty loved well?

267

O where has gone that country, where free were each and all?
Where? I know: 'tis sadly held in thrall
By tyrants merely, whose shame I shame to tell!"

The lines drew thunderous applause.

"When there is no longer Engañada, how can we be Engañadans? We cannot, yet we tried to preserve that fatherland, and asked respectfully of the usurpers that they treat us as equals, and what was their answer? Threats, and insults! Did they think any Engañadan would tolerate this? Much less an Alcalán?"

As Espejo went on justifying their cause, his words reaching out as easily and luxuriantly as jungle foliage, Max gazed at the surrounding floodlights on the plaza, fast becoming the only focal points in his vision. Darkness came swiftly at this latitude; once the sun dropped below the horizon, full night was only fifteen minutes away. He could see few of the people now, but he could hear and even sense their energy: not as a crowd, but as a human force that Espejo stimulated, calmed, and guided at will. Soon Max saw only the floodlights and the insects that flew against them, and Espejo's back silhouetted by their glare, and the bats, shadows or silhouettes of bats, that swooped suddenly across the plaza and disappeared again.

So this is a declaration of independence, and Max Lacey a founding father, or a guest founding father. Lafayette might be the better parallel, except that I'm no soldier. No matter. Present at the birth of a nation where its real father describes himself as a political joke, and where the citizens have no idea how variously they're used for their own good by some, for less noble reasons by others. Where the insects beat against the floodlights, and the bats swoop. Where the father of the new country and the midwives on the platform deliver it in the hope it will meet a negotiated death within weeks.

And yet it wasn't laughable. It was terribly important to these people and now to Max. He thought it strange that he should feel a part of it. Rosa's hand lay contentedly in his, but it was still more of a contact than a root. His practical self recognized all this, yet did not object to his being here, caught up in something probably absurd yet innocent and pure. At peace, Max felt neither scorn nor envy for anyone. *God bless America. North and South.*

A change in Espejo's tone caught his attention; he was coming to a conclusion. Max listened to the words now not as music, but in their less wonderful aspect, as politics, and bluff.

"So today we begin as a new and sovereign country. Our success is assured by God and our arms" –he indicated the Archbishop and several military officers behind him— "by justice, and by our dedication to the cause of Alcalá. Indeed, so just is our cause, and so certain, that already our great enterprise has been recognized and endorsed by two sister republics: Italy and the United States of America!"

The crowd cheered wildly as Max and Mr. Mazzini stood and nodded somberly. "With our Cause just, our friends true, and our hearts bold we shall see our country prosper whatever our enemies may plot against us! But we seek no enemies: let San Genesio accept us as a neighbor, in peace, and we shall be good neighbors. Then anything is possible—we shut no doors. Should the true Engañada, like Lazarus, rise from the dead, none would rejoice so much as we. But if they choose War, than woe unto them!"

The crowd seemed more ready for war than for peace. Espejo finished by leading them in singing the new national anthem, which was the traditional song of the city but with new lyrics by Blanco. It began:

Where dwells my heart? In Alcalá,
Where bones of all my fathers lie.
While I have life to guard it,
Your sacred flag shall fly!

Max looked around the well-lit VIP platform as they sang, wondering where all these people he knew had come from. There on the stage with him were Jorge Pinzón, who used to work for Gandig, and Mariana and Dr. Ramírez and Washington, now Max's Deputy Chief of Mission. And Cheryl Fletcher, wearing a pantsuit, invited both because Gonzales wanted the daughter of a

U.S. senator present and because Max had insisted she'd earned the honor. And the University Rector, Carlos Ibarra, the man who had to calculate political consequences before leaving his office. Yet this should be safe enough for him: Maoists and Rusos and Fidelistas all seemed behind Espejo now. The officers of the Historical Patriotic Society were there, with tears in their eyes as they sang Blanco's lyrics, and the poet himself wept in their midst.

Maybe this is how revolutions are made.

Benjamin Franklin must have found his bickering colonial committees as ridiculous as Max found the *Sociedad*. Bats like those present tonight had witnessed the declarations of Bolívar and San Martín, who no doubt delivered speeches as bombastic as those of Espejo and swatted away mosquitoes as annoying as those Max chased away now. As he signed, Franklin had joked to others about hanging together lest they all hang separately.

Max felt a new appreciation of Franklin and Adams and the rest. To risk comfort and security trying to construct something only imagined, is absurd. But hold to that, and New York remains governed from London. Franklin, like Max, had opted for poetry.

Chapter Twenty-Seven: The Bluffing Ambassador

Max arrived at the Center late the next morning after walking far out of his way, strolling down the riverbank to the packing plant and then from park to park, stopping twice for coffee. He wasn't in a mood to work, whatever that work might now be, and he wanted to see and hear this place that was now his at least for the duration. Alcalá was nicest in the morning when the air was almost fresh and the people more cheerful.

There was also the suit, which was less uncomfortable at this hour. Max had decided that if he were to play Ambassador, certain standards of dress must apply. The delay also afforded him time to read all about the big event in the papers, particularly his own role. His picture was on all the front pages, accompanied by the statement he had composed with Gonzales. Digested, it said: 'While the United States didn't initiate the independence movement, it has recognized the *de facto* existence of a legitimate government. Ambassador Lacey looks forward to good relations.'

Another piece in the paper said that the Citizens Committee for the Restoration of Alcalán Dignity, the interim governing body, would elect an interim President that day, to act until regular elections could be scheduled. Max had a pretty cagey idea about whom they would choose.

Meanwhile, his slow progress to work would also give Rosa and the others time to transform the Center into an Embassy, or at least the office once again his own. When at last he opened the door, they had nearly finished. Espejo had moved to the Provincial

Government Building, now renamed the Executive Building, leaving the Center his new furniture. Manuel and Juan had put up appropriate signs, with Manuel even devising the Great Seal as best he could from materials in the storeroom. In seeking an eagle, he had found only an old Thanksgiving poster that he proceeded to touch up, so that Max found his office door guarded by a turkey with arrows and palm branches under its feet. *If Benjamin Franklin proposed it, how can I object?*

He swiveled around in his chair, quite impressed. It almost felt like a real ambassador's office. What if Florence, his old girlfriend who thought he lacked ambition, could see him now? *Well, she's a law student. Probably quibble about legalities.* Florence was doubly dropped from his mind when Rosa bounced in with no diplomatic business, but plans for remodeling classrooms and replacing student desks with their newfound wealth via the subtraction of red ink: Gonzales had called to say that among the President's first acts would be the cancellation of the Center's debt and the dismissal of Braden's lawsuit as well as the inquiry into the Center's hiring Braden illegally. It seemed rather high-handed but Max asked no questions. After lighting his candle, he'd left the details to St. Jude. Rosa suggested that the beauty shop, at least, could now be invited to find new premises—nicely, though, since they had been there when the Center needed them. While Max rehearsed polite phrases to use with Señora Hernandez of the beauty shop, Washington rushed in to report what had just come over the radio: the Citizens Committee for the Restoration of Alcalán Dignity had just elected an interim President! The name of the winner was no surprise; Max wondered if it would count as Espejo's thirteenth presidency.

Diplomatic business arrived soon enough in the person of Jorge Pinzón, who came from the Executive Building to ask that Max prepare a statement about U.S. military intervention in case it might be needed.

"In case what is needed? The statement or the intervention?"

"Just the statement. We really don't expect you to arrange the other. Not that we want Marines shooting up the place, God help us."

"You've seen the movies," Max smiled.

"I've seen the Marines. I was in the Reserves while I went to school in Wisconsin. Business School," he added, seeing Max's surprise. "Got me more scholarship money from the Ministry of Education. I went to work for Gandig when I got back."

"And now you're on the other side." Max felt he had something in common with this prosperous-looking fellow.

"Always was. I'm a Pinzón Gonzales, Lucho's nephew."

Max sighed. "I should have known."

"Anyway, Uncle Lucho asked me to get into business, American business, to learn what really goes on. It will be useful in dealing with U.S. companies. Besides, I liked most of it. Even setting up fronts for Gandig's English academies around town had its fascination."

"You set up that one in San Genesio, for Braden?"

"No. That came up about the time Gandig was catching on to my connections with politics. But we parted amicably. He figured I thought there'd be a big payoff for me in this and said he understood. So someone else set it up."

Just when I thought nothing could shock me anymore, Max mused, shaking his head ruefully. *Our Treasurer was competing for our students.*

"But we're off the point," said Pinzón like an American businessman. "Look, you've seen the papers? General Madera has declared Alcalá in revolt, so he can send troops to 'restore order.' But it looks like they haven't really decided what to do yet, and our people in San Genesio think the same. They're moving troops around, and will send them sooner or later. We're trying to get our units in position before they do, but without being too obvious about it, and we have lots of problems. The spare parts for the trucks didn't arrive and we don't have enough of them running to move the tanks fast, and, well, other things. So if San Genesio starts to move too soon, we'll be in trouble. That's when we'd need some noise from you about a Marine Division off the coast ready to protect U.S. lives and property. Can you do it?"

"Nothing easier. We even have the Marines, the 7th

Expeditionary Force."

Pinzón smiled. "I hope they can handle the 3rd Expeditionary Force, if Webster succeeds in getting them down here."

"He's trying that?" Max asked, suddenly fearful.

"Some of our people in San Genesio tell us the Foreign Ministry *thinks* he is."

Max wondered briefly how many loyalists Espejo had in the capital, in the Foreign Ministry and elsewhere. *Probably a lot.*

Pinzón went on. "Other sources report that Webster's having a hard time even convincing Washington what the situation is down here, let alone that they should send the Marines. We're not worried about it, not yet. And we won't ask for your statement unless it's very urgent. We don't want to appear beholden to the Pentagon."

Max nodded, and supposed Harvey Tyrone must be their source inside the Embassy, though Espejo surely had other sources as well, maybe even in Washington.

Pinzón started to leave. "Ah, another thing: the President invites you and your party on a tour of the troops, once they're in place. You get to ride in a helicopter, see some of the country. Okay?"

"Did the spare parts for the helicopters arrive?"

"For *the* helicopter," Pinzón corrected. "Don't worry: we have the best one in the country, the one Madera ordered for himself. His personal pilot is Espejo's grand-nephew. He flew it down here."

"A defector," Max mused. "We've already attracted a defector."

"More than one. And this," he said, watching Washington stride through the door wearing a suit, of all things, and a *Viva Espejo* button, "must be your military attaché."

"I thought I was the Deputy Chief of Mission," Washington protested.

Max clarified the point for him. "That's only on Mondays and Thursdays. We'll be visiting the troops and I'll need a military attaché. Maybe Jorge here can fix you up with a uniform."

"No problem," agreed Gonzales' nephew. As Max began to

accompany him down the hall they heard the phone ring in Rosa's office and her crisp greeting, "*Oficina del Embajador.*" The HA! from the other end could be heard in the next room. "That will be for me," Max predicted, returning to his desk and picking up the phone. "Lacey here."

"Hello there, Mr. Lacey. Or should I say, 'Mr. Ambassador'?" The voice drooled in anticipation of feasting on sarcasm and ridicule.

"Jethro, among old friends 'Max' will do just fine."

"Oh. Real nice of you. I called yesterday, you know, but it seems you weren't in. Which would have been right because I *tole* you we didn't want you in that Center! But of course, Max Lacey don't believe in following orders."

"Well, I really do. But yes, I was out. We had quite a day here yesterday, Jethro. You wouldn't believe. And I have another full calendar today."

"Oh, I believe. Things've been pretty busy up here, too. Now, I'm not going to ask you how things are going down there, and I won't ask you for an explanation of what you were doing on a platform with a bunch of seditionist communist terrorists, or why you're passing yourself off as a U.S. ambassador. I'm not going to ask you any of that. And you know why I'm not?"

Sounds like Jackson has exchanged his usual accent for something more formal. "Well, Jethro, I'd guess it's because you don't even want to hear it."

"That's right. That sho' is just exactly right!" His heavy breathing roared in the phone as he slipped back into his proper voice.

Max changed to a businesslike tone and said, "Well, Jethro, I see you still haven't got the word and I'm busy, so I'll just ring off and you see if you still feel the same way in, say, twenty-four hours."

"Whoa! What you say? Don't go ringing off on me, boy! I got a message for you from the Ambassador, and I mean the *real* Ambassador. He says for you to get your ass up here to San Genesio right now! He want to see you before you shipped home, you hear?"

"Aside from everything else, Jethro, the airport's closed."

"Then you can take a bus. Or drive. Or walk! Or crawl on your goddamn belly like a reptile! Just get your ass up here!"

Max sighed. "Look, tell Brad something for me."

"Who?"

"Brad. That's 'Mr. Ambassador' to you. You just tell him I'm sorry his embassy hasn't been clued in yet, but if he'll just tie into the Delta Channel like I suggested he do some time ago, he'll get the word. He could also check with the Senator. Now maybe it's not his fault; the Department is probably screwing this up, too. But if Brad ran a tighter ship up there, I'm sure he'd have picked up something. Meanwhile, as long as I have this appointment from the President in my hand, I don't take orders from Brad, or anyone else at Embassy San Genesio. That clear?"

Only Jackson's labored breathing broke his long silence. "Max? What are you talking about, huh?"

Lacey answered in a hard, even voice: "Jethro, this is not a secure line. I have told you that before. Now look: I'll send a copy of the appointment as soon as the mail is reestablished, just so Brad will stop making a fool of himself. By that time, though, this should all be clear to everyone."

"Now look here, Max, if you think I'm gonna believe—"

"Jethro, considering everything, I think I'd better insist on a little more formality after all. It helps keep things in perspective. So make it 'Mr. Ambassador' and we'll get on better." He hoped his voice was the audio equivalent of cold blue eyes.

"Uuuh. Hell look here, Max, I don't know what—"

"Jethro..."

"Oh, now damn it all, Max!"

"Very well, Mr. Jackson," Max snapped. "This conversation is at an end. I'm making a note of it."

"Wait! Oh, all right...Mr. Ambassador." There was an audible swallow. "But we never got no word like that up here and the damned Department sending down telegrams all time asking what the hell going on, goddamn it!" Jackson whined. "They wouldn't go and appoint no ambassador in Alcalá without even telling us!"

"Jethro," asked Max in a softer, almost paternal voice, "how long have you been with the government?"

"Going on twenty-eight years...sir."

"And you still believe the government can't get things this fouled up and worse?"

"Well now, I see your point."

"Now I'm sure they'll get the word to you soon. The problem is probably in the White House. And given the speed with which it all happened, they probably didn't get the word to all the right people in State."

"Oh yes, yessir—I seen that every time. Get a new Administration and they get all these hotshots in there don't know nothing about the government or diplomacy or nothing and they get to sending letters and memos and they make one hell of a mess, don't nobody know what's going on!"

"Precisely. But you–and I'm sure Brad will back me on this– you know that this fact doesn't help us career people. Our job is to stay one jump ahead of the politicians' blunders. If we don't, well, they raise hell about the unresponsive bureaucracy. Isn't that so?"

"Oh, yes sir! You sure hit it right on the head!"

"So, in the present case, you can imagine what hell there'll be to pay if Brad is found to be undermining White House decisions– never mind that the NSC staff handled it badly."

"I'm real glad you pointed that out, Mr. Ambassador, and I'll sure tell the Ambassador here. Sure will."

"Good. Now as I told you, I've a very full schedule. Good talking to you, Jethro."

"Good talking to you, sir. Real nice of you to take the time. 'Bye now."

In the days that followed, Max kept abreast of world reaction to Alcalá's declaration of independence via short-wave broadcasts from the BBC and Voice of America. Fictions that were born in his own head now beamed back to him from the ionosphere, as if his prayers had been answered.

Not that the reports were always clear, especially at first. An early report spoke of disturbances "in the coastal city of San Genesio, capital of Nueva Alcalá," and another described a visit some weeks before by the American Ambassador to Mr. Espejo in the American Cultural Center, in which the two men seem to have discussed a possible visit by Espejo to Washington to discuss cultural exchanges. After the airport reopened under the new flag, even more misleading reports appeared in U.S. newspapers.

And I used to think I knew what was going on by watching the news.

Questions had been raised in the Senate about U.S. complicity in coastal massacres and other systematic violations of basic human rights "in that impoverished land-locked country," and one Senate committee had voted to investigate a certain "Plan Delta" with suspected links to the Miami Cuban exile community. Another committee was to hold hearings on contingency plans for the use of American forces in "brushfire wars." The chairman of this second committee noted dryly that, "If it's too much to expect to keep the Pentagon out of these things, maybe we can at least see that the Marines go in on the right side for a change."

The State Department denied any knowledge of a Plan Delta, while an anonymous source at the CIA insisted that the last agents in the Mekong Delta had been evacuated long ago. However, a lower-level source at State suggested that all this might involve a certain 'Delta Report,' but said that he could give no information since it was a Defense Department initiative. Pentagon spokesmen refused comment on either the Delta Report, the existence of which they would neither confirm nor deny, or the whereabouts of the 3rd and 7th Marine Expeditionary Forces. They did admit that military aid was "in the pipeline" to Engañada. Asked whether it was destined for the government or for the rebels, the sources indicated it was "just helicopters and support equipment, mostly." Later in the day, another Pentagon source said shipment of the supplies had been temporarily suspended at the request of "someone on the Hill."

The White House had no comment germane to the actual matter. At the President's biweekly press conference, a *New York Times* reporter asked him about the AP story on U.S. support of indigenous forces in Nueva Alcalá, and why U.S. recognition had not been announced in the usual way. The President reiterated the policy of his Administration, "as indeed of all previous administrations, to support the right of people everywhere to seek that form of government that best answers their aspirations for a richer and happier life for themselves and for their children–just as we Americans wish the same things for ourselves." He added that the United States neither could nor should be "the world's policeman," but insisted that he should not be interpreted to mean that his Administration would not honor the treaties and other commitments to which the United States was a party: "treaties approved, I might add, on both sides of the aisle." The White House Press Office later clarified that the President of course meant that the United States could not be the world's police *officer*.

The contingency plan for Max's report about the Marines did not materialize, thanks to the confusion in both Washington and San Genesio, which allowed the Alcalá troops ample time to get into position. In fact, Espejo began to worry that his troops would get an obvious advantage: questions about possible U.S. reaction handicapped General President Madera's planning so severely that he couldn't even decide how many troops to mobilize. By whatever channels, reports from the Embassy reached Alcalá and Espejo and eventually Max. One of them said Ambassador Webster was getting frantic and angry messages from the Foreign Ministry, but for the moment he could do little more than to repeat that "I have received no instructions from my government that would lead me to believe that the fundamental relationship between our two governments has changed in any significant way."

Somewhat more gracefully, the Italian Ambassador announced he was seeking guidance from Rome, while reports from Rome said the Italian government was seeking clarification from San Genesio. The Vatican declined comment, except to say that His Holiness urged all Christians and others of good will to join him in praying for peaceful and just solutions to conflicts everywhere. The Foreign Office in London also declined comment, reportedly in deference to Washington. Moscow denounced U.S. support of reactionary fascist elements without identifying the latter.

279

By the time the confusion began to sort itself out in late October, the Alcalá troops were fully deployed. Espejo's initial strategy had worked, and Max had the satisfaction of knowing he had done his part. He also had the satisfaction of seeing an end to his frustrations with the Center. Money cured the most vexing problems, and now only the limitations of imagination restricted the contribution it could make to international understanding.

Most of the artful plywood panels that had covered the broken windows now hung in the auditorium; almost every artist and intellectual in town attended the opening of the exhibit. University faculty who wouldn't have come near the Center a few weeks before posed for photos with Max, and even with other academics and artists with whom they normally feuded. In this time of danger, almost all the coast rallied around Espejo and his "friendship between equals" policy toward the United States.

Some, of course, rallied less enthusiastically than others, and some hardly at all.

At the exhibit opening, Raúl Rojas glumly sipped his drink alone in a corner of the auditorium. Max felt sorry for him, and when the University Rector excused himself from the party to browse through the Library's economic section, Max carried a fresh drink over to Raúl.

"If you'd be more comfortable," he suggested, "we could step out to the street and throw rocks at the place."

Raúl smiled bitterly. "Some *compañeros* who aren't here tonight, who wouldn't come, would join us in throwing rocks."

Max nodded.

"Always the United States," said Raúl in a low angry voice. "For good or bad, nothing can happen here without the Yankees having a hand in it!"

Max said nothing, just sipped his drink and nodded again in agreement, seeing the matter through Raúl's eyes. The United States could destroy Engañada from afar, or it could shower aid on the country, and neither would impact Americans very much. But Engañada could barely make Washington aware of its existence. The discrepancy had to be humiliating.

"At least," said Max hopefully, "we're on the right side this time—and for the moment, the United States is paying attention to Engañada."

"So much the worse for us," responded Raúl. "What does this Delta Plan really involve?"

When not drinking and chatting, Max oversaw the continuing renewal of the Center. Classrooms were remodeled as fast as the workers could do it, with Washington watching costs, the accountant watching Washington, and Max watching the accountant. The Center bought back the rental contracts of the beauty shop and the karate school, not so much to polish up the image as to make room for new students. Young people, and some not so young, flooded in as if studying English at the Center had become a patriotic duty. Max raised teacher salaries another twenty-five percent, inspiring gratitude and contentment for nearly a week. He retained an architect to study how the last bungled remodeling of the entire building could best be repaired and completed.

The librarian dug out the long lists of books she had been unable to buy over the years of drought. Now, with her own budget of fifty thousand *honores* a month, she began to import the many titles not locally available. As fast as she could get books on the shelves, university students checked them out. Even Raúl came in, though his tastes ran to old Senate Committee hearings on the CIA. "See?" he said to Max, pointing at efforts to assassinate Castro. "You see?"

"Maybe it's a false report?" Max suggested.

"How false? Look! It's the U.S. Government Printing Office!"

"You believe *them?*"

But there came a day when Raúl admitted, after reading a biting criticism of U.S. multinational corporations in the imperialist *New York Times,* "I don't know. I don't understand your country."

Max shrugged, hiding his satisfaction that Raúl had taken the first step. Now he could learn something. "Neither do I," he sympathized. Too many contradictions. Just like Engañada"

Indeed, Max now so enjoyed his days in the Center that he almost regretted sacrificing one to join the military inspection tour that Espejo's staff had arranged. Gloria would remain in charge of the

Center, but her mind wouldn't be on it. After she and Washington had learned their new salaries, they had announced a wedding. Nonetheless, Max looked forward to riding in a helicopter and seeing the troops, and this was likely his only chance. Everyone agreed that within a week or two at the most, Madera would have to accept reality. The armies would go home, elections would proceed, and Max would be a private U.S. citizen employed by the Center. Probably. For now, he refused to think about loose ends.

Like a CIA hit team on my tail.

Chapter Twenty-Eight: You're In the Army Now

Amid the camera clicks of a dozen photo-journalists, the Inspection Party left from the Plaza in front of the Presidential Palace (formerly the Governor's Mansion) in the one large and luxurious helicopter Alcalá possessed (formerly General Madera's). Its ample passenger compartment easily seated Espejo, a general and aide, Max, Washington, and Manuel (as Air Attaché). Rosa flew as well; she had begged to come, so Max promoted her to the Embassy Alcalá Political Officer.

Max had second thoughts about the joy of helicopter rides. *This thing can't glide. If the engine fails, we're toast.* He comforted himself that the expedition gave him a rock-solid excuse to skip the afternoon lecture of Dra. Esperanza Romero Ycaza. He had finally scheduled it when all the money began flowing, and after Espejo reminded him that they owed the *Doctora* something after her help with those confusing AP articles. Max could only agree, and had ordered materials for her directly from Miami.

As they lifted off, Espejo joked that such helicopters were one of the few good legacies of military governments. The general responded with an uncertain smile. They flew northeast in a more or less straight line, climbing slowly. When they were past the foothills of the mountains, General Lincoln Villacis, Supreme Commander of the Nueva Alcalán Army and their guide for the day, began to explain the military situation below them as his aide, Major Rodríguez, held the map:

"You see, Mr. President, if the *Centralistas* attack in this sector they must come down that road— "he pointed below them— "and

283

here it is on the map. So, they come here, to there, and *boom!* We have tanks covering that space there. So they must go back to here, on the map, that is over there—" he pointed out the window at a ridge— "and then try to come cross-country, so. But with artillery covering at this angle and with infantry there, we stop them. The only other way they can come across is up here, and that is very difficult. We have there a few fieldpieces and one rifle company, which would slow them until our other forces, deployed here, could come up like this and so block them again." He smiled with professional satisfaction.

Washington, looking like a WWII Air Corpsman in a rakish uniform that Pinzón had dragged up somewhere (with a matching uniform for Manuel), tried to look as if he understood. Max and Rosa, dressed for the day in borrowed Army fatigues, tried to look understanding. Max wished he'd paid more attention in ROTC classes.

But Espejo only glanced at the map politely, and continued looking out the window. "Whose troops are we visiting first?" he asked.

"Those of Lieutenant General José Drango, Mr. President."

"Drango Molinos?"

"Yes, Mr. President."

Espejo nodded and shut his eyes. "His father was my first military aide," he said softly, "and the youngest general ever to overthrow me."

"This General Drango is a very loyal officer, I assure you," said Villacis.

"I'm sure he is," smiled Espejo. "But to what?"

They landed in a small clearing atop a broad-backed ridge. Tents and trucks and tanks were scattered through the jungle on both sides of a dusty road. Two companies of soldiers stood in formation, squinting against the dust blown up by the helicopter. When the rotor slowed enough, Espejo and the others climbed out to be greeted by General Drango, a balding middle-aged officer with a pleasant drinking man's face. He invited them to inspect the troops.

The soldiers, most with Indian features beneath helmets that seemed too big, made a great show of spit-and-polish as they shifted their rifles around in response to commands barked out by a captain who simultaneously whipped a saber to and fro. Max was mainly impressed with how young the soldiers looked, and felt old for the first time in his life. *What if this farce collapses and some of these kids die?*

Espejo must have felt infinitely older, but did his part well, turning the sad-looking camp into something special. He greeted each soldier as Max imagined Washington or Lincoln or Bolívar might have greeted them. Espejo took an avuncular interest in each, asking where they were from and how things went, and asserting that the *Centralistas* would have a nasty surprise if they tried coming through here! The boys laughed and looked proud. However much they wanted to return to the farm or the barrio, they would be glad they had been here now, when *El Presidente* came.

Espejo made a short speech in which he referred to a tattered flag that hung with others from the company standard: it had been the flag of a Spanish regiment defeated long before, in the Battle of Santa Mercedes. As the sons of the patriots who had won that flag, Espejo told them, they would know how to defend it. The soldiers stood a little straighter as Max studied the faded prize, now little more than a blue rag with crossed swords poorly represented, and "XIV" in pale yellow numerals.

The Presidential party was shown around the camp, past neat rows of pup tents and then to a row of tanks. Espejo stopped to look inside one, helped up by strong hands, and asked if its cannon could shoot as far as San Genesio and so save them all a lot of trouble. Others laughed, but the young tank commander solemnly answered, "No, sir; we'll take it closer."

In the command tent they sat amidst maps and radio equipment and drank coffee. Max was glad to hear Espejo remind General Drango that the supreme mission of this Army was not to fight. If they were absolutely forced to fire their guns, they were to aim high or low, anywhere but at their "brothers from the mountains," unless their lives were in immediate danger.

"I understand, Mr. President," confirmed Drango. "If they advance, we shoot to let them know we're awake, and no more. I think it should work, and yet..."

He looked at Washington, one military man to an apparent colleague, for support. Washington hit his mark on cue: "It could be a problem, Mr. President. How can one order the troops to miss when all their training is to hit the target?"

"Those aren't targets, they're Engañadans. And the answer is easy: order your troops to fire before they're in range." Drango promised to do his best as the Presidential party rose to board the helicopter again.

They visited another camp as they flew north along the mountains, this one also located in front of one of the few passes down which a military force might attack. The routine was the same as in Drango's sector, save that Manuel was invited to try driving a tank and nearly took it off a cliff, inspiring jibes against the Air Force. But here, ominously, General Bernardo Verde Campos seemed eager to fight, resentful of Espejo's orders. He asked Villacis sarcastically if they were simply to wait for the *Centralistas* to work up their courage, or if they couldn't instead seize the initiative. The Army commander answered sternly that he would be the one to decide when they took the initiative and got a sullen, "Of course, my General," from Verde. As they flew further north, Espejo twice reminded Villacis to keep a close eye on this man.

The last camp, where they were to spend the night, was highest in the mountains, and yet the most civilized, for it lay on the main coast-to-capital highway surrounding the village of La Subida. There were fewer troops here than in the other positions; as they circled above the town, General Villacis explained that while the main highway might seem the most logical invasion route, it was not. It passed over the narrow steep canyon of La Subida, and could be easily defended or even closed with a few well-placed cannon shots.

"Where are the *Centralistas*?" asked Rosa.

"Up above, just a kilometer or so. If the President weren't with us, we'd fly up and take a look."

Max peered out the window. "Those look like elephants down there."

"So they do," agreed Villacis. He looked at Espejo and

shrugged.

The helicopter did another half-circle over the area and descended toward a field several hundred feet from the town square. It was still some two hundred feet above the ground when a muffled explosion directly above them shook the aircraft. The engine noise changed from a steady roaring whine to an uncertain growl.

"They shot us!" announced Manuel, and scrambled toward the door until he remembered where he was, then crossed himself and began praying *Ave Marias* as fast as he could. Rosa grabbed Max's arm. Everyone turned pale.

"Anti-aircraft fire?" asked Villacis doubtfully.

"No, sir," offered the crew chief. "It's the motor, something in the motor."

They dropped quickly. No one said anything, but if their thoughts were anything like Max's, they were all confused. He alternated between cursing the stupidity of dying like this, and praying, and wondering how his death would be reported by the Embassy. Then the engine roared more loudly, their descent slowed and even stopped for a brief second. Then it coughed and they fell again. It roared, and they slowed, then hit the ground violently. Something broke beneath them. The crew chief had thrown the door open just before they hit and now yelled, "Out! Get your asses out of this thing! Quick! Mr. President, sir!"

They scrambled out and away from the aircraft, which fortunately leaned away from the door. Max glanced at the rotor blade describing a high arc over his head and guessed it must almost hit the ground on the other side. They joined the reception committee fifty feet away, and then turned to look at the disabled helicopter and sigh in thankfulness. Rosa crossed herself. General Figueroa, the local commander, asked solicitously if they were all right.

"Quite all right," Espejo assured him, "though perhaps we shouldn't drop in on you quite so suddenly."

Only a president could get away with that.

General Villacis called the pilot over, and Captain Gutiérrez apologized jokingly for not having defected from San Genesio in a more reliable aircraft. "I'm afraid we'll be here for a while. It will be impossible to fix the thing before late tomorrow, if then. We won't even know what it needs until we get the motor torn down."

Espejo tousled the Captain's hair. *"Mi'jito,"* he smiled, "I hope all my troops are so skillful. Thank you for getting us here alive." Then, turning to General Villacis, "We'll have to drive back, then. I must be back by tomorrow noon. Not that I wouldn't enjoy staying with you longer, General Figueroa," he said to the local commander. "The town looked absolutely festive from the air, with the circus here."

"Yes." Figueroa had a pained smile on his face. "We have a circus whether we want it or not. They want to go to San Genesio, but the *Centralistas* won't let them through. In the meantime, my camp looks less military than it might, and for that I apologize."

Max sympathized as their guides led them through the town and camp, recalling the last time he saw these jugglers and clowns, in the Center patio. *Wonder if the elephants remember me?*

The Presidential party had nearly finished the inspection and was looking at a howitzer "already locked in on the pass" when they heard a motorcycle approaching from that same pass. No one could mistake the deep arrogant roar of the Harley-Davidson.

"How did that fellow get through?" asked Villacis.

"I asked Harvey to meet us here," said Espejo, obviating all need for further explanation. They watched Harvey get off the cycle in front of the circus wagons and embrace the juggler, the Fat Lady, and the elephant trainer. Other circus people waited to greet him.

"Ask Harvey to join us when he can," smiled Espejo. "We'll be in the Command Center." They went to Figueroa's headquarters at the police station, where the general briefed them on the local situation, pointing at a dusty torn map with his swagger stick. Simply put: the pass was the only way down, and as long as Figueroa's troops stayed awake, the *Centralistas* were stymied.

Espejo was upbeat, expressing confidence that the San Genesio forces wouldn't try coming through. There was no easy way, thus they would not try. No reasonable Engañadan soldier would risk the consequences, he assured them all.

A lieutenant entered and whispered something to Figueroa, who turned to Espejo and said, "Harvey Tyrone to see you, sir."

Harvey entered wearing a white shirt and tie with his faded jeans. "Mr. President," he said with a touch of awe, "what a pleasure to see you again!"

"And it's good to see you, Harvey," announced the President gravely, embracing him Latin fashion, "and to thank you for your help in making this—" he gestured widely—"possible. And for coming now to tell me the latest from the capital."

"Happy to help, sir."

"Did you know," asked Espejo, turning to bring Max, Rosa, and the rest into the conversation, "that Harvey here was the first U.S. cultural attaché in Engañada after the war?"

"And here I am in the same job again," Harvey jumped in. "And just where I want to be, even though it doesn't reflect a meteoric rise in the Foreign Service. Not like Max here, who has made Ambassador in record time! Congratulations, Max!"

"It's nothing, Harv," said Max.

"Jethro Jackson thinks it is, or he did when I left him. He even had Webster wondering. However, Mr. President, I'm afraid they just about have it figured out now. I can tell you one thing you'll want to know, sir: there's no way the U.S. is going to send any guns to Madera, much less Marines. Webster's madder than a hornet. If he sent home every Embassy officer he's threatened to fire, or everyone that wanted to get out of there, he'd have the whole place to himself!"

"But excuse me," interrupted Villacis, "may I ask how you got down that road?" He then smiled, abashed. "Everyone knows you could talk your way out of a school of sharks. I mean, who did you talk to?"

"Why, General," answered Harvey, "don't you know who's in command up there?"

"Of course—Bolívar Guzmán Blanco. But did you to talk to him?"

"Precisely. My *compadre*. His oldest boy, Pablo, was born during my first tour here, when Bolívar was a 1st lieutenant in the

2nd Artillery, the old Invincibles, and my partner in the tennis doubles tournament at the Army Club. We were celebrating the arrival of little Pablito for five days."

"Ah," added Figueroa, "that was when Bolívar pulled a howitzer into the town square and shot off six rounds at midnight. Half our ammunition."

"Right! Well, old Bolívar wouldn't stop a *compadre*, and I hope he won't refuse me one more favor: Carlos Ruales has to get this circus of his up to San Genesio by tomorrow night."

"I'm sure he won't refuse you," said Espejo. "If all else fails, invoke the disappointed children."

"That's just what I'll do, sir. And anyway, he probably won't give it much thought. They're going crazy up there, turning themselves around and waiting for something. More transportation, I think."

"What?" Villacis frowned. "That's what I want to know! What are they doing? How many are they, and how disposed?"

"I've never been much of a military man, General," confessed Harvey, "but when I see the troops throwing their rucksacks up on a deuce-and-a-half, and breaking up their card games, I guess they're planning to move."

"To where?"

Harvey shrugged. "I heard something about Las Cuevas, but I don't know why they're so rushed. They don't have nearly enough trucks for the troops I saw. But that's the Army: hurry up and wait."

Figueroa and Villacis both frowned and stepped over to consult the map. "Why would they go there?" asked Figueroa, fingering a spot in the midst of a solid green section of the map.

Harvey shrugged again. "Maybe to guard the bridge. You military men, you get pretty excited about bridges."

"What bridge?" demanded Villacis.

Harvey looked puzzled and turned a little pale. "You mean you don't know? The bridge over the Rio Diablo that a Dutch company built a few years back, then abandoned after their mining project didn't work out. The road to it isn't much, and I guess just locals use it because it wanders all over nowhere, but Christ! From the bridge you can get down to the San Luis road, and then to the Alcalá highway."

"That's in General Verde's sector," observed Espejo gloomily.

Harvey looked from the President to the generals. "You didn't know? You don't have it guarded?"

"Goddamn maps!" cursed Figueroa.

"Apparently they didn't know about it either," mused Espejo, "not until recently."

"General Verde, he's the one who wants to fight," Max reminded them, gratuitously.

"But Bolívar doesn't." Harvey's hopeful tone sounded forced.

"No," allowed Figueroa, "but he's a soldier. If an opportunity like this presents itself, to cross our border unopposed in less than two hours..." His voice trailed off.

Max looked at Rosa, saw fear and anger. All their political, diplomatic, and military maneuvering could founder because of one obscure bridge. Figueroa called in several other officers to update the old map per Harvey's descriptions. According to Nueva Alcalá's new government, Rio Diablo formed part of the border with Engañada, "but there's no way to get there from here, even though it's only about seven miles away."

Sheer cliffs stood between La Subida and the bridge. "Look," Figueroa pointed out, "you'd have to descend this cliff which is some sixteen hundred meters, and then climb the other that is even higher."

"That's for sure," agreed Harvey. "I went down there once with César Ayala. Friend of mine who lives right here in La Subida, but has some land down there. We were looking for a stray goat, and took us two days to climb out."

"But when will they advance?" asked Villacis. "Or have they done so already?"

Harvey shook his head. "I don't think they'll be ready for a while yet. Not enough trucks. They were just waiting around in a hurry, some at the pass and some back by the road that turns off to Las Cuevas, back there by Jorge Monda's sawmill. Unless they got some transport down from San Genesio, of course."

"How many troops?" asked Figueroa.

Harvey thought a moment. "Two or three companies maybe, if you put them all in one place."

"Ha!" said Figueroa happily. "Not enough for an advance. Of course not! They never planned to advance from there and they knew this pass was impregnable. So now, having found another way, they're waiting for reinforcements as well as for transport."

"Then," said Villacis, "maybe we have time to blow up that bridge. We can't defend it, since we can't get there in time. And radioing General Verde wouldn't be a good idea, because our radios have the same frequencies as the *Centralista* radios. We've only had time to develop codes to trigger pre-planned movements."

"Besides," said Espejo glumly, "if General Verde knew about the bridge, he just might charge across the damned thing."

"You're right, General," said Figueroa to Villacis. "It must be blown, but how can we get a commando team there? I have no airworthy helicopters and no fighter-bombers–the six U.S. surplus planes are based in San Genesio. So we have no air power and it would take days for them to hike there."

They all looked gloomily at the map. "You see..." said Figueroa, "there is only one route that would allow a team to arrive in time. It would require them to start from a point on the highway three kilometers above the pass, above the *Centralista* troops. I don't suppose General Guzmán would be so kind as to permit it, even if he is Harvey's compadre—and mine."

There was a dejected silence until Rosa asked, "But if Harvey can arrange for the circus to go up there, why couldn't someone sneak up with them?" The rest looked at each other, then at Rosa and Harvey. "Could be," allowed Villacis. "A small team, hidden in the wagons, or disguised. And then..." he turned to the map again. "It would be a hike of some four hours, more or less. Yes."

But Figueroa shook his head. "There's no place to hide a commando team in those wagons. I know; we searched them when they arrived here. And at least half my troops and officers have served with Guzmán, or with his officers, and some of his men have been in my unit in the past. So whomever we send would surely be recognized. Even worse, my one explosives expert, Captain Hernández, was with that unit until a month ago. He'd never make it."

"Is it that hard to blow up a bridge?" asked Rosa. "Couldn't Captain Hernández explain to someone else how to do it?"

Figueroa shook his head again. "It's not like making a *tortilla, Señorita.* If one doesn't know what he's doing he will probably just kill himself."

"That's for sure," agreed Max, immediately wishing he hadn't.

"That's right," said Rosa excitedly. "Ambassador Lacey was a soldier—he knows about bombs!"

"Is that right?" Espejo looked at Max.

Max remembered the look. He'd seen it when Espejo asked him to become the U.S. Ambassador. "No, not really," he answered in haste. "I was never a soldier—I was just in ROTC for a while."

"What's that?"

"That, Mr. President," interjected Harvey, "is one of the great traditions at American universities, a program that has produced some of the finest officers in the U.S. Army."

Goddamn you, Harvey! "I almost blew myself up," offered Max, as if it might be helpful.

"That's the way you learn," Villacis nodded.

Espejo turned to Harvey. "We'll need your cooperation too."

"Mr. President, you know I'm a cultural representative and you just can't mix culture and politics. Of course, a circus is a cultural event and I'd be happy to assist in any cultural movement."

"You've always been discreet, Harvey."

"I just hope Bolívar doesn't take it the wrong way when he finds out."

"I hope he'd cooperate if he knew," answered Espejo solemnly. "His Pablito is in the Army too, as I recall. So, Max, are you ready?"

Good lord. I don't remember agreeing to this! But if I refuse, I lose their respect and my own. And maybe some of those kids get killed.

He permitted himself a small sigh. "I can't do it alone," he said.

"No one would recognize your Military Attaché here," said

Figueroa, looking approvingly at Washington's rakish uniform.

"Me? Hey, I'm getting married and I don't know anything about blowing up bridges. Besides, I finished my military service five years ago."

"Then you're in the Army again," Espejo informed him. "The reserves and veterans have been called up, have they not, General?"

"Yes, sir. I just heard the call," answered Villacis. Washington went pale. Then Manuel volunteered, though he looked as if his second thoughts began the moment Villacis accepted. Harvey suggested asking César Ayala and his son. "I saw them before I came in here, and no one knows this country better than César." Figueroa sent an aide to fetch them.

"I want to go too," said Rosa.

"No way," said Max.

Espejo looked thoughtful, turned to Figueroa. "General, can we speak with Captain Hernández?"

When the explosives expert arrived, he explained what would be needed, what it weighed, and how many people it would require. "Six people to carry the munitions and equipment, perform the minimum tasks involved, and guard the operation."

"Well, surely we can find another *campesino!*" Max insisted.

Figueroa considered it. "I don't want any more of these locals to know about it than necessary. Right on the border like this, you can't be sure where their loyalties lie."

Espejo laughed softly. "Their loyalties are to their village, before anything else."

"Max, I want to go," Rosa told him in the voice she had used when he broke the door.

"Well, you can't," he answered, as if that were final. Espejo intervened.

"It would be easier getting through the lines," he said. "Rosa could pass as an acrobat. And," he judged, "my goddaughter looks fit enough. Women are in armies everywhere now, Max. Don't be more *machista* than we Latinos!"

Rosa beamed.

Captain Hernández drew a diagram of the bridge according to Harvey's description, and showed Max where the dynamite should be placed and how to connect and operate the detonator, a funny-looking tube with a handle that one twisted. It didn't look like the thing he'd practiced with in ROTC. "Be sure the handle is all the way to the right before you connect these wires," he cautioned. Max nodded vigorously as he waved goodbye to Harvey who now set off to see Guzmán up the road.

"And be sure you're behind a boulder or something," Hernández continued, "because there will be rocks and wood flying all over the place. And you'll probably have to wait for morning. By the time you get there, I expect it'll be dark or nearly so. This business is dangerous enough in broad daylight."

Max carefully wrote down all Hernández's instructions. Of course, the whole plan depended on Harvey's getting permission for the circus to pass through the lines, and on the cooperation of the circus people. Sure enough, about an hour later Harvey roared back down the pass to announce that the circus could pass if he went with it. "That Bolívar," he said, shaking his head, "is he just one hell of a nice guy or what?"

Meanwhile, they had talked to Ruales, the circus owner, who wasn't at all enthusiastic at first. But Figueroa fed him a line about an urgent wedding for Max and Rosa, and Ruales pretended to believe it; he could cite it as an excuse if need be. The circus workers didn't believe the story about six new workers, but said nothing. Ruales suggested hiding their clothes in the false roof of the lion's cage, and the explosives and weapons in the false floor of a flatbed truck. He added that they'd made these hiding places to safeguard cash. Max was probably not the only one to doubt that cash was all they ever hid.

The six then dressed as various members of the company. Manuel and César and his son looked authentic as roustabouts. Rosa was fetching as a trapeze artist, but Washington and Max looked ridiculous as clowns.

"Clowns are supposed to look ridiculous," observed Ruales. "And you, Mr. Whatever, you're a mute clown. A mime. If they hear you say anything, they'll want to know what an American tourist is doing here."

"Thanks," grumbled Max. "But why do we have to ride dressed up like this? Clowns get time off too, don't they?"

Ruales' expression withered him. "We always travel in costume, as anyone knows. We stop at all the little villages and maybe earn a few *honores* selling candy, or at least get some publicity. Anyway, the kids expect it. A circus cannot tell children that working hours are over, and to go away."

Harvey ran his motorcycle up a plank onto the flatbed truck where Rosa, Washington, and the other clowns sat atop bales of hay and canvas tarps covering circus paraphernalia. Meantime, Espejo took Max aside. His voice was serious, and for the first time, fearful and urgent.

"Max, I never thought you'd end up in anything like this, and even less did I expect to send my goddaughter on such a mission. You know I wouldn't do so if it weren't necessary."

Max nodded. What could he say?

"It's maddening," Espejo sighed. "We had this absurd thing so gracefully under control. We still do—if that bridge is destroyed. Well, we can laugh at this hereafter, if you succeed. In any case, I thank you now."

Max nodded, feeling embarrassed, deceived, and ennobled all at once.

As he climbed aboard the truck and settled next to Rosa, it lurched forward and bounced onto the highway to take its place in the caravan. Max and Rosa waved goodbye to Espejo, who stood alone by the side of the road, a brave smile on his face, waving back to them in benediction.

They climbed up the pass slowly in first gear, the growling engines protesting against the steep grade, but even so they reached the enemy lines within ten minutes. Immediately they were stopped and surrounded by dozens of soldiers, indistinguishable from those they had just left, and made to get down. Riflemen guarded them suspiciously while other soldiers climbed onto the trucks and looked under the canvas and poked bayonets into the hay.

"Mi General!" shouted Harvey to a friendly-looking officer who walked over. "You see? Just as we agreed: a circus. And I

know for a personal fact that when the people in San Genesio hear about that soldier, about that, that..." He shook his head, looking for the words. "About that *mensch,* that patriot and that hombre, General Bolívar Guzmán Blanco, who had the humanity to let a circus pass through his lines at a time like this, just so the kids in San Genesio could see it!"

"All right, Harvey, all right!" The General laughed despite himself. "My God, *compadre*, but don't you ever change?"

"No. Just age."

"I even wonder about that. But for now . . . Sergeant, how's it look?"

A soldier jumped down from the truck. "Nothing so far, my General. Just a circus."

"All right," said General Guzmán, scribbling on a piece of paper and handing it to Harvey. "When they've checked the other trucks, you can go. Show this at the next checkpoint," he added, "and do drop by when this business is over. And next month, plan on a baptism. Pablito and Elena are expecting their fifth."

Well, that went well. I hope we'll be out of here soon. Some lieutenant was talking to Rosa the acrobat, smiling and trying to look martial, while a couple of soldiers stared rudely at her. Before Max could worry more about it, children appeared from God knew where. They began pointing at the clowns and laughing.

The real clowns acted as such, dancing around and saying funny things. One of then juggled oranges. Soon there were children in front of Washington and Max.

"What do we do now?" whispered Washington.

Max noticed some soldiers, larger versions of the children, also smiling in anticipation. He tried dancing a bit himself, but did it very badly and got his feet crossed, falling heavily to the ground. The children and soldiers laughed. Washington came over to help him up, Max pushed forward and they both fell down. Now Rosa laughed too. They did a few similar pratfalls, buying time.

Max glanced at some clowns farther up the road and saw they were mixing with the children. So he went over to a little girl, opened his eyes as wide as he could, feeling the paint and grease moving on his face. He held out a hand, inviting her to dance to the balalaika music that now drifted down from the truck. She squealed happily and backed away. Max sat down and pretended to cry until she timidly stepped forward and took his hand. They then danced in a slow circle while Max, finally remembering he was a mime, put on the most exaggerated look of contentment he could muster. Another little girl came close and watched until Max danced with her, too.

Washington had begun juggling oranges, and rather well. Max grabbed some and did it very badly without effort, hitting himself in the face and on the head. The children found it hilarious, as did the soldiers. He was almost sorry when Ruales passed, shouting for everyone to get back on the trucks. Max and Washington looked very sad as they shook hands with the children, gave them oranges, and then waved goodbye. *They look so disappointed.*

Max guessed this might be as much of a circus as these country kids would ever see. They must have scurried down from scattered huts in the mountains to see things strange and wonderful, soldiers on their road, and clowns.

"That wasn't bad, Max," allowed Harvey when they were out of earshot. "You may make a Foreign Service Officer yet."

"Not until I learn to play a musical instrument."

As he rubbed the grease off his face, he looked at the mountains on both sides of the road. He couldn't imagine how they could get anywhere walking through such country, or if he'd even be able to try for long: some of his falls had been all too realistic, and his back hurt. But they must get through, and quickly; he'd seen soldiers do more than laugh, had seen them loading trucks and rolling up tents. And Guzmán's caravan was pointed uphill, in their direction.

Feeling ashamed that he wasn't more enthusiastic, Max reminded himself that he'd been fantasizing adventure and roles for years. *On the freighter down here, I saw myself as an intrepid agent, or a jungle explorer or guerrilla fighter. But those were just daydreams. After seeing Gandig, I imagined myself a businessman. With Harvey, I even imagined playing a banjo. Then*

Espejo made me see myself as an Ambassador. But a real commando? How can klutz Max Lacey get there in real time, place a real bomb, and stop a real war?

"Harvey," he asked, "want to blow up a bridge?"

"Can't." Harvey pulled a piece of paper from his shirt pocket. "Bolívar gave me this pass here, that says Harvey Tyrone can accompany one circus to San Genesio. I've got to arrive with it. Anyway," he smiled, slapping Max on the back, "it's your turn. I did my bridge in Spain." He shook his head at the memory. "Funny the way things work out. Story about that job got around until Hemingway got hold of it and created this big deal about a general offensive. There wasn't any offensive, but old Papa, he knew how to dress up a story. And to tell the truth, I wasn't that proud of it later, not after I saw the Republicans were at least as bad as Franco. I got out. Well." He finished with a shrug.

For the first time Max saw something like regret on Harvey's lined face. Tyrone shook his head, smiled wanly, and began again to pluck his balalaika. "Didn't have any Maria with me, either. Wish I had!"

I have, Max thought, imagining Rosa with close-cropped hair as Ingrid Bergman had worn it. Max Lacey, bureaucrat, couldn't do this job. But he could imagine himself as someone who could. Espejo inspired a whole country to believe in what they could imagine, even if they had to imagine they believed it. Max would act and see and hear in imagination until he had done this thing.

Chapter Twenty-Nine: Nature Takes Its Course

Max stood with the others and watched the circus trucks disappear slowly around a curve in the road. Max, Rosa, and Washington quickly changed out their circus costumes for olive-drab military fatigues under a steep rise in the terrain that ran for several hundred meters back toward La Subida. They had backpacks heavy with equipment and food, and they were armed. Washington, Manuel, and Pancho all looked awkward holding their old submachine guns, while Max almost tilted from the weight of the .45 pistol at his side. Only César liked his weapon, a bolt-action Springfield 30.06. Captain Hernández had told him that it was still the best rifle, the most accurate for long distances, a weapon once treated with almost holy regard by the *Norteamericano* Marines. César polished it with his shirttail.

Max hoisted his backpack and looked again at the curve in the road. The circus trucks were gone. César led them away from the road about three o'clock in the afternoon.

The walking began easily, except for the thin air at seven thousand feet above sea level. "It not too hard, Patrón," César said, "except for the climb on the other side. If God wishes, we will be there before it is dark. There are two huts that the pickers use in the season, a large one and a small one. There we can sleep until the morning."

César led them south over rocky ground, through a mixture of muddy clearings and patches of forest. Once they crossed a wide lava field where nothing grew and footing was iffy. Now and then they would pick up a visible trail; it would soon vanish, but César seemed to know every foot of the way. Max's pack bothered him, then didn't, then bothered him again. After about an hour, César turned to the right and they began to climb down.

Now the trail grew steep, rocky and loose. Max held Rosa's hand to help her where the trail was steepest, and when the trail was easy again he did not let it go. After a long descent, the bottom of the gorge came into sight. César advised them that the Rio Diablo crossing, when it came, would not be difficult in this season.

They descended in silence now, except for short warnings about loose rocks or long steps. The last part of the trail was the steepest, and was where the backpacks caused the most trouble. When they had to use their hands to climb down, the packs would shift and pull them forward. Max, whose pack held the dynamite, was especially nervous. There was much relief when everyone reached the bottom of the gorge.

Max stopped and told the others to rest by the river, have something to eat, and drink the cool water. All were already tired except César and Pancho, with the hardest part yet to do. Max's back was killing him, but he said nothing. When it was time to cross the river and move on, Max carefully handed the pack with the dynamite across to Washington. "We can't let this get wet," he cautioned.

"Not to worry. We can dry it over the fire," said Manuel. Everyone laughed, and so did Manuel after thinking about it for a moment.

Their path now led uphill through some jungle toward a ridge. In places, the jungle was dense enough for vines and branches to slap their faces. The air was full of mosquitoes. The grass moved on both sides of them as crickets jumped away. Max asked César if there were snakes here. César laughed and said they had only good snakes.

"How are they good?"

"Here they are the one-minute snake. Very painless!"

Everyone laughed; they laughed to hide their fear.

Each time they stopped to rest, it grew more difficult to resume the climb. Only César and his son Pancho did not seem to tire. All agreed at last that it was better not to rest so often, but to go slowly and steadily up the mountain.

"Oh, Max, I'm so tired I think I'll die!" said Rosa the last time they stopped.

"I know, my little rabbit, but we must be brave and do this thing."

"Your what?"

Max didn't answer.

At last, César stopped on a hump on the ridge and announced they need climb no more. There below them lay the bridge, just where Harvey had said and as César had confirmed. They looked around for any sign of Centralista soldiers, but the bridge seemed deserted.

Looking down, Max felt queasy as he focused on the bridge high above the river at a point where the gorge was narrow and steep. It didn't look quite like Hernández's drawing. The supports, the ones leaning out from the sides of the gorge, were different. So where was he to put the explosives?

As they climbed down to a small clearing almost directly above the bridge, he found the mountains felt both strange and familiar. The pine trees and their scent were familiar from American forests, as was the soft carpet of needles. But these mountains also had trees he did not recognize, except for the eucalyptus and the banana trees. He hadn't thought bananas could grow at this altitude, but this was a different sort of banana tree. Above them, he could see peaks where nothing grew.

In the clearing were two huts that the banana pickers sometimes used. "There is where we will sleep," said César, and Max nodded. Both huts stood a meter above the ground on bamboo legs. Max put his pack in the smaller hut and then went to study the bridge, taking Captain Hernández's drawing with him. Washington, Manuel, and César joined him, while Pancho stayed to help Rosa make dinner.

A nearby rock outcropping afforded Max and the others a fine vantage from which to study the bridge more closely. *This feels so, so weird. This bridge looks so peaceful, and I'm going to blow it up. All those birds over there are going to get the shock of their lives. I hope it doesn't kill them.*

"That bridge is nothing," scoffed Washington. "Look! It's like matchsticks! We'll blow it up easily."

"No, Don Washington," said César. "The bridge is very strong. I watched the foreigners who spoke strangely come with machines and build it. With iron they fastened the beams and supports. It is a serious thing, this bridge."

"It is a matter of placing the charges correctly," said Max. "It does not matter how strong the bridge is. If we place the charges correctly then the bridge will fall."

Manuel looked troubled. "I do not like this thing. The Director—*perdón*, I correct myself—the *Señor Comandante* will have noticed that the bridge is very high. How will he place the charges without falling into the great abyss that is below?"

"By climbing very carefully."

"Would it not be safer," Manuel continued, "to place the dynamite on top of the bridge? Is it not as well to blow the bridge down as up?"

You're a fool born of fools. "No, Manuel. In that way the bridge will not fall." But where was he to place the charges? In Captain Hernández's drawing, the bridge's supports formed one long inverted V. He had been told to place the dynamite at the apex of that V. In the actual bridge before him, a very large beam ran directly across the chasm, and on top of this beam were three small inverted Vs that supported the roadway. Where should he place the dynamite? At the base of the beam, where it was anchored in the earth? He studied each of the supports and tried to imagine which of them held the most weight, to visualize the absence of each in turn and the effects that must follow. *I'll place the charge where the beam comes out of the ground. If that's gone, the bridge can't hold up. But how do I climb down there?* Before he could study his route carefully, the sun dropped another degree and the shadows crept up to the bridge.

"I will put it on this side, under the main beam," Max announced. "Washington, tomorrow you cross the bridge to watch for Centralistas and warn us if they come. I'll summon you back before I set off the charges. Manuel, please stay close. César, I would like you to cover us from here with your rifle, in case the Centralistas show up."

The idea of Centralistas caused him to study the east end of the bridge more carefully. They had seen no one so far and that seemed odd. Surely General Guzman would have sent some guards to hold the bridge until he was ready to cross it? Indeed, a few seconds of intense study revealed two figures in green sitting, barely visible, in the shadows a few feet back from the bridge on the other side. So far as Max could read their body language, they looked bored. There had to be more soldiers farther back. He pointed the two out to Washington and the others as Rosa joined them.

"What can we do now?" asked Rosa in a despairing voice.

Max was probably not the only one with an answer: *shoot them.* But he wouldn't say it and didn't even want to think it.

"We'll place the bomb very early in the morning. I won't let them see me, and we'll warn them before we set it off. Washington, instead of crossing the bridge, stay here. If they do see me, all of you fire your guns – into the air or into the river – so they will stay under cover until I finish."

"I wish we could do it now and get it over with," said Washington.

"So do I. But Captain Hernandez was right: it will be dangerous enough in daylight. Now let's go eat and rest, to be ready early in the morning to do what we must."

The others looked at him curiously, wondering about his strange way of talking. *Of course they wonder. But there's no time to explain why I need to be Robert Jordan. They'll just have to live with it.*

They went back and sat around the fire that Pancho had made in front of the huts. Rosa brought Max a plate of meat and something that had arrived in a can. It was hot from the fire and Max was hungry. "It is very good, Rosa," he said.

"I am glad," she said, and looked at him with soft eyes. "Would you like some wine?"

"Yes, I would like wine."

She took her plate and the wine bottle and sat beside him. "The bridge—you can blow it up?"

Max was chewing on a bite of meat. Manuel answered first: "With the help of God and all the saints! But it's very dangerous, because it is so high up. I do not like this thing, with your permission, Don Max. What if the Centralistas start shooting while you are hanging there?" He shook his head and took a long drink of wine from the bottle beside him.

"It's not so bad," said Max.

"I am afraid for you," said Rosa, with feeling.

Max shrugged. "It will be as it will be." It was very dark now, and cold. Beyond the fire they could see nothing. There was little post-dinner conversation. Soon Manuel went to the big hut to sleep, then Washington, César and Pancho joined him.

"I will clean up these things," said Rosa. Max nodded and went to the little hut where he had left his backpack. There was another pack there. He flipped on his flashlight and arranged the two sleeping bags. Soon he heard Rosa's voice by the door. "Max?"

"Here," he said, taking her hand to guide her into the hut. They sat together on the sleeping bags.

"Max," said Rosa softly, "this may be our last night—our only night."

"Yes," he agreed, swallowing hard.

She leaned over and put her head on his chest. "You must promise me you'll be careful."

"Yes, very careful," he answered, "and very gentle." He began to nibble her earlobe. She giggled at first, and then sighed.

"And we will go to Father Pedro when this thing is over, and he will say the blessing over us. Many do it that way. Some bring their children."

"Of course." Vague memories of some theology class spun through his head, something about a man and a woman on a desert island with no priest who nonetheless truly marry each other. He continued to nibble. She moaned softly and lay down on the sleeping bags, pulling Max after her. He began to kiss her neck, and she kissed him in turn as if she were drinking after long thirst. Slowly and gently his hand began to seek the buttons of her shirt.

Suddenly she stiffened and said, "Max! I feel something!"

"That is well, my little one."

"The earth—I feel it moving!"

"Already?"

"There! Don't you feel it?"

"Oh. Oh! Oh my God!"

The hut swayed drunkenly. Pieces of thatch fell on them from the roof. The bamboo supports squeaked as they rubbed together, and behind that cacophony came a dull ominous roaring crescendo that filled the hut and the whole world. The earth moved, and moved again.

Max dragged Rosa out of the hut. He'd always heard you were supposed to get under a doorframe or a table during an earthquake, but the flimsy structure was already tipping and there was no table. They stumbled through the darkness as Washington and the others joined them, tripping through the shuddering night and cursing one another for forgetting the flashlight. Then the huts collapsed, first one and then the other, and the little company gathered around the embers of the fire. It wasn't the chill that drew them, but rather that ancient instinct to join together near fire in time of fear and darkness.

No one was hurt, at least. *Which is fine, but goddamn the luck! Of all times! What damn thing can go wrong next?* As if in answer, they heard a new sound. A loud shrieking and splintering of wood echoed through the gorge, followed by a dull crash and then another, two more, another, and finally a terminal collapsing roar and roiling of water.

"The bridge!" cried César. "The bridge has fallen!"

Max knew it was so, knew he had been cheated. He thought, *I obscenity in the milk of the earthquake,* but it didn't help. The moment was past. He would have to seek another. Only in the light of day would he feel relief and gratitude.

Chapter Thirty: The Burden of Command

It was a chilly night, even with sleeping bags salvaged in various states of repair and arranged around the fire. In the early morning light, they went shivering to the edge of the canyon to look down at the scattered timbers and chunks of asphalt that had been a bridge. Unmoved, the Rio Diablo continued its course over and around the wreckage.

"The bridge is well and truly destroyed," said Manuel.

You got that right. Wish I could take credit for it.

Everyone but Max was jubilant, exchanging congratulations. They had to know, as did he, that the bridge would have fallen in the earthquake even if they had never left Alcalá.

But do they?

Maybe the fatalism that allows them to accept so many things also lets them take credit for the earthquake. If what must be must be, then maybe we had to hike up into the mountains, and if we hadn't done what fate wanted us to do, maybe the tectonic plates deep in the earth wouldn't have done their job either. The more he thought about it, the more appealing this idea became. He felt himself halfway to belief. After a few more years in this country he would believe it entirely.

Rosa leaned more heavily against him and shivered. "It's cold! I've never been so cold!"

It made sense. She had spent her whole life on the coast, where neither the temperature nor the humidity ever dropped much. He actually welcomed the chill; it *should* be cold on the last day of October, and he was glad something agreed with his old notion of normal. Manuel was not glad at all as he hugged himself to stay warm. "Well, we'll soon be back in Alcalá," Max assured them, then immediately wondered how he would keep that promise. They had passed the *Centralista* line coming here. How would they go back through it without benefit of a circus?

Washington had the same thought. "What do we do now?"

"Ask César if there is another way to the coast, I guess. And why didn't we think about this before? I mean, it was our damn plan to be here this morning with the bridge gone!"

Washington's look said, *You're in charge. Why didn't you think of it?*

Max knew he was right. The commander should indeed have thought of it, should have remembered that lesson on tactics back in ROTC. The instructor had gone on and on about identifying possible retreat routes, or the way to your next checkpoint. *Damn.*

He walked over to ask César. "Yes, there are other routes to the coast. The problem is that they are almost impossible." They could follow the Rio Diablo to the coast, but there were gorges with sheer cliffs on each side that would oblige them either to try walking in the river itself, with all its rapids and boulders, or spend days climbing up and around the narrow places. "Or we could go overland," César continued, "but there are few trails. We would have to cut our way through the jungle in many places. Many days."

"Whatever we do, we have to eat first," Rosa cut in. "I'm hungry."

They returned to the hut wreckage, built up the fire again, and sat close to it as they ate bread and bananas and eggs, of all things, which Rosa had somehow carried here intact in her backpack. They drank coffee and discussed their options. It seemed they had to choose between impossible routes for which they were not equipped, or to return the way they had come and hope that the San Genesio troops had gone away because there was no longer a bridge for them to cross. Except, they had apparently come there before they knew about the bridge, just to guard the highway. So they were probably still there, Max's little group would have to slip carefully around them somehow. His instinct was to decide democratically, but they all looked at him, expecting a decision.

"Back the way we came," he said.

The return trip was the mirror image of their hike the day before: back to the steep slope and down, across the river, up the other side to walk north over clearings and through forests and rocky ground. But now the air was cool and Max might have enjoyed the trek were it not for the nagging feelings of failure and futility and uncertainty about the dangers that might lie ahead. *Maybe the soldiers will be gone, for some reason I haven't thought of? Maybe we should take it slow, to give Guzmán more time to pack up and leave.* His swirling thoughts now served up a mocking voice: *a couple weeks should do it.*

He and his little squad made even better time than he had expected. Midway through a stand of eucalyptus trees, César turned and put his finger to his lips, then came back to Max and spoke in a low voice.

"We're almost there. Just a few hundred meters." He pointed ahead and to the right, toward the place where the circus trucks had stopped to let them off the day before. "You must stay here and remain quiet while we see if there are soldiers there. We should be back soon."

"Right," Max agreed. Then he thought about it. "There shouldn't be any. They were all camped farther down the road. But, anyway, you and Pancho could walk right out there. You live here, so if they are there you can just tell them you were doing... whatever you do."

"Looking for a lost goat!" César caught on quickly.

"But then..." Max frowned. If there were no soldiers, César could just come back and tell them. But if they did encounter troops, it would arouse suspicion if the two *campesinos* returned the way they had come. He shared his doubt with the others who were now gathered around.

"If they don't come back," Washington shrugged, then we'll know the troops are still there and just stay out of sight."

"For how long? And then what?" Rosa asked. "Don't we need César and Pancho to show us a way around them?"

She and Washington and Manuel and the two *campesinos* stared at the ground and then looked at Max, who sighed. *Everything has to be so damned complicated!* He thought it through again. *If there are no soldiers, the six of us could just walk down the road or, rather, across it and into the forest on the other side. No. Wait. There's a cliff there, or something. We'll have to walk down the road some distance. But if there are soldiers, and César doesn't return, we'd be guessing and might wander in the woods for days, or blunder out into an army camp.* He finally decided: "Right. Forget what I said about just walking out there. Sneak up there and peek, then let us know."

César smiled and nodded patiently as Max shut his eyes and wondered at his own idiocy. *Brilliant. El Comandante has just countermanded his own dumb idea and opted to do the sensible thing that campesino Cesar had first proposed.*

He felt a wave of sympathy for all the captains and colonels and generals who have to make decisions about such things when they never have enough information and when their ignorance or stupidity works against them. And their vanity. *Now I'm worrying about my image rather than about the problem.*

As César and Pancho disappeared into the woods, Max and the others sat down and broke out snacks. They needed cheering up.

"With any luck at all," Max assured them, "we'll be able to just walk through the woods to meet up with General Figueroa and the rest. Maybe they'll have whatever part they need for the helicopter and we'll fly home, be there almost by lunch time— maybe before President Espejo gets there by truck!"

"Unless they all decided to leave in trucks," Washington cautioned.

"Why would they do that?"

Washington shrugged.

As it happened, they had barely finished eating before Pancho burst through the trees smiling. "The road is clear! No soldiers anywhere! My father says for you to come now."

The company tied shut their packs and set off. César awaited them some 200 feet from the highway, mostly concealed by the woods. "I saw no one," César advised in the same low voice he had used before, "but you never know. It is better not to make noise, and not to walk on the road but beside it, in the woods, until we reach a point where we can get to the trees on the other side."

I knew that, Max thought. He remembered that much from ROTC. He nodded agreement and started walking toward the highway until he was within fifty feet of the pavement, and then staying parallel to it.

"Everything's turned out wonderfully!" Rosa gushed as Max pushed aside some branches that barred their way.

"Ssshh!" he whispered. "Let's not mess it up now."

It was not always possible to maintain an exact distance from the highway, but César guided them well. "The road doesn't move," he said, and so it proved. But then they came to a deep stream that ran as far as he could see in both directions. César shrugged. "It gets even deeper and faster that way," he said, pointing north. "There's a big culvert at the highway." He let Max draw the inevitable conclusion: they had to cross the road.

Following the stream south to the highway, Max stopped to have a good look. No one was around as far as he could see, but he couldn't see very far to the east. Perhaps two hundred feet from his position, the road curved out of sight. Still, it would take only a few seconds to run to the highway and over the culvert, past the high bank that ran along the highway, and back into the woods. Nothing to it. And he felt something like satisfaction that there was now some slight risk, as if confronting any danger at all would restore the honor that the earthquake had stolen from him.

"One at a time," he told the others, "but quickly."

"Why one at a time?" asked Washington.

So one grenade doesn't get us all? "Because if anyone's watching, they are less likely to spot one person than six in a group."

"It seems kind of silly," Rosa complained, peering up and down the road herself. "There's nothing there."

"There's nothing you see," Max amended. "Nothing now."

"*Bueno,*" she shrugged, and got in line behind César and

Washington.

Max peeked out again. Seeing nothing he pointed to César and said, "Go!"

The faithful guide was an incredible walker, but evidently didn't do much running. His short-legged lope seemed painfully slow as he moved down the road and disappeared into the woods behind the bank. Washington did better without waiting to be told, following César into obscurity in perhaps twenty seconds. After looking again, Max waved for Rosa to follow. She was not as fast as she was graceful. Pancho proved the fastest, disappearing in the time it took Max to study the road east and west.

"The Señor Director is sure it is safe?" asked Manuel.

"The Señor Director is sure," Max answered, studying the road. "Go!"

Manuel was the slowest of all, pushing his usual shuffle into an ungraceful trot. He stumbled halfway across and his backpack went flying; he ignored it and scurried on. When he was out of sight, Max looked again and then started running, a smile forming on his lips as he imagined a new requirement for joining the Foreign Service: a 40-yard dash of no more than six or seven seconds

Do army trucks have a distinctive growl? That sound reminds me of my days at Summer ROTC. Could be just a farmer's truck, he told himself as he tried to run even faster. The noise grew louder and he turned his head to look. The olive-green color was unmistakable. And in looking back, he had failed to see Manuel's backpack. He now tripped over it, banging the side of his head against the pavement. He tried to get up, grew dizzy, began to run, then lost his balance. Brakes squealed beside him, then soldiers with guns helped him to his feet.

They seemed to spin slightly as he looked at their dark faces very like those of César and Pancho, adding to Max's sense of unreality. *This can't be happening! Manuel, you dolt. Thank God Rosa and the rest got away. But now I'm a prisoner? Me?*

As they helped him into the back of the truck he felt terribly lonely, his friends off there in the woods somewhere watching, but able to do nothing as he was taken off to...what? It was rather exciting in a horrible way, but he'd rather be bored. Still, it could have been worse. *At least I didn't have a horse fall on me.*

Chapter Thirty-One: They Shoot Spies, Don't They?

Max's claims of diplomatic immunity fell not so much on deaf ears as on informed ones. General Guzmán laughingly advised Max that there was no Republic of Nueva Alcalá, and no U.S. Ambassador to this fictitious country. Nor was he impressed by the alternate claim, that Max Lacey was the Branch Cultural Affairs Officer of the U.S. Embassy to Engañada.

"I'm advised that the Embassy has cancelled your assignment, and asked that we look for you and return you to them. You may take some satisfaction," he smiled, "that by falling so conveniently into our hands you have contributed to U.S.-Engañadan relations."

Max looked through the flaps of the tent at the same soldiers and jeeps and crates that he had seen the day before. It was little satisfaction to know that he had surmised rightly, that Guzman hadn't left but stayed in place for the reasons that brought him there in the first place. He must have learned from the guards at the bridge that the bridge had fallen in the earthquake, but that changed nothing except to let the soldiers stand down from their preparations to move.

Now Max wished he could appreciate Guzmán's sarcasm, or even join in it by predicting that there would be no award for Max Lacey for improving relations. But that he couldn't do.

"Of course, we could shoot you," Guzmán added thoughtfully. "Since your diplomatic assignment was cancelled, you're now just a tourist. Well, not even that. You have no tourist visa. You're in the country illegally, and engaging in subversion. The laws of war permit summary execution of spies and subversives."

"But," Max objected, "that would not be...Engañadan!"

315

"True, we haven't shot each other much for a long time. But that's because any Engañadan we took prisoner would turn out to be related to ourselves, or to someone we knew, or to the President's brother-in-law. Maybe this country wouldn't be so screwed up if we had. Anyway, you have no family here."

"But I have, well, a fiancée, sort of. In a way."

"Don't we all?" the general laughed. "They don't count."

Surely he's teasing. But I hope Webster didn't tell them 'dead or alive.'

"And just were you doing, walking around up here in the mountains?" Guzmán studied his prisoner's face.

Max tried to look innocent as he explained that he had come on an inspection tour with President Espejo, taken a hike to enjoy the scenery and gotten lost. He didn't expect anyone to believe it, but better to be known as a liar than to tell them he had planned to blow up a bridge and ruin their plans.

"It's a beautiful country," he shrugged. "One should take advantage of any chance to see more of it."

"I see. And do you always carry explosives on your nature hikes?"

Max began to mumble something about not knowing what was in the pack someone loaned him, but the General cut him off.

"Well, well. I think the earthquake saved you some trouble. But why would they send you?"

Max fidgeted and finally shook his head, saying, "Me? Explosives? These are very confusing times."

Guzmán waved his hand and stood up. "Indeed they are. But I've no time now to sort out your part in all this. My orders are to send you on at once. Now you'll have the chance to see the capital of our beautiful country. Or have you already been to San Genesio?"

"Briefly. I didn't get to see much."

"A pity. You won't see much from an embassy window." He studied Max again. "Seems like I've seen you somewhere. Were you at the Embassy reception last month?"

Max started to deny it and then checked himself. "Yes." It wasn't even a lie. He had been at an Embassy reception, even if it was informal, unofficial, and not the event the general remembered. He was happy to let the General believe he'd seen him there, lest he ponder it until he remembered a clown who passed through his lines with Harvey Tyrone. Max wouldn't want to hurt Harvey's relations with a compadre or, worse, see the general get mad for having been tricked.

"Ah," Guzmán sighed, happy to have made a connection. "Well, have a good trip, and give my best to Harvey Tyrone when you see him."

Guzmán walked out, leaving Max to speculate that maybe the tectonic plates had been watching out for him. Had they blown the bridge up as planned, Guzman might have been too angry to turn the bomber over to anyone. *Of course, in that case, there'd have been no explosives in my pack . . .*

A tall young lieutenant entered the tent, introduced himself as Tomás Gonzales Espejo, and announced in formal Spanish, "I have the honor to deliver you to the U.S. Embassy. Please come with me."

As he followed the formidable lieutenant, who looked as though he lifted weights while running marathons, Max thought that if you are going to be taken prisoner or even executed, you should hope it will be at the hands of someone who speaks the old formal Spanish like this fellow. He couldn't imagine an American cop telling a suspect that he had now the honor to read him his Miranda rights. On the other hand, the American cop would put you in the back of a sedan. Lt. Gonzales led him to a two-ton truck and directed him to take a seat between two infantrymen on one of the wooden benches in the back, while Gonzales himself got into the cab with the driver.

It was a bumpy, noisy ride, but nonetheless the soldiers began trying to converse with Max. They kept their voices down; probably they had been told not to speak with him, but couldn't resist. In a way they almost followed orders, for Max had to listen carefully to understand them over the noise of the truck and through an accent he couldn't place. He inferred they were drafted from small towns somewhere in the mountains. They didn't sound

Alcalán, and they look more Indian than coastal people. Short, maybe 5'5" on average, with black hair and brown eyes. Most Engañadans had native blood in their veins, usually mixed with that of Europeans or, especially on the coast, of Africans. He caught their names, at least: Bernardo Gómez Echeverría and José Pacheco Ruiz. They understood "Max" easily enough, but had more trouble with the last name.

"Lah-sí?" repeated Bernardo.

Close enough. Max nodded.

"You are a foreigner." José put it as half statement, half question.

"Yes."

"From...Brazil?"

"No, *estadounidense.*" Max supposed these two had come from a world as closed in upon itself as Rosa's village of San Andrés, and had perhaps never spoken with a foreigner.

"Ah, *los Estados Unidos,*" repeated José, as if it rang a bell.

Bernardo asked, "What did you do that you're in trouble?"

Max sat back. There was no way he could make it clear over the truck's noise, especially in a Spanish that probably sounded confusing and strange to them. He shrugged and said, "*Complicado.*" To their expectant gazes he responded with a small clarification yet a vast understatement: "*un malentendido.*" That satisfied them. They knew about misunderstandings.

After two hours they stopped climbing and headed north up a long valley. Not long after, the truck stopped at a collection of huts beside the road. Everyone jumped down to stretch legs, visit the trees and buy a cup of tea or a piece of pork from the vendors who stood before the huts. The pork smelled wonderful, and Max paid a few *honores* for a large piece wrapped in a leaf of some kind. It proved as delicious as the aroma had promised. As he ate he looked around at the mountains to the east and west, the two Andean *cordilleras* that formed the valley where the Spanish had established their capital centuries before. Looking up the road he guessed they still had a long way to go, for he saw no sign of anything that looked like suburbs. He didn't know whether or not to be happy about that; he was sick and tired of bouncing on that wooden bench, but in no hurry to meet Ambassador Webster and Jethro Jackson.

As he climbed back on the truck, Max remembered the proverb about spilt milk. But intrepid agents don't cry anyway.

Some thirty minutes later they began to pass small houses, more like huts of stones and mud, then some little stores and a gas station. The truck slowed as traffic grew denser. A small truck came up behind them, or sort of a truck: a three-wheeled Vespa scooter with a small bed in the back. As it passed them, Max noticed large milk cans in the bed.

He didn't think they were close to the Embassy yet. It all looked unfamiliar. The airport lay north of the city, and his path then had led through relatively prosperous middle-class neighborhoods. Entering from the south was very different, with mules hauling firewood or sacks of flour, passing humble homes with little gardens and barefoot children playing beside the street. Just as many children were working in gardens, feeding pigs, or busy with other chores. The midday sun made it stifling hot in the truck, all the more so due to the altitude and thin air. He welcomed the clouds now coming in from the west. Someone had related the old saying that in San Genesio they had four seasons every day: spring in the morning as the sun began to warm the cold mountain air; summer at noon as it beat directly down, followed by fall rain in the afternoon and winter at night. He glanced at his watch, saw it was almost two o'clock.

It seemed about the right hour to arrive. Afternoon was the time for crucifixions.

Chapter Thirty-Two: *Semper Fi*

Rain began to fall as the truck turned onto a major avenue with upscale apartments and stores on either side. They went past a park and the conservatory, and then the upper half of the Embassy came in view. A high adobe wall hid the bottom half. The truck stopped in front of the gate.

Max heard the cab door open and close, and then Lt. Gonzales said something Max couldn't catch to someone he couldn't see. He guessed Gonzales was telling one of the Engañadan guards at the gate that he had a delivery. A radio squawked, and within thirty seconds two Marines in dress blues appeared at the back of the truck and peered in at him. The taller of the two asked, "You Lacey, Max?"

"That's me." Max reflected that he was sort of a prisoner of war and need provide only his name, rank, and serial number. He had a Foreign Service rank, FS-5, but no serial number unless he used the one from ROTC that he didn't remember. Maybe his Social Security number would serve.

"Stand by one second, sir."

Max felt a touch of sympathy with the young Marine. He didn't remember his name, though he was sure he had greeted him on his previous visit, and he couldn't make out the name tag from the back of the truck. But the kid was trying hard to put a firm Marine Corps front on his uncertainty. He had an Embassy officer here, arriving as a prisoner. So what's the drill? Of course he had to kick it up the chain of command.

Three links in that chain arrived next: Jethro Jackson and two crew-cut guys in dark suits. Max didn't recognize one of them, but thought the other was the Security Officer he had met on his visit. Guarini? Whoever it was spoke quickly to Lt. Gonzales and the Marines, while the other dark suit and the Public Affairs officer turned toward Lacey.

"Well, well, well, what have we got here?" Jackson almost drooled as he peered into the truck. "Damn if it ain't the U.S. Ambassador to Alcalá!" *My ill wind has blown some satisfaction to Jethro. I knew it would.*

"Get out of the truck, Sir," said the shorter Marine. Max sighed and pushed himself up from the seat, shook hands with José and Bernardo, and walked to the back and climbed down. He could read the insignia and name tags now: the tall one, Sgt. Breen, got right next to him on his left and Cpl. Mendez, the shorter one, on his right. Without putting a hand on him, they made it clear he wasn't going anywhere until they took him there. They stood while the dark suit signed something on a clipboard, which he handed back to Gonzales.

People had come out of the embassy building and now stood on the steps or in the parking lot watching it all, as did passers-by. Max found himself looking at one woman who resembled Rosa. She looked back and shrugged as if to ask, "What's going on?" He shrugged in reply, just as a young man with a big video camera pushed his way past her and pointed the camera at him and the Marines and the Americans standing around. Max imagined himself on the evening news, in the tradition of suspects being hauled into jail. But he wasn't hauled. The man in the dark suit gestured and Breen put a hand on Max's arm, directing him toward the front door. He nodded at people he knew: Mike Black the Press Officer, who looked worriedly at the TV camera; Assistant Cultural Attaché Barbara Deedy, who stared at him with a mixture of pity, disbelief, and disgust, and Jerry the Consular guy with whom he had played charades, whose face looked thoughtful.

I suppose Jerry is wondering what consular services he's supposed to provide to Americans jailed in the American Embassy.

He himself wondered where Harvey Tyrone might be. It would be nice if he were to ride his Harley to the rescue, or just convince these guys it's all a misunderstanding. *I wouldn't count on it. Not all the bullshitting back-slapping camaraderie in the world can help me now.*

Max noticed something strange: just to the side of the Embassy entrance sat several large cardboard boxes. A couple were open with the contents, costumes, draped here and there as if someone had opened the boxes to check. One costume looked like that of a witch; another had a white skeleton on a black background. "What's that?" he asked Cpl. Mendez. The Marine thought a second, then answered, "For the Halloween party tonight." Seeing Max's puzzled look he added, "They don't do trick-or-treat here, so they get this on for the Embassy kids."

Max nodded. The day before All Saints, to be followed by the Day of the Dead. He thought his timing perfect. He considered asking for a lawyer. *If this is a little piece of America, then surely Miranda rights and the Constitution and all that apply.*

Yes, but 'all that' includes obscure legalities and paperwork to document all the procedures that produced unending delays. He saw no way he could get out on bail, not from here. *Maybe when I'm back in the U.S. But I don't want to go back there. I'm guilty as hell of something. Still, if I end up under the American legal system, a clever lawyer could get me off, though that could take a very long time.*

This embassy felt strangely foreign to him. His sojourn in Engañada hasn't been very long, but it's been intense, and changed his sense of how things work. Outside this building, someone could make a phone call to a relative or compadre and get him set free while the case sank into a quagmire of a legal process even more arcane and complex than the American justice system.

In the Embassy lobby, a portrait of President Ford looked down on him. Ford had always seemed to Max like just one hell of a nice guy. Was a pardon too much to ask? Nixon got one. Besides, Max and Ford had something in common: circumstances had elevated both of them unexpectedly to high office, to which they devoted their best efforts.

He stumbled as they started up the stairs, past a placard that announced "Embassy Halloween Party 7 – 9 PM!" Strong hands on either arm pulled him upright as they followed Dark Suit up another flight of stairs and down a hall to an office marked "Legal Attaché." The Marines walked him in, set him down in a chair in the middle of the room pointed out by the man in the suit, and left when he said, "Thank you, Sergeant. I'll take it from here," and sat down at the desk.

Jethro Jackson had followed them in and now stood nodding as if to say, "I knew it would end like this. Knew it all along." What he actually said managed to surprise Max: "You know your monthly report is more than a month late?"

For a moment Max felt like crying. Oh, to be back in the day when all he had to worry about were pointless monthly reports and pointed financial problems and broken doors and flaky air conditioning! He would gladly sit down now and write reports for the past six months, and the next six months too, if it would make all this go away. He got control of himself and said, "Sorry, Jethro. Been busy. And I don't think the mail's running anyway."

"Oh, well, you don't have to worry." Jethro's mock-comforting tone was just right.

"Jethro," said Suit, "why don't you go back to your office? I've got some questions for Mr. Lacey here."

"Oh. Well, so do I–"

"Jethro, I'll handle it."

Max liked the way the man's cold authoritative voice silenced Jackson. He didn't like the knowledge that it would soon be turned on him.

Jackson reluctantly went out the door after making way for a young woman who walked over to a sofa and sat down. Dark Suit settled behind a desk and glanced over some papers.

"All right," he sighed. "You're Max Lacey, Branch Cultural Affairs Officer, right?"

"Right."

"And you've been in-country for six months, right?"

"A bit more. Who are you? We didn't meet when I was up here before."

"Bernard Bettaluci, Legal Attaché. This is the Assistant LegAtt, Maureen Kelly."

"Good to meet you," Max said, then smiled with the other two at the grotesque lie.

"You want to explain what's been going on?" Bettaluci asked.

Max remembered every TV cop show he'd ever seen. *Don't say nuttin'!* "First," he said, "am I under arrest?"

"Under arrest?" The man repeated it like he'd never heard the phrase before. "Why would you think you're under arrest?"

Max told himself he was too smart to fall for that. He wasn't going to make the guy's job easier for him by declaring, *Because I passed myself off as a U.S. Ambassador and disobeyed orders and undermined U.S. foreign policy and...didn't get my monthly report in on time.* Instead he said, "I sort of felt like I was when the Marines trundled me in here."

"We're not a police force," the LegAtt said easily. "I have no power to arrest anyone in this country, do I, Maureen?"

"No, you sure don't." She said it like it was funny.

"But we do have some legal issues to sort through. I'll have to send a report on them. Other people will decide the next steps, if any. There's a place on the report where we indicate whether a witness was cooperative or uncooperative." He let this sink in for a minute.

Before it could, the door burst open and Ambassador Webster strode in, followed by two others. Max recognized one of them as Political Officer Terry Gaines. He didn't know the guy in the Army colonel's uniform.

"Well, Lacey. Looks like your stupid little game is up." Ambassador Webster's satisfaction was cold and clinical, like a surgeon who had determined that amputation was the only option.

Having nothing useful to say, Max said nothing.

"Now before we put you on a plane to Leavenworth, we want to know just what sort of scam you arranged with Espejo and what he's trying to do here. And you're going to tell Bob what you know about their military units." He sat on the sofa next to Kelly and crossed one leg over the other without taking his cold blue eyes off Lacey.

All sorts of things ran through Max's head, about whether anything he said could be used against him, if it would make any difference, and that the Ambassador shouldn't be worrying about Max Lacey when the fate of Alcalá and Engañada hung in the balance. *Might as well answer the man's question.*

"Seems to me like what Espejo wants to do has been pretty clear from the start," he began. "Save the country."

Following the Ambassador's snort, Max recounted what Espejo had told him about forcing President Madera to return to Engañadan-style democracy by declaring Alcalá's independence, though of course Espejo had no wish to break up the country. He certainly didn't want a civil war, but only a military stalemate as a prelude to negotiations. All that stuff about the U.S. recognizing Alcalá was meant only to confuse Madera enough so he'd hesitate to send in the army before Alcalá could block all the roads and create a standoff.

"How could you ever imagine such a hare-brained scheme would work?" asked Webster.

Max was tempted to say that if the Ambassador got out of the capital more often, and saw another Engañada, he'd understand the power of imagination. Terry Gaines interrupted the temptation. "Looks like it did work. My contacts didn't know what the hell was going on and were afraid to push for any action. From what they say now, I'd guess the government will try to settle this embarrassment as soon as they can."

"They could have been on the coast in a day," added Colonel Bob, whose nameplate said MICHAELS. "Looks like old Espejo outfoxed them again."

Ambassador Webster scowled at both of them. "His 'outfoxing them' involved making the United States–and me–look ridiculous." Turning again to Lacey he told him coldly, "You may think you played some clever part in all this. Maybe you'll change your mind halfway through your thirty-year sentence for treason."

He stood up and walked stiffly out of the office.

Col. Michaels then asked about military matters. Max was happy he really couldn't tell the colonel anything new and useful. He mentioned the bridge, and that Generals Villacis and Figueroa had been very worried about it.

"And they should have been," the colonel agreed. "Talk about dumb luck! If the earthquake hadn't taken it down, Guzmán would have been around their flank by noon."

Probably not the time to point out that I myself was about to take out the bridge. I wonder what they'd charge me with for that.

The Legal Attaché gathered his papers and stood up. Apparently Max's narrative had told him all he needed to know. "You'll leave on the afternoon plane tomorrow," he said. "Washington will handle it from here."

The name of the city reminded Max of his Activities Director. *Where in the hell is* my *Washington? Back in Alcalá? Consulting with Espejo on how to arrange my release? Or my escape?* He tried to imagine Washington and Rosa and Manuel in black ninja outfits, rappelling down from a helicopter above the embassy to pluck their leader to freedom. Though Rosa looked as fetching in the ninja outfit as she did in everything else, he couldn't picture her throwing those little pointed stars to neutralize the Marines. Not that Max wanted Sergeant Breen neutralized. He was probably a real fun guy when he wasn't wearing his *Semper Fi* face.

The Sergeant and Cpl. Mendez appeared in response to the Attaché's call. They escorted Max to a small, furnished but unused ground floor office in the Consular Section. Max asked whom it belonged to.

"The new consular officer coming in next week."

Max noted that Breen didn't call him *Sir* now, as if he understood that his prisoner was a brig inmate rather than a Foreign Service Officer.

"We'll get you a cot later," Mendez said. "You need to use the head, you dial 999."

They went out. Max heard a key turn in the lock. He sat down at the desk, thinking it strange that the GSA-issue furniture could seem at once so familiar and so foreign. Had he known in his GSA days what he lived through now, he would have taken more time to appreciate the lack of impending doom. And the freedom to go to the bathroom without dialing 999.

He glanced around at the filing cabinet, the stapler and telephone on the desk, the typewriter beneath a plastic dust cover, and the pencil sharpener fastened to the wall. His chair was much like his old GSA chair, with casters enabling one to glide back and forth on the large thick clear plastic mat that lay behind and partly under the desk on the off-white carpet. The office almost sang the virtues of practicality and of process carried out as methodically as the GSA clock on the wall ticked off the seconds. A man could produce reports here.

But its song sounded increasingly more foreign than familiar.

I don't want to produce any reports. I do not want to file anything. I want to go home to Alcalá.

He looked out the window through the security bars into the Embassy garden, and remembered the line from some English poet: "Stone walls do not a prison make. Nor iron bars a cage." It sounded like something an Engañadan would say. What came next? Something about innocent minds. If Max didn't feel exactly blameless, he could work on becoming innocent in the sense of *naïve,* which might lead to some sort of inner peace. He thought he might as well start practicing in preparation for entering a real cage behind real stone walls.

Soon he stopped seeing the door and the filing cabinet and the desk. He saw the jungle and Rosa and books of poetry on a shelf above a table laden with bananas and *linguado.*

Chapter Thirty-Three What Would James Bond Do?

The imagined *linguado* didn't satisfy the hunger that soon destroyed the reverie of life in the jungle. He didn't want to dial 999, which had to be the Marine station, and ask for dinner. He didn't want to accept his helpless situation. Yet his hunger said there's no point pretending he was anything but helpless, so why suffer?

He decided to compromise. He'd ask for food when he was *really* hungry. But soon he had to dial 999 anyway and ask to use the bathroom. Nature trumps pride. When he got back, he turned on the light and looked around the office again.

The bars on the window, which didn't yield a millimeter, ended any idea of climbing out to the garden and seeking a spot to climb the high razor-wire-topped wall. The garden definitely had security lights, and probably a surveillance camera. And if he got over the wall, where would he land? He tried to remember how the Embassy was laid out. He thought one side was next to a home or business. At least two sides bordered streets. There might be a chance if there were a way through the window.

Start a fire and set off the alarm, and try to get away in the confusion? The Marines would be at the door. He climbed on the desk and pushed against a ceiling tile, which moved. He pulled the desk light up—the cord barely reached—to survey the area above the tiles. Thin aluminum braces held by wires; it would never support his weight. Max tested that by pulling on a brace, which bent toward him.

No go. Maybe I could hide in a file cabinet? But that was no good either. He'd have to take the drawers out, a dead giveaway. He had seen plenty of movies where the hero waited behind the door, knocked out the guard, took his pistol and escaped. In the movies, those who are knocked out just take a nap and wake up with no damage other than a slight headache. To knock out Sgt.

Breen, Max would have to hit him hard enough to do serious damage—if he could manage that with the heavy GSA tape dispenser, or something else. Otherwise, the encounter could go south very quickly. He remembered a billboard he had seen once with a photo of a grim-faced Marine and the legend, "No one wants to fight. But someone has to know how."

I don't. And even if I did, what if I really hurt this Breen kid?

Then he studied the door itself. The hinges were on the inside! But upon closer inspection, they weren't like the doors in a house, with a slender pin holding the door to a piece of iron on the sill. Instead, this had some kind of bolt with a strange head that required a special tool. There probably wouldn't be such a tool in the desk, but maybe a key to the door? Could they have been dumb enough to lock him in with the key?

No. He found keys to the filing cabinet, and to the desk drawers that locked, but no others.

Maybe tomorrow. He didn't think they would march him around in public in irons. So why not just jump out of the car at a traffic light on the way to the airport and run for it? He tried to picture himself in the back seat of an embassy sedan. Alas, the picture that came to mind had a Marine on either side of him.

An unmistakable voice beyond the door interrupted his meditations.

"...the *carabineros* didn't care if it was his wedding night! They dragged Sgt. Grimes off to jail and we figured poor Margarita would just have to pine away for a long time, 'cause the Ambassador was sure as hell going to have him shipped back to Quantico in the morning!"

"That would be the drill," answered a voice Max didn't recognize.

"So his friends figured they'd just have to get him out."

"Hold on here a second."

Max heard a key slide into the lock. The door opened to reveal a Marine corporal he hadn't seen before, bearing a tray with some bread, cheese, cake, and a bottle of water. "Got your dinner here," he announced as he came into the office and set the tray on the desk. "Got what we could find in the kitchen, leftovers from lunch. And some cake the staff made for the party before they left."

Max nodded. Embassy cafeterias existed only to serve lunch. "And I take it you relieved Breen or Mendez?" Looking past the Marine he saw Harvey Tyrone looking at him and mimicking a man dressing. Something big and clumsy sat on the floor beside him.

"Right. Came on at six. I'm Dougherty."

"Good to meet you. Except..."

"Yeah." Maybe there was a trace of sympathy in Dougherty's voice. "I heard you're in deep shit."

"That would be the legal definition."

Dougherty chuckled. "Got you a cot here too."

As if invited, Harvey wheeled in the awkward bundle that proved to be a portable bed frame with a thin mattress. A blanket and pillow were on top of the bed, which was folded in on itself to make almost a triangle. "Don't know if you'll get much sleep tonight, Max." Harvey shook his head and sighed. "All my years in the Foreign Service, I never saw anyone get his foot in it like you have."

"Well," Max smiled sheepishly, "at least they won't say I didn't make a difference."

"For sure! But hey, I've got some good news for you. You know Charlie Brown the Admin guy?"

"Think I met him."

"Says your car finally arrived! Seems it got sent to Surinam or someplace by mistake."

"So can I pick it up and drive away?"

"Hah! Not any time soon. And worse, now you're going to miss the Halloween party! Damn shame. Hey, Dougherty, you think you could let him out about 8:15 to hear me do my thing?"

"No way!" the Marine snorted. "But maybe afterwards you can come down here with your balalaika and sort of serenade him, like, from in front of the door!"

Harvey laughed louder than the jest merited, while Max took comfort in thinking that even in Leavenworth he would live on in

South America, as a subject in one or more of Harvey's tales.

But what was that dressing gesture?

He looked at the cot and frowned. "How's it work?"

"You'll figure it out," Harvey assured him quickly. "Not like it's hard–not like stringing a hammock up in a *baobao* tree so the snakes don't get you!"

"Snakes?" Dougherty asked, setting Harvey off on another story. Before it ended, Harvey had worked his way to the door and out, drawing the Marine after him as if by magnetism. Before he disappeared behind the wall, Harvey looked at a corner where the wall met the ceiling of the office and stared for two seconds. At the same time, he held his hand up briefly as if signaling someone to stop, or wait.

"Sleep tight," Dougherty said as he turned and followed Harvey out the door. The lock turned again.

Max looked where Harvey had stared and saw a fire alarm, a little box with a red light that flashed when there was an emergency. *That and "wait" add up to...what? Wait until the fire alarm goes off? Can't think of anything else, unless he wants me to set off the alarm. There's a panic button right below it, but I already dismissed that idea. So, wait until the alarm goes off. But when? Ah,* he thought, and remembered Harvey's mentioning he'd do his thing at 8:15. But then? So what if the alarm went off? Maybe he'd figure it out when he'd eaten something.

Hunger's the best chef, he thought as he made a sandwich from the dry bread, sat at the desk and bit into it. The cheese was good and the cake moist. He washed it all down with the bottled water within minutes.

Harvey had something in mind. *What?*

He glanced around the room as if some explanation might be there in plain sight. Maybe it was: his eyes fell on the folding cot.

He found the bars that held it together, pulled them out and let the two halves of the bed frame and mattress fall open revealing a costume–the skeleton outfit he had noticed outside, or one just like it. He picked it up and held it against his body. It looked a bit small, probably made for a child, but a fairly large child. Maybe he could squeeze into it. And then? Looking back at the bed he saw a key. He walked quietly to the door and slowly slipped it into the lock. It went in well enough, but he dared not try turning it, not with the Marine right outside.

As he stuffed the costume under the mattress and spread out the sheets and blanket, the light dawned. *Good old Harvey! A genius! Or, a guy who will do anything to add another story to his repertoire–a better one than some tale about a guy just getting bundled on a plane back to the States. No matter. He's welcome to it.* He sat down to wait for 8:15.

Time passed very slowly. Starting at 6:50, he went to the door periodically to put his ear against it, hoping to hear something that would give a clue about what was happening. The lobby was some distance from the Consular Section and he remembered turning a corner or two when they had brought him here. Mainly he heard a vague hum that might have been anything, maybe machinery running somewhere, maybe the heating system. But the total volume seemed to increase after seven o'clock. He went from the door to the chair, got up and stared at the few books in the bookcase, took a history of Engañada and sat down and tried to read. Insofar as he could concentrate on reading anything, the book seemed to provide a bunch of events without ever bringing the real Engañada to life.

At 8:10 he got out the skeleton suit and tried to pull it on over his fatigues. This proved impossible, so he took off the fatigues and squeezed into the suit, hoping the flimsy seams wouldn't burst. What do to with the fatigues? Leaving them here might provide a clue that would lead the security people to Harvey. But Harvey could deal with that, probably. Still... He rolled them up as tightly as he could and, opening the shirt of the skeleton suit, stuffed them underneath. He had barely finished when the red light of the alarm began flashing and a loud bell sounded right outside the door.

Over the racket, he could hear feet hit the floor and move quickly down the hall. *Precisely! Marine Dougherty has a station to man somewhere!* He grabbed the key from the bed and quickly inserted it in the door and turned it. A satisfying *click!* told him it was the right key. He opened the door and peered out; no one in sight. He stepped out, the key in his hand. What to do with it? He ran back into the office and threw the key into a bottom drawer of the desk, then went out and moved toward the lobby. Above the din he heard voices, one of which might be Dougherty's, and thought they were coming towards him. He glanced around frantically, saw a door he had visited earlier marked MEN/HOMBRES, and ducked inside. In a moment, a loud knock on the door startled him. "Sir? Got to evacuate the building. Right now!"

Max opened the door and visibly fumbled with his pants. "*Bien, gracias,*" he mumbled, barely glancing at the Marine who was not Dougherty but another he'd never seen. *I'll have to light a candle somewhere in thanks.* The Marine headed back toward the lobby and Max briefly resented the idea they would let him burn in the locked office. He told himself to be thankful the Marine had not gone to get him, found him missing, and raised another alarm.

Old bureaucratic thinking dies hard. Max mused that the Marine's command to evacuate constituted an official order— something he could cite if caught. He went hurriedly to the lobby, which was mostly empty already except for a dozen or so people crowding toward the exit. He put himself in the middle of them, avoiding eye contact with anyone, as Marines and other staff pointed urgently toward the door and waved people on. Harvey's amplified voice urged everyone to stay calm and everything would be fine. "*Todo estará bien!*"

As the human current carried him to the exit, Max noticed Bettaluci and Jethro Jackson standing off to one side. It seemed to Max that one of them must recognize him at any second. He turned his face away, that being all he could do. The sound of his heart beating grew until it drowned the sound of the fire bell, and he was aware he had not dared to breathe. But apparently those two Americans saw nothing but a skeleton. A third American near the door stared at him more searchingly.

Braden? The guy was tall and gaunt, yes, but that clean-shaven pale face looked completely foreign. *If it's really Braden, then that gray business suit must be his Halloween costume. Great costume!* Two small, absent, hazel eyes drilled into him and, staring back, Max had no more doubts that it was his former Academic Director: those eyes could belong to no one else. Max hoped Braden was in his usual stoned state, and slow to act.

Yet Braden acted now. He began moving toward Max, cutting off his exit route. In a moment Max was standing in front of him.

"You fired me," Braden said in his normal sepulchral voice.

Max tried to push around him but Braden, surprisingly, moved with him, still blocking his way. Any scuffle would call attention to them. Max had no choice but to try to address Braden in his own terms. "Yes," he said. "I have so much to answer for."

The vacancy in Braden's eyes changed slightly, admitting a touch of puzzlement.

"As you see," Max continued, gesturing to the bones painted on his costume, "death comes to all men. Pray for me."

It took Braden a moment to respond. "I don't pray."

"Then at least let me rest in peace."

Finally Braden nodded and stepped aside. Max waited no longer.

In two seconds he was in the courtyard beneath a perfect full Halloween moon in the cloudless sky, where Marines and Engañadan contract guards encouraged the people to keep moving, to get a safe distance away and wait; the party might resume. Max obeyed. Reaching the sidewalk, he turned right and walked north, staying in the middle of the crowd.

There were shouts from the embassy now. Something was going on back there. Bettaluci might have talked to Braden, who would have told him about the walking dead. *And maybe they've discovered I'm gone.* Max began pushing through the people in front.

Only on the next block, after he had left the high Embassy wall behind, did he slow down. He got behind a tree and peeked out to see if any Marines were running up the sidewalk. None were, but he clearly saw Jethro Jackson's white hair moving through the crowd of those hoping they could soon return to apple-bobbing and costume contests.

Max moved quickly to the next block. *What now?*

A horn's beep provided the answer as a small pickup pulled up next to him. "Need a ride to the cemetery?" asked a familiar voice in Spanish. Washington was behind the wheel and Rosa beside him, both of them smiling and laughing. Max climbed in and Washington gunned the engine as Rosa embraced Max eagerly and began to cry.

"I thought I'd never see you again!" she said.

"*¿Pero cómo,*" asked Washington. "How could you worry about Max when Harvey was on the job?"

"Harvey's not God," she answered from Max's shoulder. "It might not have worked."

"I guess he's not." Washington seemed to mull over deep theological issues. "So did you pray to God to get Max out?"

"Of course."

Washington thought some more. "So God sent Harvey."

Chapter Thirty-Four: At Home with the Ceibos

Washington drove the pickup through the city as quickly as the roads and traffic allowed, then west on the highway to Alcalá. Every pothole made a hundred things rattle, but as far as Max was concerned, the truck was a beautiful thing with only pleasant sensations. As they drove, Washington and Rosa filled Max in on the development of the escape plan. "I thought of the costume," Rosa said proudly. "General Figueroa let us use his phone and we talked to Harvey, and he mentioned this Halloween party."

Washington claimed credit for the fire alarm. "I've always been good at distractions. But Harvey had to figure out a way to make it all work. Looks like he did!"

"And now," Max asked, "Where are we going?"

"First, as far from here as we can. We should meet up with the Alcalá army just where we left them, before we set out with the circus."

As for politics, they told Max that the threat of civil war seemed to have vanished. General President Madera of Engañada had made another speech, but this time it was all about reconciliation among brothers and mutual respect and the need to honor sacred national traditions. That translated to 'Espejo wins again.' They would talk and talk and fudge things, and eventually have elections that Espejo would surely carry. The military units had been told to open the roads ("We were the first ones through!" Rosa exclaimed) and stand down, and many were already returning to their barracks. As if to emphasize the point, a convoy of military vehicles went past them, heading east, jeeps and truckloads of soldiers and cannon and tanks on flatbeds. Max and Washington and Rosa studied them carefully in the moonlight which, at this altitude, cast a soft glow across the landscape.

"Those the ones that we went through earlier?" Max asked.

"The ones blocking the pass? Yeah, I think so."

"I'm sure," Rosa insisted. "I think I recognized a couple of the soldiers who were flirting with me."

"That will make things easier," Max said. "If there were still a blockade I'd probably have to walk around it. They might have been told to watch for me."

Washington thought it unlikely. "The military can't communicate that fast, not when everything has to go through ten layers of command."

There were no blockades, and the road was almost deserted when they arrived at last at General Figueroa's La Subida encampment around 2 AM. Some tents had been taken down, suggesting that some of the Alcalán troops–or once again, loyal Engañadan troops–had already returned to their barracks. A sleepy guard approached the truck and asked what they wanted, telling them they couldn't see the General until the morning. Washington turned up the heater full blast, let it run for a few minutes, and shut off the engine. The three former commandos leaned against each other as comfortably as they could and fell asleep.

After what seemed like only minutes, Max opened his eyes to find the sun almost up over the eastern cordillera, bathing the camp in soft dawn light. A cook was fixing breakfast over a huge camp stove while soldiers busily rolled up tents, gathered equipment, and loaded everything on trucks. Max shook his head. *Soldiers do spend a lot of time packing.* Soon the three of them were invited to breakfast with General Figueroa. Max ducked into the bushes to change from his skeleton suit to his fatigues. The skeleton suit now went under his shirt: it seemed ungrateful to just throw it away.

As they entered Figueroa's headquarters, the General looked up from his coffee. "Hello, Rosa, and Washington! Good to see you again!"

"Max is here too," pointed out Rosa in a puzzled tone.

"Max? I don't see any Max!" said Figueroa blankly. "If there were a Max here, the same one that I've been told to arrest should he show up, I'd have to do my duty to General Madera, whose authority we of course recognize anew after the happy resolution of the late misunderstanding!"

Max thought Washington should apologize to the military, who could communicate faster than he had thought.

They kept up the fiction of "No Max here" through a breakfast of eggs and ham, during which Figueroa happily described the relief that he and all his troops felt when Madera and Espejo had reached an agreement to avert the prospect of fratricidal fighting. He thanked the two of them for their efforts at the bridge. "Had Guzman and his troops crossed it..." He shook his head. "Things would be very different. I'd thank that Max fellow too, if I saw him, before I arrested him. Oh, and I'd give him this, something former President Espejo sent to me this morning." He reached out, pulled a duffel bag over, removed a bulky parcel, and placed it on the table. None thought to remind the general that their expedition to blow up the bridge was pointless because an act of God had done it for them.

The brown paper package, bound with twine, was addressed to *Sr. Max Lacey.* Max undid the twine with some difficulty and pulled away the paper to find a book, a fat envelope, and a note:

Dear Ambassador Lacey:

I'm sorry I could not now arrange things more gracefully for you; be patient. Time erases resentments, or takes the resentful away. Meanwhile I hope the enclosed book will help you make peace with your situation, and that the envelope will enable you to make arrangements until better days arrive, as they surely will. Thank you for your part in making them so.

JFES

P.S. Don't worry about your Center. It will be funded one way or another, and if elections go as we hope, I will emphasize its importance to the U.S. Ambassador. Besides, how could we ever neglect an institution that helped save the country?

The book was *The Complete Works of Woodrow Lively,* while the envelope was stuffed with *honores.* Max felt at once grateful and betrayed.

Espejo was generously telling Max to get lost, that he could or would do nothing else for him.

After breakfast they went out to find the trucks nearly loaded. "*Los muchachos* are eager to get home," Figueroa chuckled. "They don't usually work this fast."

"I'm eager to get home too," noted Rosa.

"You and Washington can ride in one of the staff jeeps. You're heroes. Anyone else would have to ride in a truck, hidden amid the troops."

"I have to return the pickup to my cousin," Washington said. "Five kilometers down the road. I'll join you there."

"No problem." Figueroa's answer was drowned out by a familiar roar. They turned to watch Harvey arrive. He pulled his Harley up next to them and got off laughing.

"Did that go like clockwork or what?" he asked.

"It did," Max allowed. "But what in the world are you doing here, and so early?"

"Looking for you, Max."

"Who? If you mean that Max Lacey wanted by the authorities, I'm looking for him too." Figueroa delivered the line straight-faced. Harvey picked up on it.

"Right. You and the CIA and spare Marines and everyone else the Ambassador could get. Doesn't matter that the war won't happen. That Max guy is a criminal and a fraud and traitor and the U.S. government wants him bad! I hear they'll offer a reward for anyone can finger him."

Max shrunk back a couple steps.

"If he's smart he'll head for the jungle." Figueroa frowned. "Too many people in Alcalá know him."

"That's what I'd do," Harvey agreed.

Figueroa went off to talk to some officers. Around the Harley, Max, Rosa, Washington and Harvey looked at each other. "So," Max said at last, "off to the jungle."

"You'd best," Harvey emphasized. "Word is the Ambassador pressured Madera to insist that Espejo let the Americans go wherever they wanted to find their fugitive."

"And he agreed." Max had known it more or less since he read the note. Still, he couldn't keep the disappointment from his voice.

"Big picture, Max. Gotta see the big picture. Good of the country versus one little Branch Cultural Officer. A bunch of dead soldiers versus one unhappy Center Director. He did what he had to do."

"I guess."

"It's not fair!" Rosa complained, stamping her foot. "Max risked so much to help us! How can Espejo turn his back on him?"

"No," Max objected. "What Harvey says makes sense. And he hasn't abandoned me." He held up the letter and money.

"Hey, hey!" Harvey exclaimed. "What a guy! Sure, he agreed to what he had to, but he's not about to help them look. Oh, no! He'll do all he can to make sure they don't find you and in the meantime, looks like he gave you enough to live on for a long time. At least, if you stay in the jungle. Webster and company will figure out you're there somewhere probably--where else would you go?—but it's a big jungle."

"You could go to San Andrés," Rosa suggested. "My family would hide you."

Max pondered. He had never been to San Andrés, of course, but imagined a small village. *All the residents would have to be in on it, and immune to the offer of a reward. Not too promising. Someone, maybe that anti-Espejo guy Don Jorge, would be glad to turn me in. Maybe not. He has to live there. Damn! You never know!*

Harvey voiced similar doubts. "That wouldn't be safe, at least not right now. Maybe not the village itself, but there's lots of country there, lots of little places with a hut or two and no roads. We'll find something."

"And what do I do? How do I earn a living? The money won't last forever." He stared at the ground for a moment and then asked Rosa, "Can you pass a message to Jorge Caballero for me?"

"The President of the Board? Of course," she assured him.

"Tell him I'm interested in the banana business."

Washington made the connection. "Great idea! You know Pepe Maldonado? Works for Caballero, guy in charge of all these little stations around the coast, little banana operations, load up bananas on the boat he sends around. Bet Caballero will tell him to give you one. And don't worry, Pepe's an *Espejista* to the bone, just like Caballero."

Washington's confidence was encouraging, or should have been. But Max had asked out of desperation. "Great. Even though I never really pictured myself as a banana counter."

"Come on," Washington urged. "Better off counting bananas in a jungle hut than sitting in jail, and anyway, why worry about things you can't do anything about? You've been in Engañada longer than that!"

Washington was right. And the more Max thought about it, the more he could picture himself and Rosa living amid banana trees. He'd still have plenty of time to read Livesly, or even write his own poetry. Anyway, other people might have problems too. "Harvey," he asked, "how did you do that last night? I mean, how can you know they won't trace it to you–the key and the alarm and all that?"

The Cultural Officer looked ecstatic at the question; he could tell another story. "Good question! You can thank old Francesco Gómez the artist–you know his work?"

"Don't think so."

"Wood carvings. Doesn't just carve them, he paints 'em. Statues of Don Quixote or St. Francis or a llama, stuff you pick up in the Indian markets. Anyway, I invited him to the party, told Jethro this guy was into folklore, and what more authentic American folklore than Halloween, right? He was pretty drunk when he got there and I kept him drinking. Five minutes before my gig I took him to the hallway where those controls are, you know?"

Max didn't, but Harvey didn't pause.

"Asked him to turn down the house lights when I went on. I meant the overheads. But I pointed to the fire alarm that's close to that big switch. So as I go out with my old balalaika to do my thing, Francesco does his thing and the bells go off and I'm out there in front of God and everybody, innocent as a lamb! Later on, when Guarini the security guy is trying to figure out what happened, I explain about the lights and he concludes the drunk just mixed up the switches!"

"Nice. But how about my getting out of the office? They had to figure someone helped."

"We got lucky, or maybe you got smart. They found a key to the door in the desk, figured it was an extra they overlooked. What they can't figure out is how you got out of the place without anyone recognizing you. Everyone had to go through the lobby." Harvey shrugged. "Told 'em that in all the confusion, crowd like that, we must have just not seen you in the middle of all the people. I'm not sure they believe it; Guarini's no fool. But they're at a dead end."

Max wondered what good angel had urged him to drop that key in the drawer.

"I'd better get going," Washington said, noting that soldiers were now climbing into the trucks. "So, Max, what..."

"I'll give him a ride. To a safe place, right on my old Harley."

"And the Center?" Max asked. "In this note, President Espejo promises it will be funded somehow and he'll do all he can to keep up the American connection. But what happens now, while I'm off in the jungle?"

"We'll get by," Washington assured him. "We've had lots of gaps when there was no American Director."

Max thought about it. They didn't really need an American Director. Many Engañadans could do as well or better. But a live Foreign Service Officer represented an official blessing on all that friendship and good will. "Maybe they could assign Harvey for now?" he suggested.

"Nothing would make me happier!" Tyrone agreed. "But, well, hey; what have you learned here about things you can't control?"

"That there's no point in worrying about them. Guess you're right."

Max turned to Rosa. "Well, you know the way to San

Andrés," he smiled wanly. "Harvey or someone will let you know where I am. Come soon."

Rosa and Max exchanged a long kiss, which Rosa interrupted to say brightly, "*el naufragio!*"

"The shipwreck?"

"Yes. Perhaps ten kilometers before San Andres, near the coast on the *Estuario San Miguel*. Someone can tell you where the old ship is, though almost no one goes there. Only my Aunt Inés and Uncle Hernán live nearby—he fishes, mostly. Tell her that her goddaughter needs her to help you. No—wait. Give me a pen and paper!"

Max fumbled in the package Espejo had sent him, where the best paper he could find was the flyleaf of Livesly's *Complete Works*. He held the book open, Washington provided a pen and Rosa wrote a brief note to her aunt, asking that she help her *novio* for a few weeks, and to tell no one.

Max took the book back and studied the word *novio*. Seeing himself described as a fiancé in writing made it seem official as well as real. "Come soon," he told her again, this time adding, "*mi novia.*" They renewed the kiss.

Harvey groaned playfully. "Ah, isn't that sweet? Hey, I'll get Chiquito and Poquito and some other musicians there for the wedding. Let me know when. And where: I never heard of this shipwreck."

"Soon," Max answered, thinking the place must be a great hideout if Harvey knew nothing of it. Rosa smiled and blushed.

"Hey, you want a backpack?" Washington asked, pointing to the package Max held under his arm. Max did, and Washington plucked one from the cab of his truck; it was just like the one he had carried to the bridge and then had taken from him by the army.

After Washington had embraced Max, wishing him all the best of luck, he had taken off in the truck. Rosa, after a tighter embrace, had climbed into a jeep, Harvey and Max stood and watched as the army vehicles crawled onto the highway and formed a convoy heading west toward Alcalá.

After the last truck turned the corner, Harvey climbed on to

343

the Harley and waited for Max, who had leafed through the book and stopped to read a poem he hadn't seen before:

The Ceibo Knows

Midway 'twixt earth and sky
The Ceibo does not brood;
Branches seeking light on high,
Roots downseeking food.
Fat twisted limbs appear absurd
To all right-angled thought;
The poet sees instead the Word
And joins what God has wrought.

"Come on!" Harvey shouted. "Fugitives gotta keep moving!"

Max stuffed the package into the backpack, slung the pack over his shoulders and got on the back of the bike. One kick and the motor roared. The next minute, they were heading west, Harvey keeping his speed down so as not to overtake the convoy. "Just as well no one can say they saw us going toward San Andrés!" he shouted over the subdued roar.

"Good thinking!" Max shouted back.

They stopped trying to talk over the roar of the motor, which let Max try to impose order on all the conflicting ideas and hopes and fears in his head. The prospect of living in the jungle seemed increasingly attractive, and even what he'd always wanted, as if his daydreams were really choices. Rosa clearly had a shrewd practical side that might compensate for his own lack of experience in jungles, or with bananas. He could get letters to his parents–he'd have to be careful how, lest the FBI was watching them–and assure them he was well, and that somehow someday all this would be forgotten as Espejo predicted and Max could go home. He imagined a visit rather than resettlement, could more easily picture himself returning to a banana station than to a GSA office. He felt better, yet something bothered him, something about his own autonomy, resentment at feeling dependent. God knows we're all dependent upon someone always, but it seemed newly important that he seize as much responsibility as he could.

Five miles on they came to a village just big enough to have a gas station and a small store. Said station consisted of a hut with a pump in front. Max pulled on Harvey's shoulder and indicated he should stop.

Harvey pulled into the gas station. "What's up, *compadre?*"

"Such a deal," Max answered, getting off the Harley and walking toward a medium-sized battered Yamaha, something between a scooter and Harvey's hog, with a sign on it: "For Sale – H/4300."

"Looks like it's seen better days," Harvey opined as he walked to the other side of the bike. A small old man emerged from the hut to greet them affably and ask if *los señores* were interested in this excellent machine.

To Max's surprise, Harvey hurried to introduce himself and Max to maybe the one Engañadan unacquainted with Harvey Tyrone. The old man, Paco Maldonado, seemed pleased to meet gentlemen capable of seeing the merit in a fine machine, one which had acquired a few dents over the years, but still ran as well as on the day it left Japan. He happily demonstrated, swinging a leg over the bike, flipping a switch that Max supposed had long ago replaced a keyhole, and jumping on the starter. The engine roared loudly to life on the third kick.

"Sounds great," Harvey allowed. "But why...?"

Max looked seriously at the older man. "Harvey, you are one hell of a friend and I'm more grateful than I can say for what you've done. But it's time I drove my own motorcycle."

Harvey's face rapidly registered surprise, a touch of offense, and finally understanding and approval. "Yeah. Well, let's see you start with the haggling!"

Max knew what custom required of him. Mr. Maldonado would be shocked if anyone paid the posted price. Harvey would probably have got the guy down to H/3000; Max could get him only to 3600 *honores*, but that included a full tank of gas. He handed the money to Maldonado in exchange for a scribbled receipt. "What about the license?" Max asked.

The old man pulled a folded piece of paper from his pocket and handed it over. "You take this to the municipality somewhere and change the name."

Harvey snorted. "Good luck finding a municipal clerk where you're going! But who's gonna ask for your license anyway?"

The old man invited them in for a beer before they left, talking non-stop about the excitement of army movements up and down his highway in the last week. Harvey matched him wonder for wonder until Max started glancing at his watch and they bid farewell to Maldonado.

Max had another stop to make: the small store that sold electric fans and shoes and clothes and chicken feed and more. He picked out a mosquito net, a blanket, two *guayaberas*, two pair of short pants, and a pair of flip-flops. When he asked about a map, Mrs. Maldonado--as it happened--seemed puzzled at first but finally found an old one in a drawer. "No one ever asks for these," she observed with a shrug. Max thanked her, paid the bill she summed up in her head, and went outside.

"These fatigues don't feel like me," he told Harvey. "And too warm, anyway." He stuffed his purchases in the backpack. He thought about consulting the map but decided it was too early, that planning a route at the outset would violate the spirit of the occasion.

"That would be your road," Harvey advised as they climbed onto their respective motorcycles, "there on the right."

Max nodded. "Don't know where I'll end up, whether this shipwreck place will work out or not, but I'm sure you'll find me even if Webster can't. And if you don't, I'll get word to you somehow. You'll always be welcome."

"Rosa will find you sooner, wherever you hide!" Harvey laughed, then kicked the Harley to life and roared back up the highway, waving with his left hand as he went around a bend.

Max got his own bike started, experimented until he heard the transmission click into first, and started down the dirt road Harvey had indicated. It headed west and north, and within a couple miles began descending sharply through increasingly thick jungle. The rear wheel slid as Max maneuvered through hairpin turns that kept surprising him because his mind kept wandering. He began to feel that he was the only thing in motion in this world in which trees kept stubbornly in their place forever. With every mile, his confidence in his ability to handle the small motorcycle increased, and his mind roamed the more freely. He had an image of the trees and plants declaring a sort of sovereignty over their places: pine trees up higher, with *paramos* and passionflowers, and as the road led down toward the coast, palms, orchids, and ferns. And those were only the plants Rosa or Miguel had named for him. There were thousands more that were just green things, bushy or branching, claiming the land as far as he could see.

There were also Ceibo trees, trees who knew. Perhaps Max would learn their language. Maybe they would tell him where and when to hide if Webster's guys got close, or where Livesly was buried. His reverie produced an image of himself reading Livesly as he sat by the poet's grave, beneath a Ceibo, gazing now and again at a shipwreck. From that, he latched on to a memory of himself on the day he arrived in Alcalá through the estuary, seeing a solitary thatched *Lord Jim* hut perched high atop thin bamboo legs, embraced by the jungle. And a pair of dark eyes following him, and whether fierce or soft, they allowed him to be there too, to imagine himself. Of course they would be soft, usually. Rosa's eyes.

A log lay suddenly across the road. Max jerked the motorcycle to get around it and returned to full consciousness, though his reverie stayed in memory. Looking ahead, he caught a glimpse of the Pacific before the road turned again. He gazed at the walls of green flashing by, studying them rather as a man might study the neighborhood into which he was moving.

Yes, he could make a home here. He imagined he was home already.

About the Author

James F. O'Callaghan served in the U.S. Navy 1960-63 before attending Seattle University where he received a BA in English in 1967. He earned his MA and Ph.D. from the University of Washington, and taught at the University of Idaho from 1970 to 1974, when he joined the U.S. Information Agency.

After serving in Latin America, Italy, Africa, and Washington D.C., he retired in 2000 and lives with his wife Giovanna in Maple Valley, Washington. They have three grown sons.

He has published short stories, articles, and poems in various publications including the *Foreign Service Journal, Homiletic & Pastoral Review, The Latin Mass, New Oxford Review, First Things, Curitiba in English, PAWA Quarterly,* and *Naples and Beyond* (anthology of the Naples Writers Circle).